AT HOME
with the WORD
2003

Sunday Scriptures and
Scripture Insights

Michael Cameron
Mary Katharine Deeley
Kathy Hendricks

LTP

LITURGY
TRAINING
PUBLICATIONS

Acknowledgments

Scripture pericopes contained herein are from the New Revised Standard Version of the Bible, © 1989 Division of Christian Education of the National Council of Churches of Christ in the U.S.A. All rights reserved. Used by permission. Text emendations as found in *Readings for the Assembly, Cycle B* © 1996 Augsburg Fortress. All rights reserved. The NRSV without emendations appears in Rdg. I, pp. 12, 24, 40, 42, 46, 60, 84, 86, 96, 100, 104, 134, 140 and 150; in Rdg. II, pp. 24, 28, 42, 80, 116, 118, 120, 122 and 136; in the Gospel, pp. 54, 56, 88 and 100.

Roman Catholic parishes in the U.S. proclaim the Sunday scriptures using the *Lectionary for Mass, Volume 1: Sundays, Solemnities and Feasts of the Lord,* copyright 1998, 1997, 1970 Confraternity of Christian Doctrine, Washington, D.C.

Psalms are from *The Psalms: Grail Translation from the Hebrew* © 1993 by Ladies of the Grail (England). Used by permission of GIA Publications, Inc., exclusive agent. All rights reserved.

Seasonal prayers, Preparation and Thanksgiving for the Word were written by Gabe Huck.

AT HOME WITH THE WORD 2003 © 2002 Archdiocese of Chicago: Liturgy Training Publications, 1800 North Hermitage Avenue, Chicago IL 60622-1101; 1-800-933-1800; fax 1-800-933-7094; orders@ltp.org; www.ltp.org. All rights reserved.

Visit our website at www.ltp.org.

The art for this year's *At Home with the Word* is by Oregon artist Vicki Shuck. The book was edited by Lorie Simmons with assistance from Margaret Brennan, Peter Mazar, Elizabeth Anders and Laura Goodman. Audrey Novak Riley and Theresa Pincich were the production editors. The design is by Anne Fritzinger, who typeset the book in Matrix and Minion. It was printed by Von Hoffmann, Inc., of Eldridge, Iowa.

ISBN 1-56854-398-0

AHW03

New for 2003

Welcome to *At Home with the Word's* new design!

SCRIPTURE READINGS

Now the full texts of the three Sunday readings are given, as well as parts of the responsorial psalm. On many Sundays of the year, the readings of other Christian churches (found in the *Revised Common Lectionary*) are the same or simply different in length from those proclaimed in Catholic communities. When the lengths differ, if the *Revised Common Lectionary* reading is printed, the citation of the Roman Catholic reading is provided, and vice versa. However, sometimes the readings of the two groups differ significantly. In a few of these cases, the Roman Catholic reading is printed and only the citation for the *Revised Common Lectionary* is given. Otherwise, both sets of readings are included.

Although Roman Catholics hear the New American Bible translation in their liturgy, the NRSV translation is used here to provide a common experience for all Christian readers of *At Home with the Word.* In scripture study, it can be helpful to read more than one translation, and the NRSV is recommended for study by many Catholic and Protestant scripture scholars.

SCRIPTURE INSIGHTS

This year, two scripture experts share the fruits of their studies. They encourage you to dig deeply into the texts and discover how flavorful scripture can be. Approached with the reverent attention these writers give, even familiar passages cannot be exhausted.

Mary Katharine Deeley is the pastoral associate at Sheil Catholic Center in Evanston, Illinois. She has a doctorate in Hebrew Bible and early Christian literature from Northwestern University, Evanston, Illinois, and has taught scripture to seminary students. Mary has written scripture insights for Winter, Summer and Autumn Ordinary Time.

Michael Cameron teaches scripture and early Christian studies at the University of Portland in Oregon. He has a doctorate in historical theology from the University of Chicago Divinity School.

Michael has written scripture insights for the seasons of Advent, Christmas, Lent and Easter.

PRACTICE OF PRAYER

In previous years, several pages of *At Home with the Word* were devoted to prayers. They set a prayerful context for the readings but also lessened the space available for scripture, which really is the point of the book! This year under the heading Practice of Prayer you will find an additional element from the Sunday scriptures: the responsorial psalm (or at least part of it). Prayers for opening and closing your study are also provided (see below).

PRACTICE OF VIRTUE (PRUDENCE, TEMPERANCE, FORTITUDE OR JUSTICE)

Previously, *At Home with the Word* writers explored the practice of the theological virtues—faith, hope and charity. Beginning this year they will focus on the essential human virtues: prudence, temperance, fortitude and justice. Kathy Hendricks has written about one of these virtues for each week. She is a speaker and writer specializing in spirituality, catechesis, family and leadership development, and has served for twenty-five years in pastoral ministry in Colorado, Alaska and British Columbia, Canada.

WEEKDAY READINGS

Some people want to read more than the Sunday scriptures. At the beginning of each season, see the list of scripture texts read at Mass on weekdays and on feasts falling on weekdays.

PREPARATION FOR THE WORD AND THANKSGIVING FOR THE WORD

At the introduction to each season of the year are prayers with which to begin and end your scripture studies: Preparation for the Word and Thanksgiving for the Word. They will make your time with the readings more prayerful. Gabe Huck, a master prayer-crafter, is the author.

ART FOR THE YEAR OF MARK

Vicki Shuck has given readers a cover to gaze at all year long. As you read more of Mark's gospel and more about its writer you'll recognize visual clues to Mark's style, to the circumstances in which he wrote and to the gospel's characters and stories. Despite a few light-hearted modern touches, there is much here that comes from serious scholarship. In illustrating our Introduction to the Gospel of Mark (page 8) the artist zooms in closer on the cover scene to reveal even more.

The text illustrated for the table of contents comes from the Proclamation of the Date of Easter, traditionally chanted during Mass on Epiphany. Find the entire beautiful chant in *Sourcebook for Sundays and Seasons 2003,* an LTP publication.

Except for Christmas, where we see the venerable prophets Simeon and Anna from the gospel of Luke, all of the introductions to the seasons feature an image from a story that Mark tells distinctively. For Advent, the artist evokes the suspense of the parable Jesus tells in Mark 13:33–37; for Winter Ordinary Time, the drama of Jesus' first public healing described in Mark 1:21–28; for Lent, the desolation of the wilderness in Mark 1:12–13. For Easter, she gives a fresh view of the three women at the tomb, Mark 16:1–7. In Summer Ordinary Time, we see a healing described only in Mark, at 7:31–37, and in Autumn Ordinary Time, the healing of Bartimaeus in Mark 10:46–52. Visual images provide another way of contemplating scripture. Vicki Shuck's art will call forth new insights as you examine it during the year.

YOUR RESPONSES INVITED

The LTP staff would appreciate your feedback. How do you use *At Home with the Word?* Alone? In a group? How are the new features working for you? Send responses to: ahw@ltp.org.

Table of Contents

THROUGH·THE RHYTHMS·OF TIMES·AND SEASONS LET·US CELEBRATE THE·MYSTERIES OF·SALVATION

4

The Season of Lent

The Paschal Triduum

The Easter Season

Summer Ordinary Time

Autumn Ordinary Time

The Lectionary and At Home with the Word

by Martin F. Connell

WHAT IS A LECTIONARY?

A lectionary is an ordered selection of readings, chosen from both testaments of the Bible, for proclamation in the assembly gathered for worship. Lectionaries have been used for Christian worship since the fourth century. Before the invention of the printing press in the fifteenth century, the selection and order of the readings differed somewhat from church to church, often reflecting the different issues that were important to the local communities of the time.

For the four centuries between the Council of Trent (1545–1563) and the Second Vatican Council (1963–1965), the readings in most Catholic churches varied little from year to year and were proclaimed in Latin, a language that many Catholics no longer understood. Vatican II brought dramatic changes. It allowed the language of the people to be used in the liturgy and initiated a revision of the lectionary. The Bible became far more accessible to Catholics and once again a vibrant source of our faith and tradition.

THE THREE-YEAR LECTIONARY CYCLE

The new lectionary that appeared in 1970 introduced a three-year plan that allowed a fuller selection of readings from the Bible. During Year A, the gospel readings for Ordinary Time are taken from Matthew, for Year B from Mark, and for Year C from Luke. This liturgical year 2003 begins on the First Sunday of Advent, December 1, 2002. It is Year B, the year of Mark.

YEAR B: THE GOSPEL OF MARK

Most of the gospel readings proclaimed in your Sunday asssembly this year and printed in *At Home with the Word 2003* are from the gospel of Mark. This gospel will be proclaimed on most Sundays from the First Sunday of Advent to the celebration of Christ the King, November 23, 2003. The introduction to the gospel of Mark on pages 8–9 and the commentaries on the gospel each week will help you appreciate the contribution of this gospel to our faith.

The Gospel of John

You might ask: What about the Fourth Gospel? The gospel of John is not excluded from proclamation during the three-year cycle. Though it does not have a year during which it is highlighted, the gospel of John punctuates certain seasons and times of the year.

The readings from Year A on the Third, Fourth and Fifth Sundays of Lent are from the gospel of John, and they are proclaimed every year in parishes celebrating the Rite of Christian Initiation of Adults (RCIA) when the elect are present. These three wonderful stories from the gospel of John—the woman at the well (on the Third Sunday of Lent), the man born blind (on the Fourth Sunday) and the raising of Lazarus (on the Fifth Sunday)—are important texts to accompany the celebration of the scrutinies in the process of Christian initiation. During Years B and C, you will find two sets of readings on these Sundays in *At Home with the Word:* one set for Sunday Masses at which the scrutinies of the RCIA are celebrated and another set for Masses at which they are not celebrated.

The gospel of John also appears for the Mass of the Lord's Supper on Holy Thursday and for the long passion reading on Good Friday. And on most of the Sundays of Easter—during the fifty days from Easter Sunday until Pentecost—the gospel of John is proclaimed at the liturgy.

The Difference between the Bible and the Lectionary

Because the lectionary uses selections from the Bible arranged according to the seasons and feasts of the church year, the assembly often hears from a mixture of appropriate texts "out of order" from their position in the Bible. However, the overall shape of the lectionary comes from the ancient church practice of *lectio continua,* a Latin term that describes the successive reading through books of the Bible from Sunday to Sunday.

You can see such a *lectio continua* in practice if you flip through *At Home with the Word* and, for example, consider the gospel texts assigned to the Sundays from the Fourteenth Sunday in Ordinary Time, July 6, through the Thirty-third Sunday in Ordinary Time, November 16. Though not every verse is included (and excepting Sundays when feasts interrupt the flow of Mark with other gospel texts), the lectionary moves from chapter 6 in Mark through chapter 13.

Although Christians hold the gospels in particular reverence, the first two readings provide strong teaching as well and comprise nearly two-thirds of the material in the lectionary. The first reading often echoes some image, character or idea in the gospel, as is the church's intention. The second reading stands on its own and comes from a letter of Paul or some other letter of the New Testament. Notice, for example, that the second readings from July through November come mainly from Ephesians, James and Hebrews. (Again, this sequence is interrupted by several feasts.) The stretch of Ordinary Time in summer and autumn provides an opportunity for sustained attention to one or a few sections of the Bible.

Unity with other Christian Churches in the Word of God

The basic plan of the lectionary for Catholics is universal. The readings proclaimed in your church on a particular Sunday are the same as those proclaimed in Catholic churches all over the globe. The lectionary is one of the main things that makes our liturgy so "catholic," or universal.

The revision of the Roman Catholic lectionary has been so well received that other Christian churches have adopted its three-year lectionary cycle. Many Christians are hearing the same word of God proclaimed and preached in their Sunday gatherings.

May your celebration of the liturgy in your parish be deepened by the preparations you make with this book. And may your work with scripture during the liturgical year help you feel ever more "at home with the word" of God.

An Introduction to the Gospel of Mark

by Michael Cameron

In the late 60s of the first century, nearly forty years after the Lord's resurrection, he had not yet returned. Jerusalem was under Roman siege, and persecution of Christians in Rome itself was intensifying after the fire of 64. Peter and Paul had died, and few eyewitnesses to Jesus' ministry were left. The stories of Jesus' ministry, death and resurrection had been told and retold in the intervening years, but Christians began to feel the need for written instruction. In those years Mark, leaning on the teachings of Peter and others, was the first to write a gospel. It is likely that he wrote for his suffering community in the environs of Rome. His concern was to record basic facts and stay faithful to the tradition, but Mark also wrote with a flair for the dramatic and a rich theological sense.

Suffering had thrown Mark's community into a spiritual crisis. The crisis came not through weak faith, but a strong faith too focused on the privileges and glory of being the community of the resurrection: Being disciples meant enjoying the benefits of Jesus' victory (see 10:35–45). By contrast, Mark refocused on Jesus' death as the foundation of discipleship (8:31–35). Mark's primary themes of the kingdom of God, the identity of Jesus and the call to discipleship each undergo dramatic development in the gospel in light of the cross. For Mark, everything, even Jesus' glorious return, stands in the shadow of his crucifixion. The German New Testament scholar Martin Kähler aptly called Mark's gospel "a passion narrative with an extended introduction."

JESUS PROCLAIMS THE KINGDOM

In Mark's first chapters, Jesus is a messianic figure on the move, proclaiming the nearness of God's kingdom in his words and works. As the Spirit "drove" Jesus into the wilderness after his baptism (1:12), so Jesus charges the early part of Mark with divine power and urgency. The synagogue exorcism in 1:21–28 demonstrates Jesus' mastery of the spiritual world; the healings that follow in 1:29—2:10 reveal that the kingdom's power lies in redemptive service. Jesus never defines the kingdom of God, but the parables of chapter 4 describe its characteristics. Irresistibly it comes, grows, changes everything, feeds everyone. It heals bodies, repairs hearts, defeats evil, creates community. Nothing stops its relentless coming, neither sin (2:7), disease (1:40–45), calamity (4:35–41), nor demonic forces (3:22–27). The kingdom emerges as a result of God's action, not humanity's.

The unfeeling religious leaders fail to receive the message (3:1–6). They lack the spiritual eyes and ears to perceive the new in-breaking of God's love in Jesus' ministry and the new turning to God's love that this requires. Paradoxically Jesus does find this among tax collectors (2:15–17), the sick (1:29–34), and the wretched of the land (5:1–20).

BECOMING DISCIPLES OF JESUS

Initial faith through the miracles is only a first step. The disciples struggle to fulfill the Master's hopes for them. "Have you still no faith?" Jesus asks early on (4:40). After Jesus feeds the 5000, he shows the disciples deep divine care by walking to them on the water in the midst of their midnight struggle. They merely become frightened, Mark comments, "for they did not understand about the loaves, but their hearts were hardened" (6:52). Jesus tries again by feeding the 4000, but their minds are fixed on literal bread. "Do you not yet understand?" Jesus asks (8:21).

Peter confesses that Jesus is the Messiah (8:29). But his awareness is only partial, for he needs Jesus to fit his expectations, which definitively exclude suffering. Jesus calls the idea satanic (8:33). Eventually one disciple betrays him, another denies him, and all desert him. Some readers think Mark is disparaging official church leadership. But the disciples were later reconciled to the Lord after his resurrection and lived to prove their faith. More likely Mark is encouraging Jesus' followers to take heart by the disciples' example of recovery from failure. With Peter's martyrdom still a recent memory, the story of him denying the Lord would have special power.

CHRIST THE SUFFERING SERVANT

The Son of God has a rich, deep humanity in this gospel. Mark's word for Jesus' reaction to the plight of the leper in 1:41 might be translated as "his heart melted with compassion," the same word used for Jesus' compassion on the crowds.

Jesus insists that his divinity should not be made known (1:44; 3:12; 5:43; 7:36; 8:26, 30), a motif known as the messianic secret. He refuses to be the political messiah that people expected. He was not averse to honors, but reinterpreted them in terms of his mission as suffering servant. He processes into Jerusalem, but on a donkey (11:1–10). He is anointed not by a public official but an anonymous woman, not for enthronement but for burial (14:3–9). He wears royal attire and receives homage from the Gentiles, but in mockery (15:16–20). Jesus establishes the new covenant of Jeremiah 31 by becoming the Suffering Servant of Isaiah 53. "This is my blood of the covenant which is poured out for many" (14:24).

From the beginning, the reader knows that Jesus is the Son of God (1:1). Throughout the gospel, the only voices to confess his true identity come from God (1:11; 9:7) and demons (1:24; 3:11; 5:7). Meanwhile, religious leaders call him demon-possessed (3:22), his family thinks he's a lunatic (3:21), village neighbors complain he's pretentious (6:2–3). To their credit, the disciples do begin to wonder, "Who then is this?" (4:41). But no human lips confess his true identity—until the end. Stripped of his dignity, his disciples, his life, destitute and utterly alone, Jesus draws his last breath. But at this precise moment the long-awaited confession comes from a Roman centurion: "Truly this man was God's Son!" (15:39). Jesus' death reveals the identity of God's Son, a living tableau of the disciple's calling to live the way of the cross. The resurrection cannot be described directly, but only proclaimed by disciples who have received a new life after they were willing to "lose their life for my sake, and for the sake of the gospel" (8:35).

Advent

KEEP·AWAKE!

Preparation for the Word

Like thirsty gardens long without rain,
or forests longing for winter's snow,
we wait, O God,
for your word to soak us through and through.
With your prophet Isaiah,
with the forerunner John,
with Mary and with Joseph,
may we be alert to your word however it is spoken.
Make us thirsty for its joy and its burden
through all the days and years of Advent.

God of our ancestors,
speak to us the peace you desire,
the salvation that is coming near,
the glory that is filling this ever-wandering world.
We ask this in the name of Jesus
who is Lord for ever and ever. Amen.

Thanksgiving for the Word

Your words, good Lord, are our teacher.
Season after season they engage us
as we wait all life long in joyful hope.
Give us sense to treasure these words,
to brood over them like mother hens,
to taste and to chew them over
finding a banquet unexpected.

Alone and with others
may we ever be surprised to find in our scripture
the word that rings
    through Advent's lovely darkness:
Do not be afraid!
That is our will, our food and our drink,
our constant treasure,
and amidst so much violence, our solace
    and our courage.
May this be so in Jesus who is Lord
    for ever and ever. Amen.

Weekday Readings

December 2: *Isaiah 2:1–5; Matthew 8:5–11*
December 3: *Isaiah 11:1–10; Luke 10:21–24*
December 4: *Isaiah 25:6–10a; Matthew 15:29–37*
December 5: *Isaiah 26:1–6; Matthew 7:21, 24–27*
December 6: *Isaiah 29:17–24; Matthew 9:27–31*
December 7: *Isaiah 30:19–21, 23–26; Matthew 9:35–10:1, 6–8*

**December 9: Solemnity of the Immaculate Conception
of the Blessed Virgin Mary** *Genesis 3:9–15, 20;
Ephesians 1:3–6, 11–12; Luke 1:26–38*
December 10: *Isaiah 40:1–11; Matthew 18:12–14*
December 11: *Isaiah 40:25–31; Matthew 11:28–30*
December 12: Feast of Our Lady of Guadalupe
Zechariah 2:14–17; Luke 1:26–38
December 13: *Isaiah 48:17–19; Matthew 11:16–19*
December 14: *Sirach 48:1–4, 9–11; Matthew 17:10–13*

December 16: *Numbers 24:2–7, 15–17a; Matthew 21:23–27*
December 17: *Genesis 49:2, 8–10; Matthew 1:1–17*
December 18: *Jeremiah 23:5–8; Matthew 1:18–24*
December 19: *Judges 13:2–7, 24–25a; Luke 1:5–25*
December 20: *Isaiah 7:10–14; Luke 1:26–38*
December 21: *Song of Songs 2:8–14; Luke 1:39–45*

December 23: *Malachi 3:1–4, 23–24; Luke 1:57–66*
December 24 Morning: *2 Samuel 7:1–5, 8b–12, 14a, 16;
Luke 1:67–79*

Reading I   *Isaiah 63:16b—17; 64:1—9*

Roman Catholic: Isaiah 63:16b–17, 19b; 64:2–7 (The numbering of these verses in the New American Bible differs from the NRSV.)

Revised Common Lectionary: Isaiah 64:1–9

You, O Lord, are our father;
    our Redeemer from of old is your name.
Why, O Lord, do you make us stray
      from your ways
    and harden our heart, so that we do not
      fear you?
Turn back for the sake of your servants,
    for the sake of the tribes that are your heritage.
O that you would tear open the heavens
      and come down,
    so that the mountains would quake
      at your presence—
as when fire kindles brushwood and the fire
      causes water to boil—
to make your name known to your adversaries,
    so that the nations might tremble
      at your presence!
When you did awesome deeds that
      we did not expect,
    you came down, the mountains quaked
      at your presence.
From ages past no one has heard,
    no ear has perceived,
no eye has seen any God besides you,
    who works for those who wait for you.
You meet those who gladly do right,
    those who remember you in your ways.
But you were angry, and we sinned;
    because you hid yourself we transgressed.
We have all become like one who is unclean,
    and all our righteous deeds are like a filthy cloth.
We all fade like a leaf,
    and our iniquities, like the wind, take us away.
There is no one who calls on your name,
    or attempts to take hold of you;
for you have hidden your face from us,
    and have delivered us into the hand
      of our iniquity.
Yet, O Lord, you are as a father to us;
    we are the clay, and you are our potter;
    we are all the work of your hand.
Do not be exceedingly angry, O Lord,
    and do not remember iniquity forever.
    Now consider, we are all your people.

Reading II   *1 Corinthians 1:3—9*

Grace to you and peace from God, our Father, and the Lord Jesus Christ.

I give thanks to my God always for you because of the grace of God that has been given you in Christ Jesus, for in every way you have been enriched in Christ, in speech and knowledge of every kind—just as the testimony of Christ has been strengthened among you—so that you are not lacking in any spiritual gift as you wait for the revealing of our Lord Jesus Christ.

He will also strengthen you to the end, so that you may be blameless on the day of our Lord Jesus Christ. God is faithful, by whom you were called into the communion of the Son of God, Jesus Christ our Lord.

Gospel   *Mark 13:24—37*

Roman Catholic: Mark 13:33–37

Jesus said: "In those days, after that suffering, the sun will be darkened, and the moon will not give its light, and the stars will be falling from heaven, and the powers in the heavens will be shaken. Then they will see 'the Son-of-Man coming in clouds' with great power and glory. Then the Son-of-Man will send out the angels, and gather his elect from the four winds, from the ends of the earth to the ends of heaven.

"From the fig tree learn its lesson: as soon as its branch becomes tender and puts forth its leaves, you know that summer is near. So also, when you see these things taking place, you know that he is near, at the very gates. Truly I tell you, this generation will not pass away until all these things have taken place. Heaven and earth will pass away, but my words will not pass away.

"But about that day or hour no one knows, neither the angels in heaven, nor the Son, but only the Father. Beware, keep alert; for you do not know when the time will come. It is like someone going on a journey, who leaving home and putting the slaves in charge of their own work, commands the doorkeeper to be on the watch. Therefore, keep awake—for you do not know when the lord of the house will come, in the evening, or at midnight, or at cockcrow, or at dawn, or else, coming suddenly, the lord may find you asleep. And what I say to you I say to all: Keep awake."

Practice of Prayer

Psalm 80:2–3, 15–16, 18–19

O shepherd of Israel, hear us,
you who lead Joseph's flock,
shine forth from your cherubim throne
upon Ephraim, Benjamin, Manasseh.
O LORD, rouse up your might,
O LORD, come to our help.

God of hosts, turn again, we implore,
look down from heaven and see.
Visit this vine and protect it,
the vine your right hand has planted.
May your hand be on the one you have chosen,
the one you have given your strength.

Practice of Virtue

Virtue. The word may call to mind any number of images—clean living, uprightness, austerity, saintliness, a well-ordered life. The dictionary defines it as "moral excellence or goodness" and "conformity of life to moral laws." That may sound restrictive, a way of living set aside for only the holy; yet we are each invited to live a virtuous life. Doing so keeps us from spinning out of control, grounds us, gives us guidance and insight, and helps us choose wisely. It opens up the truly good life. As we make our way through the liturgical year, we will be looking at the four cardinal virtues—prudence, justice, temperance and fortitude. Dusted off and polished up, they can offer us surprising insights.

Scripture Insights

Isaiah 63 dates from a time after the honeymoon period that followed the return from exile. The people are beginning to face the harsh difficulties of re-establishing their spiritual identity as God's people, caught in the crush between soaring hopes and paltry performance. They question and recall glories that the Lord once performed for the nation. They repent. They surrender themselves anew and despite the possibility of rejection, they plead longingly for God to appear.

Paul writes to a church that needs that perspective. Considering itself ready for the Lord's coming, the Corinthian church will learn in this letter how woefully unprepared the apostle thinks it is: theological errors, unethical practices, misplaced priorities, forgetting the poor, constant infighting, interest in self-advancement. But at the letter's beginning, Paul celebrates the fact that for all their faults the Corinthians are nevertheless a true Christian community. He reminds them that God alone keeps them faithful.

Mark's gospel stresses the need for constant watchfulness among the disciple-servants who must account for their actions. A subtle move by the evangelist should not be missed. Note how Mark deliberately juxtaposes these words of Jesus on the Mount of Olives with the disciples' failure in the garden of Gethsemane in the very next chapter (14:26–41). On the mount Jesus suddenly turns to the reader directly and says, "Keep awake!" (13:37); in the garden Jesus again warns the disciples, "Keep awake" (14:34). On the mount he warns the disciples lest the Lord come and find them sleeping; in the garden he returns after prayer and finds them asleep (14:36–41). On the mount they do not know the time that the Lord "will come" (13:35); in the garden he declares "the hour has come" (14:41). Mark portrays these sorrowful events as a warning to disciples of every generation.

Isaiah 64:3 highlights the ever-surprising element of God's actions in history. Saint Paul quotes this same verse to highlight what God has in store for our future. What is Paul referring to in 1 Corinthians 2:9?

Reading I   *Isaiah 40:1—5, 9—11*

Revised Common Lectionary: Isaiah 40:1–11

Comfort, O comfort my people,
  says your God.
Speak tenderly to Jerusalem,
  and cry to the city
that it has served its term,
  that its penalty is paid,
that it has received from the Lord's hand
  double for all its sins.

A voice cries out:
"In the wilderness prepare the way of the Lord,
  make straight in the desert a highway
    for our God.
Every valley shall be lifted up,
  and every mountain and hill be made low;
the uneven ground shall become level,
  and the rough places a plain.
Then the glory of the Lord shall be revealed,
  and all people shall see it together,
    for the mouth of the Lord has spoken."

Get you up to a high mountain,
  O Zion, herald of good tidings;
lift up your voice with strength,
  O Jerusalem, herald of good tidings,
    lift it up, do not fear;
say to the cities of Judah,
  "Here is your God!"
See, the Lord God comes with might,
  with an arm to rule;
God comes bearing the reward,
  preceded by the recompense.
The Lord will feed the chosen flock
    like a shepherd;
  God's arms will gather the lambs,
God's bosom will carry them;
  the Lord will gently lead the mother sheep.

Reading II   *2 Peter 3:8—15a*

Roman Catholic: 2 Peter 3:8–14

Do not ignore this one fact, beloved, that with the Lord one day is like a thousand years, and a thousand years are like one day. The Lord is not slow concerning the promise, as some think of slowness, but is patient with you, not wanting any to perish, but all to come to repentance.

But the day of the Lord will come like a thief, and then the heavens will pass away with a loud noise, and the elements will be dissolved with fire, and the earth and everything that is done on it will be disclosed. Since all these things are to be dissolved in this way, what sort of persons ought you to be in leading lives of holiness and godliness, waiting for and hastening the coming of the day of God, because of which the heavens will be set ablaze and dissolved, and the elements will melt with fire?

But, in accordance with God's promise, we wait for new heavens and a new earth, where righteousness is at home. Therefore, beloved, while you are waiting for these things, strive to be found by God at peace, without spot or blemish; and regard the patience of our Lord as salvation.

Gospel   *Mark 1:1—8*

The beginning of the good news of Jesus Christ, the Son of God.

As it is written in the prophet Isaiah,

"See, I am sending my messenger ahead of you,
who will prepare your way;
the voice of one crying out in the wilderness:
'Prepare the way of the Lord,
make straight the paths of the Lord,' "

John the baptizer appeared in the wilderness, proclaiming a baptism of repentance for the forgiveness of sins. And people from the whole Judean countryside and all the people of Jerusalem were going out to him, and were baptized by him in the river Jordan, confessing their sins. Now John was clothed with camel's hair, with a leather belt around his waist, and he ate locusts and wild honey. He proclaimed, "After me one who is more powerful than I is coming, the thong of whose sandals I am not worthy to stoop down and untie. I have baptized you with water; but the one who is coming will baptize you with the Holy Spirit."

Practice of Prayer

Psalm 85:9—10, 11—12, 13—14

I will hear what the Lord has to say,
a voice that speaks of peace,
peace for his people and friends
and those who turn to God in their hearts.
Salvation is near for the God-fearing,
and his glory will dwell in our land.

Mercy and faithfulness have met;
justice and peace have embraced.
Faithfulness shall spring from the earth
and justice look down from heaven.

The Lord will make us prosper
and our earth shall yield its fruit.
Justice shall march in the forefront,
and peace shall follow the way.

Practice of Prudence

The mood was glum. Three friends sat around the kitchen table talking about Christmas. One lamented that, after the baking, shopping, decorating, entertaining and gift-wrapping, she was too tired to enjoy it. "I'll be glad when it's over," she sighed.

Even cherished family traditions can become burdensome when added to an already over-crowded Christmas schedule. This stands in marked contrast to how Christians are invited to observe Advent: awake and alert. The practice of *prudence* at this time of year would help us unburden our minds and schedules in order to appreciate Advent's sacred meaning. This season of expectancy and longing is meant to culminate in a joyous celebration of the Incarnation—God with and among us in the presence of Jesus Christ. What a pity to expire from exhaustion and miss the greatest gift of the season!

Scripture Insights

Early in the sixth century before Jesus, the kingdom of Judah was overrun and its people carried into exile in Babylon. The Temple was destroyed and Jerusalem was leveled. Into this mournful situation came an anonymous disciple of the prophetic school of Isaiah preaching a scintillating message of hope. The poet-prophet recalled God's first "coming" to the people at the time of the Exodus (see Isaiah 41:17–18; 42:16; 43:16–17; 48:21; 50:2). Then, God had come to the people Israel through one of their own, Moses. But this time, the prophet proclaimed, God would come through a pagan, Cyrus, the Persian king and conqueror of the Babylonians. This second "coming" ("Here is your God!" 40:9) confronted the doubt of the exiles with a trumpet call of good news, "Comfort, O comfort my people" (40:1).

Mark used this picture of God's "second" Old Testament coming to speak of God's New Testament "coming" in the gospel. John the Baptist's appearance and thunderous preaching prepared the people for "one who is more powerful than I" (1:7). John seems to have expected the day of judgment that had been announced by the old prophets. But in the rest of his gospel Mark unfolded the unlikely story of God's anointed who came to teach, heal, suffer and finally give his life as a ransom for others (Mark 10:45).

Peter's second letter refers to a future coming of Christ. By the time the letter was written by an anonymous representative of Peter in the second century, Christ's final coming was long delayed. But the writer rekindles anticipation by speaking like John the Baptist and the Old Testament prophets. He warns that Christ delayed his second coming only to give people time to prepare and calls for urgent and active obedience. Such obedience not only prepares for but even "hastens" God's final coming.

Note the shift in the image of God from power to tenderness in Isaiah 40:10–11. Check Psalm 85:10; Romans 11:22; James 2:13; 1 John 4:17–18. What contrasts appear in these verses and how are the tensions resolved?

Reading I   *Isaiah 61:1— 4, 8 —11*

Roman Catholic: Isaiah 61:1–2a, 10–11

The spirit of the Lord God is upon me,
    because the Lord has anointed me;
the Lord has sent me to bring good news
        to the oppressed,
    to bind up the brokenhearted,
to proclaim liberty to the captives,
    and release to the prisoners;
to proclaim the year of the Lord's favor,
    and the day of vengeance of our God;
    to comfort all who mourn;
to provide for those who mourn in Zion—
    to give them a garland instead of ashes,
the oil of gladness instead of mourning,
    the mantle of praise instead of a faint spirit.
They will be called oaks of righteousness,
    the planting of the Lord, to display the glory
        of God.
They shall build up the ancient ruins,
    they shall raise up the former devastations;
they shall repair the ruined cities,
    the devastations of many generations.

For I the Lord love justice,
    I hate robbery and wrongdoing;
I will faithfully give them their recompense,
    and I will make an everlasting covenant
        with them.
Their descendants shall be known
        among the nations,
    and their offspring among the peoples;
all who see them shall acknowledge
    that they are a people whom the Lord
        has blessed.

I will greatly rejoice in the Lord,
    my whole being shall exult in my God;
for God has clothed me with the garments
        of salvation,
    and has covered me with the robe
        of righteousness,
as a bridegroom decks himself with a garland,
    and as a bride adorns herself with her jewels.
For as the earth brings forth its shoots,
    and as a garden causes what is sown in it
to spring up,
so the Lord God will cause righteousness
        and praise
    to spring up before all the nations.

Reading II   *1 Thessalonians 5:16—24*

Rejoice always, pray without ceasing, give thanks in all circumstances; for this is the will of God in Christ Jesus for you. Do not quench the Spirit. Do not despise the words of prophets, but test everything; hold fast to what is good; abstain from every form of evil.

May that very God of peace sanctify you entirely; and may your spirit and soul and body be kept sound and blameless at the coming of our Lord Jesus Christ. The one who calls you is faithful, and will do this.

Gospel   *John 1:6—8, 19—28*

There was a man sent from God, whose name was John. He came as a witness to testify to the light, so that all might believe through him. He himself was not the light, but he came to testify to the light.

This is the testimony given by John when the Judeans sent priests and Levites from Jerusalem to ask him, "Who are you?" John confessed and did not deny it, but confessed, "I am not the Messiah." And they asked him, "What then? Are you Elijah?" He said, "I am not." "Are you the prophet?" He answered, "No." Then they said to him, "Who are you? Let us have an answer for those who sent us. What do you say about yourself?" John said, "I am the voice of one crying out in the wilderness, 'Make straight the way of the Lord,'" as the prophet Isaiah said.

Now they had been sent from the Pharisees. They asked him, "Why then are you baptizing if you are neither the Messiah, nor Elijah, nor the prophet?" John answered them, "I baptize with water. Among you stands one whom you do not know, the one who is coming after me, the thong of whose sandal I am not worthy to untie." This took place in Bethany across the Jordan where John was baptizing.

Practice of Prayer

Luke 1:46—48, 49—50, 53—54

My soul magnifies the Lord,
   and my spirit rejoices in God my Savior,
who has looked with favor on me, a lowly servant.
   Surely, from now on all generations
      will call me blessed;
for the Mighty One has done great things for me:
   holy is the name of the Lord,
whose mercy is for the God-fearing
   from generation to generation.
God has filled the hungry with good things,
   and sent the rich away empty.
God has helped Israel, the Lord's servant,
   in remembrance of mercy.

Practice of Justice

"From everywhere, filling the air,
O how they pound, raising the sound,
O'er hill and dale, telling their tale."

The "Carol of the Bells" is a beloved Christmas song. Its happy lyrical image of sweet silver bells is offset by an underlying chorus, reminding the listener of the compelling force of ringing bells.

Bells are clear symbols of liberation and hope. They act as heralds, announcing vital news or sounding an alarm to those within range of their call. So profound is their ability to stir hearts that they are often silenced by dictators insistent on absolute control.

Prophets are God's bells. Their voices rise above the din of superficial noise and summon us to *justice,* to treating others with the respect and dignity that is rightfully theirs. As we enter this second half of Advent, how can we turn our attention to just ways of living?

Scripture Insights

Catholic Christians traditionally call this "Gaudete Sunday" (Latin *gaudere,* "to rejoice," from the entrance refrain) to stress the joy of anticipating the Lord's coming. Today's texts express the joy of the watcher who heralds the dawn while standing between darkness and light.

The prophet of the school of Isaiah was one returning from exile in Babylon. Our passage appears in a magnificent series of salvation proclamations (chapters 60–62) that bolstered the courage of the exiles. The prophet exults in his call as bearer of God's good tidings: "I will greatly rejoice in the LORD . . . for God has clothed me with the garments of salvation" (61:10).

New Testament readers know this text from the time Jesus stood in his home synagogue at Nazareth announcing his messianic mission (Luke 4:18–19). Here on Gaudete Sunday it characterizes John the Baptist's joy as the herald of Christ.

John is a dour man in a camel-hair tunic who eats a ghastly diet foraged from the wilderness. But a distinct joy infuses the New Testament texts about him springing from his privileged position as forerunner and friend of Jesus. His mother Elizabeth hears the greeting of Mary and says, "the child in my womb leaped for joy" (Luke 1:44). In the fourth gospel, John came "to testify to the light" (John 1:7), saw Christ's glory, "full of grace and truth" and cried out in witness to his majesty (1:14). Later, when Jesus first came to him, John exclaimed, "Here is the Lamb of God" (1:29). He then surrendered his disciples to Jesus and described his joy with a vivid metaphor: "The best man rejoices greatly at the bridegroom's voice. So this joy of mine has been made complete. He must increase; but I must decrease" (3:29–30). This is the joy in the Isaiah text applied to John today, all the more striking for the contrast between the prophet's "garments of salvation" and John's rough clothing.

Paul's letter to the Thessalonians strongly anticipates the Lord's coming, while also reminding readers to "rejoice always" (5:16). How would you describe the character of joy in a time of waiting?

December 22, 2002

FOURTH SUNDAY OF ADVENT

READING I   *2 Samuel 7:1—12, 14a, 16*

Roman Catholic: 2 Samuel 7:1–5, 8b-12, 14a, 16
Revised Common Lectionary: 2 Samuel 7:1–11, 16

Now when David the king was settled in his house, and the Lord had given him rest from all his enemies around him, the king said to the prophet Nathan, "See now, I am living in a house of cedar, but the ark of God stays in a tent." Nathan said to the king, "Go, do all that you have in mind; for the Lord is with you."

But that same night the word of the Lord came to Nathan: Go and tell my servant David: Thus says the Lord: Are you the one to build me a house to live in? I have not lived in a house since the day I brought up the people of Israel from Egypt to this day, but I have been moving about in a tent and a tabernacle. Wherever I have moved about among all the people of Israel, did I ever speak a word with any of the tribal leaders of Israel, whom I commanded to shepherd my people Israel, saying, "Why have you not built me a house of cedar?"

Now therefore thus you shall say to my servant David: Thus says the Lord of hosts: I took you from the pasture, from following the sheep to be prince over my people Israel; and I have been with you wherever you went, and have cut off all your enemies from before you; and I will make for you a great name, like the name of the great ones of the earth. And I will appoint a place for my people Israel and will plant them, so that they may live in their own place, and be disturbed no more; and evildoers shall afflict them no more, as formerly, from the time that I appointed judges over my people Israel; and I will give you rest from all your enemies. Moreover the Lord declares to you that the Lord will make you a house. When your days are fulfilled and you lie down with your ancestors, I will raise up your offspring after you, who shall come forth from your body, and I will establish his kingdom. I will be a father to him, and he shall be a son to me. Your house and your kingdom shall be made sure forever before me; your throne shall be established forever.

READING II   *Romans 16:25—27*

Now to God who is able to strengthen you according to my gospel and the proclamation of Jesus Christ, according to the revelation of the mystery that was kept secret for long ages but is now disclosed, and through the prophetic writings is made known to all the Gentiles, according to the command of the eternal God, to bring about the obedience of faith—to the only wise God, through Jesus Christ, be the glory forever! Amen.

GOSPEL   *Luke 1:26—38*

In the sixth month the angel Gabriel was sent by God to a town in Galilee called Nazareth, to a virgin woman engaged to a man whose name was Joseph, of the house of David. The virgin's name was Mary. And the angel came to her and said, "Greetings, favored one! The Lord is with you." But she was much perplexed by the angel's words and pondered what sort of greeting this might be.

The angel said to her, "Do not be afraid, Mary, for you have found favor with God. And now, you will conceive in your womb and bear a son, and you will name him Jesus. He will be great, and will be called the Son of the Most High, and the Lord God will give to him the throne of his ancestor David. He will reign over the house of Jacob forever, and of his dominion there will be no end." Mary said to the angel, "How can this be, since I am a virgin?" The angel said to her, "The Holy Spirit will come upon you, and the power of the Most High will overshadow you; therefore the child to be born will be holy; he will be called Son of God. And now, your relative Elizabeth in her old age has also conceived a son; and this is the sixth month for her who was said to be barren. For nothing will be impossible with God."

Then Mary said, "Here am I, the servant of the Lord; let it be with me according to your word."

Then the angel departed from her.

Practice of Prayer

Psalm 89:2–3, 4–5, 27, 29

I will sing for ever of your love, O Lord;
through all ages my mouth will proclaim
    your truth.
Of this I am sure, that your love lasts for ever,
that your truth is firmly established
    as the heavens.

"With my chosen one I have made a covenant:
I have sworn to David my servant:
I will establish your dynasty for ever
and set up your throne through all ages."

He will say to me: 'You are my father,
my God, the rock who saves me!'

I will keep my love for him always;
with him my covenant shall last.

Practice of Fortitude

This is the season of women who overcome fears to facilitate God's work in the world. Mary has spoken her courageous yes, visited Elizabeth and now looks forward to the birth of a strange new life. In the Roman martyrology December 20 belongs to Esther, the brave queen of the Old Testament story who prayed and fasted for the strength to save her people from an evil plot. God gave her the fortitude—courage and endurance—to triumph in a perilous situation.

For those who mourn a loss or struggle with depression and anxiety, the holiday season can feel like an evil plot. Society's expectations that everyone be "merry and bright" impose pressures on many. As the great feast of Christmas draws near, consider how you can be attentive to someone in your midst who needs to be fortified by an extra minute of attention, care and compassion.

Scripture Insights

The dynamic of prophetic promise and fulfillment is deeply embedded in the Christian understanding of the Bible. Four peak moments unify the sweeping story of salvation in the Jewish Bible, our Christian Old Testament. These are represented by the election of Abraham, the deliverance through Moses, the kingship of David and the restoration after the Babylonian exile. Christianity affirms the continuing potency and reality of these events for both synagogue and church, and adds a fifth, culminating moment in the person and paschal mystery of our Lord Jesus Christ. We believe that this final moment of salvation history was figuratively anticipated by "types" that are found in the previous four Old Testament moments and many others. These interrelationships of "typology" continue to shape Christian liturgy, prayer, theology and practice.

The third of these moments and its fulfillment in Jesus are in view today. The promise given to King David in today's 2 Samuel text assured that his royal line would never fail. Israel's king would call God "father" and be called God's "son." This promise originated the Jewish hope of a coming Messiah (see Isaiah 9:5–6, 11:1–9). But when David's royal line was broken following the Babylonian exile, this promise became problematic (see Psalm 89, used in today's liturgy). Christians found its new and deeper fulfillment in Jesus. Many New Testament texts recall Jesus' royal heritage as the "son of David" (Matthew 1:1; Acts 2:25–36; Romans 1:3). But nowhere is the fulfillment of promise of the "sure love for David" (Isaiah 55:3) more strongly invoked than in Luke's story of the annunciation, where the angel Gabriel's words to the Messiah's mother, Mary, are modeled on the promise given to David.

Reread God's promise to King David. What parts of Jesus' coming would have seemed to fulfill it? What parts might have seemed to contradict it?

ANNA·SIMEON

Preparation for the Word

We turn the pages of our ancient books,
tender and fierce God,
and here we find the amazing words:
the Word was in the beginning
and the Word was made flesh
and the Word dwelt among us
full of grace and truth.

So in these long nights and brief days
may we ever hear you speaking
in Isaiah's dream of prisoners set free
and every war weapon pounded into a plow,
in Luke's stories of the poor being first to hear
and Matthew's of outsiders paying attention,
and John's of an amazing wedding.
Amazed are we to be guests at this wedding
of earth and heaven
for in these pages we find that you, gracious God,
have made a place for us.
We pray in Jesus' name who is Lord
    for ever and ever.
Amen.

Thanksgiving for the Word

God of the shepherds and magi,
of ox and sheep, of Joseph and of Mary,
may these wondrous scriptures dwell among us,
comfort and confront us
through all the days of Christmas.
Alone and in conversation, open us to your words
proclaimed to our assemblies
and echoed in our households.

With Mary we would ponder these things
    in our hearts,
till our ears can hear and our eyes see
and our lips proclaim
what the earth itself is singing,
what the sea is roaring:
We praise you for your glory
in this Jesus who is Lord for ever and ever. Amen.

Weekday Readings

December 25: Solemnity of the Nativity of the Lord
   day: Isaiah 52:7–10; Hebrews1:1–6; John 1:1–18
December 26: Feast of Saint Stephen
   Acts 6:8–10; 7:54–59; Matthew 10:17–22
December 27: Feast of Saint John
   1 John 1:1–4; John 20:2–8
December 28: Feast of the Holy Innocents
   1 John 1:5–2:2; Matthew 2:13–18

December 30: Sixth Day in the Octave of Christmas
   1 John 2:12–17; Luke 2:36–40
December 31: Seventh Day in the Octave of Christmas
   1 John 2:18–21; John 1:1–18
January 1: Eighth Day in the Octave of Christmas,
   Blessed Virgin Mary, Mother of God
   Numbers 6:22–2; Galatians 4:4–7; Luke 2:16–21
January 2: *1 John 2:22–28; John 1:19–28*
January 3: *1 John 2:29–3:6; John 1:29–34*
January 4: *1 John 3:7–10; John 1:35–42*

January 6: *1 John 3:22–4:6; Matthew 4:12–17, 23–25*
January 7: *1 John 4:7–10; Mark 6:34–44*
January 8: *1 John 4:11–18; Mark 6:45–52*
January 9: *1 John 4:19–5:4; Luke 4:14–22a*
January 10: *1 John 5:5–13; Luke 5:12–16*
January 11: *1 John 5:14–21; John 3:22–30*

December 25, 2002

NATIVITY OF THE LORD, MIDNIGHT

READING I   Isaiah 9:2—7

Roman Catholic: Isaiah 9:1–6 (Verse numbers differ in the New American Bible but text is the same.)

The people who walked in darkness
    have seen a great light;
those who lived in a land of deep darkness—
    on them light has shined.
You have multiplied the nation,
    you have increased its joy;
they rejoice before you
    as with joy at the harvest,
    as people exult when dividing plunder.
For the yoke of their burden,
    and the bar across their shoulders,
    the rod of their oppressor,
    you have broken as on the day of Midian.
For all the boots of the tramping warriors
    and all the garments rolled in blood
    shall be burned as fuel for the fire.

For a child has been born for us,
    a son given to us;
authority rests upon his shoulders;
    and he is named
Wonderful Counselor, Mighty God,
    Everlasting Father, Prince of Peace.
His authority shall grow continually,
    and there shall be endless peace
for the throne and dominion of David,
    to establish and uphold it
with justice and with righteousness
    from this time onward and forevermore.

The zeal of the LORD of hosts will do this.

READING II   Titus 2:11—14

The grace of God has appeared, bringing salvation to all, training us to renounce impiety and worldly passions, and in the present age to live lives that are self-controlled, upright, and godly, while we wait for the blessed hope and the manifestation of the glory of our great God and Savior, Jesus Christ.

It is Jesus Christ who gave himself for us to redeem us from all iniquity and purify for himself a people of his own who are zealous for good deeds.

GOSPEL   Luke 2:1—14

In those days a decree went out from Emperor Augustus that all the world should be registered. This was the first registration and was taken while Quirinius was governor of Syria. All went to their own towns to be registered. Joseph also went from the town of Nazareth in Galilee to Judea, to the city of David called Bethlehem, because he was descended from the house and family of David. He went to be registered with Mary, to whom he was engaged and who was expecting a child. While they were there, the time came for her to deliver her child. And she gave birth to her firstborn son and wrapped him in bands of cloth, and laid him in a manger, because there was no place for them in the inn.

In that region there were shepherds living in the fields, keeping watch over their flock by night. Then an angel of the Lord stood before them, and the glory of the Lord shone around them, and they were terrified. But the angel said to them, "Do not be afraid; for see—I am bringing you good news of great joy for all the people: to you is born this day in the city of David a Savior, who is the Messiah, the Lord. This will be a sign for you: you will find a child wrapped in bands of cloth and lying in a manger." And suddenly there was with the angel a multitude of the heavenly host, praising God and saying,

"Glory to God in the highest heaven,
and on earth peace among those
    whom God favors!"

22

Practice of Prayer

Psalm 96:1—2, 2—3, 11—12, 13

O sing a new song to the LORD
sing to the LORD all the earth.
O sing to the LORD, bless his name.

Proclaim God's help day by day,
tell among the nations his glory
and his wonders among all the peoples.

Let the heavens rejoice and earth be glad,
let the sea and all within it thunder praise,
let the land and all it bears rejoice,
all the trees of the wood shout for joy

at the presence of the LORD who comes,
who comes to rule the earth,
comes with justice to rule the world,
and to judge the peoples with truth.

Practice of Temperance

"Is that all?" the children asked, sitting in a mound of torn wrapping paper, ribbons and gift tags. The frenzy of ripping open packages lasted only five minutes and the initial feeling of excitement gave way quickly to disappointment. The next year the parents decided upon a new approach, one that turned into a family tradition. Gifts were opened and admired one at a time while other family members watched. The outcome was much different. Savoring the experience brought joy and a deep sense of gratitude for all that was received.

Temperance is a virtue that urges us to hold back, to practice self-control, to resist the urge to seek immediate gratification. Thankfulness and wonder are often the end result. How can the practice of temperance enliven your own appreciation of Christmas this year?

Scripture Insights

Today's texts recall past deliverance and announce a greater salvation about to be unveiled. Some historical background: Assyria was the brutal imperial power of Isaiah's day, roughly 700 years before Christ. Having overrun the northern kingdom of Israel and carried its ten tribes into captivity, Assyria threatened Jerusalem itself. But because of the promise to David, Isaiah envisioned the birth of a son of David who would save Jerusalem and liberate Israel's captive tribes. Isaiah invokes "the day of Midian," an emotionally powerful phrase recalling the astonishing story in Judges 7, in which God granted Israel victory over the powerful Midianites. After instructing Gideon to reduce his army from thousands to only three hundred, God had the Israelites blow horns, smash jars and wave torches. The Midianites panicked and fled. The lesson was clear: The Lord, not human armies, defeats the chosen people's enemies. This remained a constant Old Testament theme (Psalm 18:18—19; Zechariah 4:6). Isaiah's blockbuster news, "a child has been born for us," meant that God was again about to overthrow Israel's much-feared enemy and lift its heavy burden of oppression.

Jerusalem was saved when Assyria was overthrown. But a new empire arose that carried the people into exile and delayed the promised appearance of the Son of David. Centuries of domination and longing heightened the drama of the Savior's birth. Luke underlined the immense significance of his appearance by placing it within a vast movement of peoples responding to Caesar's tax decree. The angel specifically recalled Isaiah to the shepherds: "to *you* is born this day in the city of David a Savior, who is the Messiah, the Lord."

The letter to Titus links Christ's first and second comings. The Christmas grace of God "appeared" in order to prepare us for the future, second "appearance" of Jesus Christ. Here the two "appearances" reflect a light that shines toward the Lord's future definitive act of salvation.

Compare Isaiah's prophecy, Psalm 96 and the angel's speech to the shepherd. What words and concepts do they share?

READING I   *Genesis 15:1—6, 21:1—3*

Revised Common Lectionary: Isaiah 61:10—62:3

After these things the word of the LORD came to Abram in a vision, "Do not be afraid, Abram, I am your shield; your reward shall be very great." But Abram said, "O Lord GOD, what will you give me, for I continue childless, and the heir of my house is Eliezer of Damascus?" And Abram said, "You have given me no offspring, and so a slave born in my house is to be my heir." But the word of the LORD came to him, "This man shall not be your heir; no one but your very own issue shall be your heir." He brought him outside and said, "Look toward heaven and count the stars, if you are able to count them." Then the Lord said to him, "So shall your descendants be." And Abram believed the LORD; and the LORD reckoned it to him as righteousness. The LORD dealt with Sarah as he had said, and the LORD did for Sarah as he had promised. Sarah conceived and bore Abraham a son in his old age, at the time of which God had spoken to him. Abraham gave the name Isaac to his son whom Sarah bore him.

READING II *Hebrews 11:8, 11—12, 17—19*

Revised Common Lectionary: Galatians 4:4—7

By faith Abraham obeyed when he was called to set out for a place that he was to receive as an inheritance; and he set out, not knowing where he was going. By faith he received power of procreation, even though he was too old—and Sarah herself was barren—because he considered faithful the one who had promised. Therefore from one person, and this one as good as dead, descendants were born, "as many as the stars of heaven and as the innumerable grains of sand by the seashore." By faith Abraham, when put to the test, offered up Isaac. He who had received the promises was ready to offer up his only son, of whom he had been told, "It is through Isaac that descendants shall be named for you." He considered the fact that God is able even to raise someone from the dead—and figuratively speaking, he did receive him back.

GOSPEL   *Luke 2:22—40*

When the time came for their purification according to the law of Moses, Mary and Joseph brought Jesus up to Jerusalem to present him to the Lord (as it is written in the law of the Lord, "Every first-born male shall be designated as holy to the Lord"), and they offered a sacrifice according to what is stated in the law of the Lord, "a pair of turtledoves or two young pigeons."

Now there was a man in Jerusalem whose name was Simeon; this man was righteous and devout, looking forward to the consolation of Israel, and the Holy Spirit rested on him. It had been revealed to him by the Holy Spirit that he would not see death before he had seen the Lord's Messiah. Guided by the Spirit, Simeon came into the temple; and when the parents brought in the child Jesus, to do for him what was customary under the law, Simeon took Jesus in his arms and praised God, saying,

"Lord, now you are dismissing your servant
   in peace, according to your word;
for my eyes have seen your salvation,
   which you have prepared in the presence
      of all peoples,
a light for revelation to the Gentiles and
   for glory to your people Israel."

And the child's father and mother were amazed at what was being said about him.

Then Simeon blessed them and said to his mother Mary, "This child is destined for the falling and the rising of many in Israel, and to be a sign that will be opposed so that the inner thoughts of many will be revealed—and a sword will pierce your own soul too." There was also a prophet, Anna the daughter of Phanuel, of the tribe of Asher. She was of a great age, having lived with her husband seven years after her marriage, then as a widow to the age of eighty-four. She never left the temple but worshiped there with fasting and prayer night and day. At that moment she came, and began to praise God and to speak about the child to all who were looking for the redemption of Jerusalem.

When the parents had finished everything required by the law of the Lord, they returned to Galilee, to their own town of Nazareth. The child grew and became strong, filled with wisdom; and the favor of God was upon him.

Practice of Prayer

Psalm 105:1–2, 3–4, 5–6, 8–9

Give thanks, and acclaim God's name,
make known God's deeds among the peoples.

O sing to the LORD, sing praise;
tell all his wonderful works!
Be proud of God's holy name,
let the hearts that seek the LORD rejoice.

Consider the LORD, who is strong;
constantly seek his face.
Remember the wonders of the LORD,
the miracles and judgements pronounced.

O children of Abraham, God's servant,
O children of Jacob the chosen,

God remember the covenant for ever,
the promise for a thousand generations,
the covenant made with Abraham,
the oath that was sworn to Isaac.

Practice of Fortitude

The Holy Family is often held up as a model of unity and fidelity. We know that Jesus was tempted—in both a garden and a desert—to turn away from his mission. What about Joseph, dogged by strange dreams and plagued by worry over leading his family to safety? Must he not have been enticed to take another, easier path? Mary, too, might have had days in which her "yes" to God felt way too impulsive and overeager. Somehow they found the fortitude to remain faithful to their individual and collective responsibilities.

Scripture Insights

"The word of the Lord (*dabar Yahweh*) came to Abram in a vision." The Bible never explains the mechanics of God's communication with the patriarchs, matriarchs, prophets and apostles. But God's word was a vivid reality to its hearers, and it caused them to act decisively, even if to outsiders that obedience appeared strange or even insane.

Abraham and Sarah set out to receive an unseen inheritance, sure of nothing except the word that had burned itself into their souls. They went out, not knowing where they were going, *dabar Yahweh* prompting them in vague but unmistakable ways. Most translations of Hebrews 11:11 say that Abraham received the power to father Isaac by faith. Some manuscripts, followed by the New Jerusalem Bible, say that it was Sarah who received this word: "It was equally by faith that Sarah, in spite of being past the age, was made able to conceive, because she believed that he who had made the promise was faithful to it." Whether or not this is the original reading, her pregnancy shows that Sarah shared Abraham's habit of trusting the word of the Lord.

Venerable Simeon and Anna represent Old Testament piety at its best, very much like Abraham and Sarah. Their hidden source of life was their expectant trust in the word given by the Lord. Simeon was "looking forward to the consolation of Israel" (2:25); Anna was counted among those "looking for the redemption of Jerusalem" (2:38). From long experience they knew and lived *dabar Yahweh* and its prophetic fulfillment as if it already existed. Because they loved and lived it, they sensed its near approach and instantly recognized the reality when it arrived.

Consider any of the special characters in Mark's gospel who also sense the reality of the word: the woman with the issue of blood (5:25–34), the Syro-Phoenician woman of faith (7:24–30), blind Bartimaeus (10:46–52), the wise scribe (12:28–34) or the widow with the penny offering (12:41–43). What do they have in common with Anna and Simeon?

January 5, 2003

READING I   *Isaiah 60:1—6*

Revised Common Lectionary: Jeremiah 31:7–14

Arise, shine; for your light has come,
    and the glory of the LORD has risen upon you.
For darkness shall cover the earth,
    and thick darkness the peoples;
but the LORD will arise upon you,
    and the glory of the LORD will appear over you.
Nations shall come to your light,
    and rulers to the brightness of your dawn.

Lift up your eyes and look around;
    they all gather together, they come to you;
your sons shall come from far away,
    and your daughters shall be carried
        on their nurses' arms.

Then you shall see and be radiant;
    your heart shall thrill and rejoice,
because the abundance of the sea shall be
        brought to you,
    the wealth of the nations shall come to you.
A multitude of camels shall cover you,
    the young camels of Midian and Ephah;
    all those from Sheba shall come.
They shall bring gold and frankincense,
    and shall proclaim the praise of the LORD.

READING II   *Ephesians 3:2—3a, 5—6*

Revised Common Lectionary: Ephesians 1:3–14

Surely you have already heard of the commission of God's grace that was given me for you, and how the mystery was made known to me by revelation.

In former generations this mystery was not made known to humankind, as it has now been revealed to his holy apostles and prophets by the Spirit: that is, the Gentiles have become fellow heirs with us, members of the same body, and sharers in the promise in Christ Jesus through the gospel.

GOSPEL   *Matthew 2:1—12*

Revised Common Lectionary: John 1:[1–9,] 10–18

In the time of King Herod, after Jesus was born in Bethlehem of Judea, magi from the East came to Jerusalem, asking, "Where is the child who has been born king of the Jews? For we observed his star at its rising, and have come to pay him homage."

When King Herod heard this, he was frightened, and all Jerusalem with him; and calling together all the chief priests and scribes of the people, he inquired of them where the Messiah was to be born. They told him, "In Bethlehem of Judea; for so it has been written by the prophet:

'And you, Bethlehem, in the land of Judah,
    are by no means least among the rulers
      of Judah;
for from you shall come a ruler
    who is to shepherd my people Israel.'"

Then Herod secretly called for the magi and learned from them the exact time when the star had appeared. Then he sent them to Bethlehem, saying, "Go and search diligently for the child; and when you have found him, bring me word so that I may also go and pay him homage."

When they had heard the king, they set out; and there, ahead of them, went the star that they had seen at its rising, until it stopped over the place where the child was. When they saw that the star had stopped, they were overwhelmed with joy.

On entering the house, they saw the child with Mary his mother; and they knelt down and paid him homage. Then, opening their treasure chests, they offered him gifts of gold, frankincense, and myrrh.

And having been warned in a dream not to return to Herod, they left for their own country by another road.

Practice of Prayer

Psalm 72:1—2, 7—8, 10—11, 12—13

O God, give your judgment to the king,
to a king's son your justice,
that he may judge your people in justice
and your poor in right judgment.

In his days justice shall flourish
and peace till the moon fails.
He shall rule from sea to sea,
from the Great River to the earth's bounds.

The kings of Tarshish and the seacoasts
shall pay him tribute.

The kings of Sheba and Seba
shall bring him gifts.
Before him all rulers shall fall prostrate,
all nations shall serve him.

For he shall save the poor when they cry
and the needy who are helpless.
He will have pity on the weak
and save the lives of the poor.

Practice of Prudence

In their eagerness to find the child Jesus, the magi could have wrecked everything. Wily Herod almost convinced them of his sincerity in wanting to "pay homage" to the infant Messiah. Cautioned in a dream, they headed home in a different direction, but not before Herod set in motion his vicious plan of infanticide.

It's a disturbing story, one with a powerful message about the need for prudence when divulging information to those who might be untrustworthy. Even our own epiphanies—our glimpses of the Divine—might need to be held in reserve as we discern how and with whom they should be shared. We might also be more discriminating when choosing what to read and whom to heed. Our "say anything" society gives us access to unlimited amounts of unfiltered gossip, opinion, conjecture and judgment.

What intake or outgo of information needs your prudent attention this week?

Scripture Insights

The anonymous disciple of Isaiah wrote just after the exile, when the prophet spoke to the shrinking hope of those who had returned to the desolate land. To them he proclaimed a lyrical vision of Jerusalem's future splendor. The opulence pictured is less striking than who it is that bears it: It is a long column of Gentiles lined up to do homage in Jerusalem. The image reflects Yahweh's glory and recalls Isaiah's prophecy that many nations will one day stream to Mount Zion to learn God's ways (Isaiah 2:1—4).

Casual readers of Matthew's gospel might focus on the exotic visitors from the east, or on Herod's anger against them. But in Matthew's gospel the appearance of the Magi represents an almost liturgical introduction of the Gentiles into the court of the Messiah-King. This is the message of today's three readings as well as the psalm.

It is difficult to overstate the complexity and importance of the question that faced the first generation of Christians, virtually all of whom were Jews. Must Gentiles become Jews in order to become Christians? A strong conservative group on one side said Yes, this was the way of salvation revealed to Moses. A more liberal group said No, Jesus offered salvation freely to everyone who responded to him, even to Gentiles.

Matthew seems to represent a middle group that insists on the integrity of Torah and includes the Gentiles by the mercy of God. In his gospel, on the one hand, Jesus insists that "not one letter, not one stroke of a letter, will pass from the law until all is accomplished" (5:18). But on the other hand, "many will come from east and west and will eat with Abraham and Isaac and Jacob in the kingdom of heaven, while the heirs of the kingdom will be thrown into the outer darkness" (8:11).

The writer of Ephesians echoes Paul's preaching of the great mystery that was made known to him by revelation: the inclusion of the Gentiles in the people of God.

What is Jesus' attitude toward the Gentiles in Mark 7:24—30?

Reading I   Isaiah 55:1—11

Revised Common Lectionary: Genesis 1:1—5

Ho, everyone who thirsts,
    come to the waters;
and you that have no money,
    come, buy and eat!
Come, buy wine and milk
    without money and without price.
Why do you spend your money for that
        which is not bread,
    and your labor for that which does not satisfy?
Listen carefully to me, and eat what is good,
    and delight yourselves in rich food.

Incline your ear, and come to me;
    listen, so that you may live.
I will make with you an everlasting covenant,
    my steadfast, sure love for David.
See, I made him a witness to the peoples,
    a leader and commander for the peoples.
See, you shall call nations that you do not know,
    and nations that do not know you
        shall run to you,
because of the LORD your God,
        the Holy One of Israel,
    for the LORD has glorified you.

Seek the LORD while the LORD may be found,
    call upon God while God is near;
let the wicked forsake their way,
    and the unrighteous their thoughts;
let them return to the LORD, who will have mercy
        on them,
    and to our God, who will abundantly pardon.
For my thoughts are not your thoughts,
    nor are your ways my ways, says the LORD.
For as the heavens are higher than the earth,
    so are my ways higher than your ways
    and my thoughts than your thoughts.

For as the rain and the snow come down
        from heaven,
    and do not return there until they have
        watered the earth,
making it bring forth and sprout,
    giving seed to the sower and bread to the eater,

so shall my word be that goes out from my mouth;
    it shall not return to me empty,
but it shall accomplish that which I purpose,
    and succeed in the thing for which I sent it.

Reading II   1 John 5:1— 9

Revised Common Lectionary: Ephesians 1:3—14

Everyone who believes that Jesus is the Christ has been born of God, and everyone who loves the parent loves the child. By this we know that we love the children of God, when we love God and obey his commandments. For the love of God is this, that we obey the commandments, which are not burdensome, for whatever is born of God conquers the world. And this is the victory that conquers the world, our faith. Who is it that conquers the world but the one who believes that Jesus is the Son of God? This is the one who came by water and the blood. And the Spirit is the one that testifies, for the Spirit is the truth. There are three that testify: the Spirit and the water and the blood, and these three agree. If we receive human testimony, the testimony of God is greater; for this is the testimony of God that he has testified to his Son.

Gospel   Mark 1:7—11

Revised Common Lectionary: Mark 1:4—11

John the baptizer proclaimed, "After me the one who is more powerful than I is coming, the thong of whose sandals I am not worthy to stoop down and untie. I have baptized you with water; but the one who is coming will baptize you with the Holy Spirit."

In those days Jesus came from Nazareth of Galilee and was baptized by John in the Jordan. And just as Jesus was coming up out of the water, he saw the heavens torn apart and the Spirit descending like a dove on him. And a voice came from heaven, "You are my Son, the Beloved; with you I am well pleased."

Practice of Prayer

Isaiah 12:2—3, 4bcd, 5—6

Surely God is my salvation;
   I will trust, and will not be afraid,
for the Lord God is my strength and my might;
   he has become my salvation.
With joy you will draw water from the wells
    of salvation.
Give thanks to the Lord,
   call on his name;
make known his deeds among the nations;
   proclaim that his name is exalted.

Sing praises to the Lord, for he has done
    gloriously;
   let this be known in all the earth.
Shout aloud and sing for joy,
   O royal Zion,
for great in your midst is the
   Holy One of Israel.

Practice of Fortitude

It is powerful to watch as someone baptized by immersion emerges from the water soaking wet and gasping for air. The catechumenate is an immersion process, plunging catechumens into the life of the church through practice, observation and investigation into its most precious stories, rituals and traditions. More than an excursion of the mind, it is a journey into the heart. This would all be daunting if it weren't for the community poised to lift and support these people as they sink into and rise up from the waters of faith. Listen carefully to the blessing offered for the catechumens who are dismissed from Mass each week. It speaks of the need for encouragement and strengthening as they make their way toward full communion with the church. How are you modeling and sharing fortitude with them?

Scipture Insights

The verses from Isaiah culminate the poetic proclamation of the prophet who preached about 550 years before the birth of Christ, in the dark days after Jerusalem's destruction and the exile to Babylon.

The prophet announces that these events were not the end; they were an astonishing new beginning in the story of salvation. "I am about to do a new thing!" declares the Lord (43:19). This prophet revels in the riches of a new version of the Davidic covenant. As David's royal line was lost during the exile, the prophet announced that the spectacular "sure love for David" was now the property of the entire people of God. He imitated the vendors' cries in the marketplace of Babylon as they sold necessities like water and bread, and luxuries like wine and milk. But this vendor was offering—for free—the blessings of the God of Israel!

Five hundred years later, a man like the ancient prophets came proclaiming God's impending judgment. John preached that his baptism would prepare people for God's rending of the heavens to mete out justice. But his word was fulfilled in a way he did not expect. The one mightier than John did indeed appear when he "was baptized by John in the Jordan." The heavens were indeed "torn apart": Mark's use of the Greek word *schizo*, "splitting," carries a threatening, apocalyptic image of judgment (Mark 1:10). But what emerged from the opening in the heavens was a dove, the Spirit of God in the form of the ancient symbol of God's peace following divine judgment (Genesis 8:8–12). The gospel changed the template of salvation: Now salvation is offered *before* rather than *after* judgment. This remarkable change marks the "beginning of the good news of Jesus Christ, the Son of God" (1:1).

". . . by water and the blood" (1 John 5:6) links Jesus' baptism with his death. Jesus himself likened his death to a baptism (Mark 10:38–39). How is death like a baptism?

COME·OUT OF·HIM!

Preparation for the Word

In these days, dear God,
when we have left behind the mysteries
of the Christmas season
and Lent is not yet upon us,
we read the early pages
of Matthew, Mark and Luke,
and Sunday after Sunday we listen
to a letter Paul wrote to the church at Corinth.

Bring us to these words as those Corinthians
    must have come:
with great curiosity,
anticipating affection but ready for reprimand,
ever at risk until we are ready to be counted
with the foolish, the weak, the despised
    of the world.
Then, O God, shall we ourselves be a letter
    to the world,
written not in ink but by your own Spirit.
This we ask in Jesus' name who is Lord
    for ever and ever. Amen.

Thanksgiving for the Word

We give you thanks and praise, O God,
for the times and ways your word comes to us:
in stories of ancestors' adventures,
in details of the covenant
and books of wisdom sayings,
in the psalms and all the holy songs,
in prophets speaking truth to authority,
in lamentation and in love songs,
in letters and at last in gospels.

May these scriptures be our shelter
and our summons,
our home and our going out from home.
We make our prayer in Jesus' name
who is Lord for ever and ever. Amen.

Weekday Readings

January 13: *Hebrews 1:1–6; Mark 1:14–20*
January 14: *Hebrews 2:5–12; Mark 1:21b-28*
January 15: *Hebrews 2:14–18; Mark 1:29–39*
January 16: *Hebrews 3:7–14; Mark 1:40–45*
January 17: *Hebrews 4:1–5, 11; Mark 2:1–12*
January 18: *Hebrews 4:12–16; Mark 2:13–17*

January 20: *Hebrews 5:1–10; Mark 2: 18–22*
January 21: *Hebrews 6:10–20; Mark 2:23–28*
January 22: *Hebrews 7:1–3; 15–17; Mark 3:1–6*
January 23: *Hebrews 7:25–8:6; Mark 3:7–12*
January 24: *Hebrews 8:6–13; Mark 3:13–19*
January 25: Feast of the Conversion of Saint Paul,
   Acts 22:3–16; Mark 16:15–18

January 27: *Hebrews 9:15, 24–28; Mark 3:22–30*
January 28: *Hebrews 10:1–10; Mark 3:31–35*
January 29: *Hebrews 10:11–18; Mark 4:1–20*
January 30: *Hebrews 10:19–25; Mark 4:21–25*
January 31: *Hebrews 10:32–39; Mark 4:26–34*
February 1: *Hebrews 11:1–2, 8–19; Mark 4:35–41*

February 3: *Hebrews 11:32–40; Mark 5:1–20*
February 4: *Hebrews 12:1–4; Mark 5:21–43*
February 5: *Hebrews 12:4–7, 11–15; Mark 6:1–6*
February 6: *Hebrews 12:18–19; 21–24; Mark 6:7–13*
February 7: *Hebrews 13:1–8; Mark 6:14–29*
February 8: *Hebrews 13:15–17, 20–21; Mark 6:30–34*

February 10: *Genesis 1:1–19; Mark 6:53–56*
February 11: *Genesis 1:20–2:4a; Mark 7:1–13*
February 12: *Genesis 2:4b–9, 15–17; Mark 7:14–23*
February 13: *Genesis 2:18–25; Mark 7:24–30*
February 14: *Genesis 3:1–8; Mark 7:31–37*
February 15: *Genesis 3:9–24; Mark 8:1–10*

February 17: *Genesis 4:1–15, 25; Mark 8:11–13*
February 18: *Genesis 6:5–8; 7:1–5, 10; Mark 8:14–21*
February 19: *Genesis 8:6–13, 20–22; Mark 8:22–26*
February 20: *Genesis 9:1–15; Mark 8:27–33*
February 21: *Genesis 11:1–9; Mark 8:34–9:1*
February 22: Feast of the Chair of Saint Peter
   1 Peter 5:1–4; Matthew 16:13–19

February 24: *Sirach 1:1–10; Mark 9:14–29*
February 25: *Sirach 2:1–11; Mark 9:30–37*
February 26: *Sirach 4:11–19; Mark 9:38–40*
February 27: *Sirach 5:1–8; Mark 9:41–50*
February 28: *Sirach 6:5–17; Mark 10:1–12*
March 1: *Sirach 17:1–15; Mark 10:13–16*

March 3: *Sirach 17:19–27; Mark 10:17–27*
March 4: *Sirach 35:1–12; Mark 10:28–31*

January 19, 2003

READING I   1 Samuel 3:3b—10, 19

Revised Common Lectionary: 1 Samuel 3:1–10, [11–20]

Samuel was lying down in the temple of the LORD, where the ark of God was. Then the LORD called, "Samuel! Samuel!" and he said, "Here I am!" and ran to Eli, and said, "Here I am, for you called me." But Eli said, "I did not call; lie down again." So Samuel went and lay down.

The LORD called again, "Samuel!" Samuel got up and went to Eli, and said, "Here I am, for you called me." But Eli said, "I did not call, my son; lie down again." Now Samuel did not yet know the LORD, and the word of the LORD had not yet been revealed to him.

The LORD called Samuel again, a third time. And he got up and went to Eli, and said, "Here I am, for you called me." Then Eli perceived that the LORD was calling the boy. Therefore Eli said to Samuel, "Go, lie down; and if the LORD calls you, you shall say, 'Speak, LORD, for your servant is listening.'" So Samuel went and lay down in his place.

Now the LORD came and stood there, calling as before, "Samuel! Samuel!" And Samuel said, "Speak, for your servant is listening."

As Samuel grew up, the LORD was with him and let none of his words fall to the ground.

READING II   1 Corinthians 6:13c-15a, 17—20

Revised Common Lectionary: 1 Corinthians 6:12–20

The body is meant not for fornication but for the Lord, and the Lord for the body. And God raised the Lord and will also raise us up by divine power.

Do you not know that your bodies are parts of the body of Christ? But anyone united to the Lord becomes one spirit with the Lord. Shun fornication! Every sin that a person commits is outside the body; but the fornicator sins against the body itself. Or do you not know that your body is a temple of the Holy Spirit within you, which you have from God, and that you are not your own? For you were bought with a price; therefore glorify God in your body.

GOSPEL   John 1:35—51

Roman Catholic: John 1:35–42
Revised Common Lectionary: John 1:43–51

The next day John again was standing with two of his disciples, and as he watched Jesus walk by, he exclaimed, "Look, here is the Lamb of God!" The two disciples heard him say this, and they followed Jesus. When Jesus turned and saw them following, he said to them, "What are you looking for?" They said to him, "Rabbi" (which translated means Teacher), "where are you staying?" He said to them, "Come and see." They came and saw where he was staying, and they remained with him that day. It was about four o'clock in the afternoon. One of the two who heard John speak and followed him was Andrew, Simon Peter's brother. He first found his brother Simon and said to him, "We have found the Messiah" (which is translated Anointed). He brought Simon to Jesus, who looked at him and said, "You are Simon son of John. You are to be called Cephas" (which is translated Peter).

The next day Jesus decided to go to Galilee. He found Philip and said to him, "Follow me." Now Philip was from Bethsaida, the city of Andrew and Peter. Philip found Nathanael and said to him, "We have found the one about whom Moses in the law and also the prophets wrote, Jesus son of Joseph from Nazareth." Nathanael said to Philip, "Can anything good come out of Nazareth?" Philip said to him, "Come and see."

When Jesus saw Nathanael coming toward him, he said of him, "Here is truly an Israelite in whom there is no deceit!" Nathanael asked Jesus, "Where did you get to know me?" Jesus answered, "I saw you under the fig tree before Philip called you." Nathanael replied, "Rabbi, you are the Son of God! You are the King of Israel!" Jesus answered, "Do you believe because I told you that I saw you under the fig tree? You will see greater things than these." And Jesus said to him, "Very truly, I tell you, you will see heaven opened and the angels of God ascending and descending upon the Son-of-Man."

Practice of Prayer

Psalm 40:2, 4, 7–8, 8–9, 10

I waited, I waited for the LORD
who stooped down to me,
and heard my cry.

God put a new song into my mouth,
praise of our God.
Many shall see and fear
and shall trust in the LORD.

You do not ask for sacrifice and offerings,
but an open ear.
You do not ask for holocaust and victim.
Instead, here am I.

In the scroll of the book it stands written
that I should do your will.
My God, I delight in your law
in the depth of my heart.

Your justice I have proclaimed
in the great assembly.
My lips I have not sealed;
you know it, O LORD.

Practice of Prudence

Being labeled a "prude" is not something most of us aspire to. It connotes, for young and old alike, someone who is uptight, overly proper and puritanical. Prudes have no freedom or joy. An unreflective reader might see in today's second reading, with its reference to the body as a temple of the Holy Spirit, a prudish attitude. But a more attentive study of this passage reveals what prudence is really about: discerning what's truly beneficial for us and refusing to be dominated by anything. Prudent people can indeed know freedom and joy.

Young people are particularly susceptible to the damage caused by labels and the pressure to conform. This week, consider how you might be a positive role model of prudence to the young people you know. It may not eradicate the term "prude," but it might shine some clearer light upon it.

Scripture Insights

As with many of John's images (light and dark, spirit and flesh), looking and seeing have a deeper meaning than ordinary usage would suggest. One has only to think of the story of the man born blind (John 9:1–41) to know that "seeing" someone implies understanding who they really are, especially in Jesus' interactions. Here in the beginning of the section of John's gospel known as the "Book of Signs" (John 1:19–12:50), the call of the first disciples challenges both the disciples in the story and the readers to see who Jesus really is and interpret properly the signs that he does.

John the Baptist points to Jesus, saying, "Look, here is the Lamb of God." He calls attention to the true nature of Jesus in the world by inviting his listeners to see him as the Passover lamb whose blood saved the Israelites from the death of the first-born in Egypt and as the lamb ritually slaughtered as an offering for sin (see Isaiah 53:7, 10). It is up to the would-be disciples to see that nature for themselves. Jesus probes their search for truth by asking: "What are you looking for?" Their response indicates their desire to follow him, and Jesus then invites them to see where he is staying. As with seeing the true nature of Jesus, seeing the place where he stays means more than we think. When Andrew and the other man see where Jesus stays, it becomes their place as well, and they leave John for the new teacher.

It is not only the disciples who look intently to discern their teacher's true nature. Jesus himself looks into Simon, Andrew's brother, and sees his deepest self, renaming him Cephas (rock), Aramaic for Peter. Peter's new name signifies his new identity and bond with the Son of God. Later Jesus astonishes Nathanael with what he knows of his character from seeing him under the fig tree. John will continue to use seeing as a code word for understanding and believing in Jesus. Those who see rightly will believe that Jesus is the one to come.

The invitation to come and see applies to our lives as well. Where might you see Jesus staying today? What does following him as a disciple mean for us?

January 26, 2003

READING I   *Jonah 3:1—5, 10*

The word of the LORD came to Jonah a second time, saying, "Get up, go to Nineveh, that great city, and proclaim to it the message that I tell you." So Jonah set out and went to Nineveh, according to the word of the LORD. Now Nineveh was an exceedingly large city, a three days' walk across. Jonah began to go into the city, going a day's walk. And he cried out, "Forty days more, and Nineveh shall be overthrown!" And the people of Nineveh believed God; they proclaimed a fast, and everyone, great and small, put on sackcloth.

When God saw what they did, how they turned from their evil ways, God had second thoughts about the calamity that God had said would be done to them; and God did not do it.

READING II   *1 Corinthians 7:29—31*

Brothers and sisters, the appointed time has grown short; from now on, let even those who are married be as though they were not, and those who mourn as though they were not mourning, and those who rejoice as though they were not rejoicing, and those who buy as though they had no possessions, and those who deal with the world as though they had no dealings with it. For the present form of this world is passing away.

GOSPEL   *Mark 1:14—20*

Now after John was arrested, Jesus came to Galilee, proclaiming the good news of God, and saying, "The time is fulfilled, and the dominion of God has come near; repent, and believe in the good news."

As Jesus passed along the Sea of Galilee, he saw Simon and his brother Andrew casting a net into the sea— for they were fishermen. And Jesus said to them, "Follow me and I will make you fish for human beings." And immediately they left their nets and followed him. As Jesus went a little farther, he saw James son of Zebedee and his brother John, who were in their boat mending the nets. Immediately Jesus called them; and they left their father Zebedee in the boat with the hired men, and followed him.

Practice of Prayer

Psalm 25:4—5, 6—7, 8—9

LORD, make me know your ways.
LORD, teach me your paths.
Make me walk in your truth, and teach me,
for you are God my savior.

Remember your mercy, LORD,
and the love you have shown from of old.
Do not remember the sins of my youth.
In your love remember me.

The LORD is good and upright,
showing the path to those who stray,
guiding the humble in the right path,
and teaching the way to the poor.

Practice of Prudence

"Gone fishing." The expression brings to mind the Huck Finns of the world, those who look for opportunities to dodge work and responsibility, if only for an afternoon.

But Jesus' familiar "fishing" call was not an invitation away from commitment, engagement and attachment; it was just the opposite. Looking back, the disciples probably saw their responses as quite impulsive. Certainly Zebedee, left behind in the boat, must have thought so.

Prudence can likewise be exercised in different ways. While prudence often calls for long, slow and painstaking discernment, it can also occur in bursts of conviction like the disciples'—in a sudden recognition of where we are to go and whom we are to follow.

Is there a decision you are considering for which, at heart, you already have the answer? If so, follow the instincts of the disciples and step out of whatever boat you're in.

Scripture Insights

Written in the period after the exile to Babylon, the book of Jonah is a prophecy to the Jews returning home. Ancient prophecies were intended to call God's people back to faithfulness. They often contained indictments of neighboring powers that defied God by conquering God's people. So it is not unusual that Jonah would be directed to pronounce doom on Nineveh, capital of Assyria. That nation had conquered the northern kingdom of Israel in an earlier period of Israel's history—722 years before the birth of Christ.

The book of Jonah is unusual, however, because the Ninevites believe Jonah immediately and repent. No prophet to the Jews had such instantaneous success. Isaiah was warned that the people won't believe (Isaiah 6:8–10); Jeremiah was thrown into a cistern (Jeremiah 38); Ezekiel found the Israelites rebellious (Ezekiel 3:27). But the Ninevites change their ways. More astounding—God repents of the punishment that was intended.

This had happened before, but rarely (Exodus 32:18 is a notable example). It had never happened with non-Jews and sworn enemies of Israel. If we read further, we find that Jonah becomes very angry with God for this.

How does this story prophesy to Jews after the exile and bring them back to faithfulness? How does it prophesy to us? The story of Jonah speaks eloquently to the constancy of God as one who is "slow to anger and abounding in steadfast love and faithfulness" (Exodus 34:6; Jonah 4:2). It also draws on a theology of creation that understands God as Lord of all. Whoever turns to God is gathered in love. Finally, the story cautions against putting boundaries on God's care and concern. Israel cannot claim God exclusively for itself. No nation can. Jonah's story suggests that if God cares for the enemies of Israel so much, then God will care for Israel that much more. (Matthew 6:26 makes a similar point.) The prophecy of Jonah teaches that God is not bound by human notions of judgment and justice and that we do not have exclusive rights to God's mercy and love.

How do we counteract the idea that we are more favored by God than others?

READING I *Malachi 3:1—4*

See, I am sending my messenger to prepare the way before me, and the LORD whom you seek will suddenly come to the temple. Indeed, the messenger of the covenant in whom you delight is coming, says the LORD of hosts. But who can endure the day of his coming, and who can stand when he appears?

For he is like a refiner's fire and like fullers' soap; he will sit as a refiner and purifier of silver, and will purify the descendants of Levi and refine them like gold and silver, until they present offerings to the LORD in righteousness. Then the offering of Judah and Jerusalem will be pleasing to the LORD as in the days of old and as in former years.

READING II *Hebrews 2:14—18*

Since, therefore, the children share flesh and blood, Jesus himself likewise shared the same things, so that through death he might destroy the one who has the power of death, that is, the devil, and free those who all their lives were held in slavery by the fear of death.

For it is clear that Jesus did not come to help angels, but the descendants of Abraham. Therefore Jesus had to become like his brothers and sisters in every respect, so that he might be a merciful and faithful high priest in the service of God, to make a sacrifice of atonement for the sins of the people. Because Jesus himself was tested by what he suffered, he is able to help those who are being tested.

GOSPEL *Luke 2:22—40*

When the time came for their purification according to the law of Moses, Mary and Joseph brought Jesus up to Jerusalem to present him to the Lord (as it is written in the law of the Lord, "Every first-born male shall be designated as holy to the Lord"), and they offered a sacrifice according to what is stated in the law of the Lord, "a pair of turtledoves or two young pigeons."

Now there was a man in Jerusalem whose name was Simeon; this man was righteous and devout, looking forward to the consolation of Israel, and the Holy Spirit rested on him. It had been revealed to him by the Holy Spirit that he would not see death before he had seen the Lord's Messiah. Guided by the Spirit, Simeon came into the temple; and when the parents brought in the child Jesus, to do for him what was customary under the law, Simeon took Jesus in his arms and praised God, saying,

"Lord, now you are dismissing your servant
    in peace,
  according to your word;
for my eyes have seen your salvation,
  which you have prepared in the presence
    of all peoples,
a light for revelation to the Gentiles
  and for glory to your people Israel."

And the child's father and mother were amazed at what was being said about him. Then Simeon blessed them and said to his mother Mary, "This child is destined for the falling and the rising of many in Israel, and to be a sign that will be opposed so that the inner thoughts of many will be revealed— and a sword will pierce your own soul too."

There was also a prophet, Anna the daughter of Phanuel, of the tribe of Asher. She was of a great age, having lived with her husband seven years after her marriage, then as a widow to the age of eighty-four. She never left the temple but worshiped there with fasting and prayer night and day. At that moment she came, and began to praise God and to speak about the child to all who were looking for the redemption of Jerusalem.

When the parents had finished everything required by the law of the Lord, they returned to Galilee, to their own town of Nazareth. The child grew and became strong, filled with wisdom; and the favor of God was upon him.

Practice of Prayer

Psalm 24:7, 8, 9, 10

O gates, lift high your heads;
grow higher, ancient doors.
Let the king of glory enter!

Who is the king of glory?
The LORD, the mighty, the valiant,
the LORD, the valiant in war.

O gates, lift high your heads;
grow higher, ancient doors.
Let the king of glory enter!

Who is the king of glory?
The LORD of heavenly armies.
This is the king of glory.

Practice of Justice

The Feast of the Presentation of the Lord has also been celebrated as Candlemas. It is traditionally a day to bless candles, symbols of the light of Christ in a dark world.

Candles are often lit during vigils or other ceremonies that memorialize victims of violence and suffering, as well as those who have died in their pursuit of justice. Just as the light of a single candle pierces even the deepest gloom, so does the life of a courageous and committed soul invigorate the rest of us with inspiration and purpose.

Light two candles today. Let one witness to those around the world who are denied their basic human rights. Let the other commemorate those who have sacrificed for justice.

Scripture Insights

Malachi's prophecy tells of a messenger who is like fire purifying the world, preparing it for the coming of the Lord. This description fits the preaching of John the Baptist, who appears in the gospels calling Israel to repent. Because Malachi names Elijah as the messenger at the end of his prophecy (Malachi 3:23), the New Testament writers take care to identify John as Elijah who has returned to prepare the way. John's clothes and diet are like those of Elijah in the first Book of Kings.

There was little in the prophets or in John's preaching, however, to prepare Israel for the tiny child who made his first public appearance in the Temple for the purification rite prescribed by the law. Jewish custom considered a woman who bore a child to be unclean. A mother of a son spent forty days being purified of her blood (Leviticus 12:1–5), then presented an offering in the Temple. Only Luke's gospel relates this story, commemorated in today's feast. This feast of the Presentation was once called the feast of the Purification of Mary. A second command (which Luke mentions in 2:23) says that the first-born male shall be dedicated to the Lord. Since the earlier form of this law in Exodus 13 does not specify any sacrifice, it seems likely that Luke combined the two laws in his telling.

What is remarkable in this story is the reaction of two old wise people. When they look at the child, they see the salvation of Israel, the Messiah who has come to redeem the world. Simeon confidently describes the child's destiny and the joy and sorrow that Mary will feel. Anna bursts into proclamation about the child to anyone who will listen. Most Jews believed that the Messiah would be a great warrior, bringing God's justice and righteousness to a sinful nation. Even the preaching of John the Baptist pointed to someone greater than he. Could this infant really be the promised one? The epistle to the Hebrews answers the unspoken question. In order to save humankind Jesus had to be human.

"Refiner's fire" is a strong metaphor for the messenger. What does a refiner's fire do? What does that mean when applied to us?

February 2, 2003

FOURTH SUNDAY AFTER THE EPIPHANY

READING I   *Deuteronomy 18:15—20*

The LORD your God will raise up for you a prophet like me from among your own people; you shall heed such a prophet. This is what you requested of the LORD your God at Horeb on the day of the assembly when you said: "If I hear the voice of the LORD my God any more, or ever again see this great fire, I will die." Then the LORD replied to me: "They are right in what they have said. I will raise up for them a prophet like you from among their own people; I will put my words in the mouth of the prophet, who shall speak to them everything that I command. Anyone who does not heed the words that the prophet shall speak in my name, I myself will hold accountable. But any prophet who speaks in the name of other gods, or who presumes to speak in my name a word that I have not commanded the prophet to speak—that prophet shall die."

READING II   *1 Corinthians 8:1—13*

Now concerning food sacrificed to idols: we know that "all of us possess knowledge." Knowledge puffs up, but love builds up. Anyone who claims to know something does not yet have the necessary knowledge; but anyone who loves God is known by God.

Hence, as to the eating of food offered to idols, we know that "no idol in the world really exists," and that "there is no God but one." Indeed, even though there may be so-called deities in heaven or on earth—as in fact there are many deities and many lords—yet for us there is one God, the Father, from whom are all things and for whom we exist, and one Lord, Jesus Christ, through whom are all things and through whom we exist.

It is not everyone, however, who has this knowledge. Since some have become so accustomed to idols until now, they still think of the food they eat as food offered to an idol; and their conscience, being weak, is defiled. "Food will not bring us close to God." We are no worse off if we do not eat, and no better off if we do. But take care that this liberty of yours does not somehow become a stumbling block to the weak. For if others see you, who possess knowledge, eating in the temple of an idol, might they not, since their conscience is weak, be encouraged to the point of eating food sacrificed to idols? So by your knowledge those weak believers for whom Christ died are destroyed. But when you thus sin against brothers and sisters in your community, and wound their conscience when it is weak, you sin against Christ. Therefore, if food is a cause of their falling, I will never eat meat, so that I may not cause one of them to fall.

GOSPEL   *Mark 1:21—28*

Jesus and his disciples went to Capernaum; and when the sabbath came, he entered the synagogue and taught. They were astounded at his teaching, for he taught them as one having authority, and not as the scribes.

Just then there was in their synagogue a man with an unclean spirit, and he cried out, "What have you to do with us, Jesus of Nazareth? Have you come to destroy us? I know who you are, the Holy One of God." But Jesus rebuked the spirit, saying, "Be silent, and come out of him!" And the unclean spirit, convulsing him and crying with a loud voice, came out of the man. They were all amazed, and they kept on asking one another, "What is this? A new teaching—with authority! He commands even the unclean spirits, and they obey him."

At once his fame began to spread throughout the surrounding region of Galilee.

Practice of Prayer

Psalm 111

I will thank the LORD with all my heart
in the meeting of the just and their assembly.
Great are the works of the LORD,
to be pondered by all who love them.

Majestic and glorious God's work,
whose justice stands firm for ever.
God makes us remember these wonders.
The LORD is compassion and love.

God gives food to those who fear him;
keeps his covenant ever in mind;
shows mighty works to his people
by giving them the land of the nations.

God's works are justice and truth,
God's precepts are all of them sure,
standing firm for ever and ever;
they are made in uprightness and truth.

God has sent deliverance to his people
and established his covenant for ever.
Holy is God's name, to be feared.

To fear the LORD is the first stage of wisdom;
all who do so prove themselves wise.
God's praise shall last for ever!

Practice of Fortitude

Upon his death, Dag Hammerskjöld left behind his diary and a note to a friend giving permission to have it published. It was a surprising document on many levels. The Secretary General of the United Nations made no reference to his distinguished career as a civil servant and world leader. The writings, published in English under the title *Markings,* contain descriptions of his despair over his own failings and his struggle to lay aside his ego in order to act as an instrument of God.

His spiritual struggle has been a source of inspiration to those who also wrestle with the cost of discipleship. Dealing with external forces or internal demons requires surrender to the One who can truly fortify us.

Scripture Insights

In Mark, Jesus' first miracle is an exorcism set in the context of his teaching. Why is this so important? When Jesus entered the synagogue and spoke, the people were already amazed at the power and authority with which he taught. The scribes quoted previous experts and authorities for important interpretations of scripture and the Law. The Greek word used to describe Jesus' teaching, *exousia,* means that he taught "out of himself." In other words, he did not use other authorities to strengthen his arguments.

Into this context wanders the possessed man. The unclean spirit, a demon in other translations, reveals the true identity of Jesus as the Holy One of God. In the Old Testament, particularly in the prophecy of Isaiah, God is the Holy One of Israel. In this passage, in Acts 3:14 and in 1 John 2:20, Jesus is the "Holy One." These similar phrases imply a connection between Jesus and God. Jesus silences the demon, not because it is wrong about his identity, but because the time has not yet come for Jesus to be revealed.

With the confidence of authority, he commands the unclean spirit to come out. The crowd watches in amazement—often a signal that they do not understand what is happening. Their remarks about a new teaching are meant for the reader. Jesus' power is greater than any other power. Even the demons obey him.

Throughout Mark's gospel, Jesus' identity is revealed by demons who are then silenced, while the people with Jesus come to know who he is only slowly, if at all. The remarkable exorcisms and healings of Jesus defeat the powers of evil that oppose God. But they will soon lead to a greater question for both his followers and his detractors: What is the source of Jesus' authority?

In Mark's gospel, things happen very quickly. Consequently, when Mark slows down enough to tell the details of a story, the reader pays more attention. What details stand out for you in this story? What do the details have to say about the nature of Jesus or the unclean spirit?

February 9, 2003

READING I   Job 7:1—4, 6—7

Revised Common Lectionary: Isaiah 40:21–31

"Do not human beings have a hard service
    on earth,
    and are not their days like the days of a laborer?
Like a slave who longs for the shadow,
    and like laborers who look for their wages,
so I am allotted months of emptiness,
    and nights of misery are apportioned to me.
When I lie down I say, 'When shall I rise?'
    But the night is long,
    and I am full of tossing until dawn.
My days are swifter than a weaver's shuttle,
    and come to their end without hope."
"Remember that my life is a breath;
    my eye will never again see good."

READING II   1 Corinthians 9:16—23

Roman Catholic: 1 Corinthians 9:16–19, 22–23

If I proclaim the gospel, this gives me no ground for boasting, for an obligation is laid on me, and woe to me if I do not proclaim the gospel! For if I do this of my own will, I have a reward; but if not of my own will, I am entrusted with a commission. What then is my reward? Just this: that in my proclamation I may make the gospel free of charge, so as not to make full use of my rights in the gospel.

For though I am free with respect to all, I have made myself a slave to all, so that I might win more of them. To the Jewish people I became as a Jew, in order to win the Jewish people. To those under the law I became as one under the law (though I myself am not under the law) so that I might win those under the law. To those outside the law I became as one outside the law (though I am not free from God's law but am under Christ's law) so that I might win those outside the law. To the weak I became weak, so that I might win the weak. I have become all things to all people, that I might by all means save some. I do it all for the sake of the gospel so that I may share in its blessings.

GOSPEL   Mark 1:29—39

As soon as Jesus and the disciples left the synagogue, they entered the house of Simon and Andrew, with James and John. Now Simon's mother-in-law was in bed with a fever, and they told him about her at once. Jesus came and took her by the hand and lifted her up. Then the fever left her, and she began to serve them.

That evening, at sundown, they brought to Jesus all who were sick or possessed with demons. And the whole city was gathered around the door. And he cured many who were sick with various diseases, and cast out many demons; and he would not permit the demons to speak, because they knew him.

In the morning, while it was still very dark, Jesus got up and went out to a deserted place, and there he prayed. And Simon and his companions hunted for him. When they found him, they said to him, "Everyone is searching for you." Jesus answered, "Let us go on to the neighboring towns, so that I may proclaim the message there also; for that is what I came out to do." And he went throughout Galilee, proclaiming the message in their synagogues and casting out demons.

Practice of Prayer

Psalm 147:1—2, 3—4, 5—6

Alleluia!

Sing praise to the LORD who is good;
sing to our God who is loving:
to God our praise is due.

The LORD builds up Jerusalem
and brings back Israel's exiles,
God heals the broken-hearted,
and binds up all their wounds.
God fixes the number of the stars;
and calls each one by its name.

Our Lord is great and almighty;
God's wisdom can never be measured.
The LORD raises the lowly;
and humbles the wicked to the dust.

Practice of Justice

Barbara Vogel, a teacher in Aurora, Colorado, has led her young students in a remarkable campaign over the past few years. Outraged and heartbroken that slavery is still practiced throughout the world, binding 27 million people, she sought to educate her fourth-grade class about this brutal practice. In the process she ignited a spark of indignation that flared into action. Their efforts have included raising more than $100,000 to free slaves in Sudan and sending a delegation to ask Pope John Paul II to lend his leadership and influence to the cause.

This week as we celebrate the birthday of Abraham Lincoln, the Great Emancipator, consider how small voices joined with others can make a difference. What injustice, near or far, enrages us? What can we do about it?

Scripture Insights

After the exorcism that is the first of Jesus' miracles, Jesus performs a physical healing on Peter's mother-in-law. Mark shows that Jesus exercises authority over both demonic possession and physical illness. Indeed, Jesus' ability to cast out demons and to heal the sick becomes the way in which the world first knows him.

The difference in the details of the two healings is significant. Jesus orders the demon out; he touches the mother-in-law and the fever leaves her. For Mark, exorcism is accomplished through verbal authority (demons respond to command) and it is often an instrument for teaching and preaching. By contrast, physical healing is brought about by the touch of one who is holy. In both of these incidents, by command and by touch, Jesus is authoritative. His cure of both victims is total.

In the evening exorcisms that follow, Jesus will not allow the demons to speak, because they know him. Mark will show this many more times as Jesus seeks to be known in the full context of the passion and resurrection and not just in a handful of miraculous healings. This "messianic secret" of Mark's gospel places the full revelation at the end of Jesus' public life, not at the beginning.

Night is the traditional time for confrontation with evil, and here the sick and possessed are brought to Jesus at sundown. The power that Jesus wields is not diminished by darkness. In fact, it offers a way to encounter God with no distractions. Jesus seizes the opportunity to pray in a deserted place apart from his disciples and the crowds. Mark connects Jesus' power to his prayer by interrupting the healings to narrate this incident. When the disciples search him out, though, he immediately returns to his work, extending his mission to the neighboring towns, proclaiming the message and exorcising demons. Jesus' fame spreads, but it also attracts the attention of the Jewish leaders who will begin to question him.

How do we experience healing today? Is it always physical? What is the role of prayer or touch?

February 16, 2003

READING I *Leviticus 13:1—2, 44—46*

Revised Common Lectionary: 2 Kings 5:1–14

The LORD spoke to Moses and Aaron, saying: When a person has on the skin of his body a swelling or an eruption or a spot, and it turns into a leprous disease on the skin of his body, he shall be brought to Aaron the priest or to one of his sons the priests. He is leprous, he is unclean. The priest shall pronounce him unclean; the disease is on his head. The person who has the leprous disease shall wear torn clothes and let the hair of his head be disheveled; and he shall cover his upper lip and cry out, "Unclean, unclean." He shall remain unclean as long as he has the disease; he is unclean. He shall live alone; his dwelling shall be outside the camp.

READING II *1 Corinthians 10:31—11:1*

Revised Common Lectionary: 1 Corinthians 9:24–27

So, whether you eat or drink, or whatever you do, do everything for the glory of God. Give no offense to Jews or to Greeks or to the church of God, just as I try to please everyone in everything I do, not seeking my own advantage, but that of many, so that they may be saved. Be imitators of me, as I am of Christ.

GOSPEL *Mark 1:40–45*

A man with leprosy came to Jesus begging him, and kneeling said to him, "If you choose, you can make me clean." Moved with pity, Jesus stretched out his hand and touched him, and said to him, "I do choose. Be made clean!" Immediately the leprosy left the man, and he was made clean. After sternly warning him Jesus sent him away at once, saying to him, "See that you say nothing to anyone; but go, show yourself to the priest, and offer for your cleansing what Moses commanded, as a testimony to them."

But the man went out and began to proclaim it freely, and to spread the word, so that Jesus could no longer go into a town openly, but stayed out in the country; and people came to him from every quarter.

Practice of Prayer

Psalm 32:1—2, 5, 11

Happy those whose offense is forgiven,
whose sin is remitted.
O happy those to whom the LORD
imputes no guilt,
in whose spirit is no guile.

But now I have acknowledged my sins;
my guilt I did not hide.
I said: "I will confess
my offense to the LORD."
And you, LORD, have forgiven
the guilt of my sin.

Rejoice, rejoice in the LORD,
exult, you just!
O come, ring out your joy,
all you upright of heart.

Practice of Temperance

After healing the leper in today's gospel, Jesus tells him not to share the news with anyone but the priest at the Temple. Since leprosy had made the man a social outcast for years, this command seems harsh and somewhat unrealistic. What deeper wisdom might lie behind Jesus' stern warning?

Many people came to hear Jesus for the wrong reasons. Those who were interested solely in miracle-watching seemed deaf to the teachings. Their absorption in spectacle and their desire to tell attention-grabbing tales may have distracted them from the true drama unfolding.

Tempering our own impulses entails enormous restraint when we're bursting with news we want to share. The leper's disregard of Jesus' instruction is understandable but, in the end, might have served the wrong purpose. This week, consider how "holding back," as temperance demands, may have larger ramifications for a situation in your own life. How can practicing this virtue help you?

Scripture Insights

For lepers, the law of Leviticus must have seemed very harsh. They could not live in the camp with anyone. They had to warn people that they were coming. Actually, any skin disease was considered leprosy unless proven otherwise. The book of Leviticus devotes two chapters (13 and 14) to laws requiring a period of separation and examination before anyone with a skin lesion is allowed back into the camp. Leprosy was worse than other ailments because the opening on the skin often exposed blood, the source of life, and any contact with blood made a person unclean.

Every Jew reading Mark's gospel would have been familiar with the laws regarding leprosy. When Jesus touched the leper to heal him, Jews collectively gasped. Not even the prophet Elisha (II Kings 5) cured a leper this way. Touching the leper made Jesus unclean, yet neither he nor Mark seem concerned. The encounter with the leper again shows Jesus confronting the conditions that separate people from each other. The possessed man was disturbed and frightening; Peter's mother-in-law could not fulfill her place in the family; the leper is alienated by the unclean nature of his disease. In each case, by word or touch, Jesus restores the person to the family and the community.

Mark adds two interesting details to this story. First, Jesus is "moved with pity" for the man. Mark, who tells the story of Jesus more simply than the other gospels, describes Jesus' emotional state. This makes Mark's portrayal of Jesus very human. But he also emphasizes the healing power of Jesus to show his divine identity. Second, as he did with the demons, Jesus urges the leper to tell no one. Jesus did not want followers based solely on his ability to heal. If we were to hear all of verse 45 in this reading, we would understand what Jesus feared. He is no longer able to move about openly because people flock to him seeking healing. In the face of their preoccupation with physical healing, his message may well be lost.

Who is shunned in our society? How might we reach out to touch the outcasts?

READING I   Isaiah 43:18—25

Roman Catholic: Isaiah 43:18–19, 21–22, 24b–25

Do not remember the former things,
  or consider the things of old.
I am about to do a new thing;
  now it springs forth, do you not perceive it?
I will make a way in the wilderness
  and rivers in the desert.
The wild animals will honor me,
  the jackals and the ostriches;
for I give water in the wilderness,
  rivers in the desert,
to give drink to my chosen people,
  the people whom I formed for myself
so that they might declare my praise.

Yet you did not call upon me, O Jacob;
  but you have been weary of me, O Israel!
You have not brought me your sheep
    for burnt offerings,
  or honored me with your sacrifices.
I have not burdened you with offerings,
  or wearied you with frankincense.
You have not bought me sweet cane with money,
  or satisfied me with the fat of your sacrifices.
But you have burdened me with your sins;
  you have wearied me with your iniquities.

I, I am the one
  who blots out your transgressions
    for my own sake,
  and I will not remember your sins.

READING II   2 Corinthians 1:18—22

As surely as God is faithful, our word to you has not been "Yes and No." For the Son of God, Jesus Christ, whom we, Silvanus and Timothy and I, proclaimed among you, was not "Yes and No"; but in Christ it is always "Yes." For in Christ every one of God's promises is a "Yes." For this reason it is through Christ that we say the "Amen," to the glory of God. But it is God who establishes us with you in Christ and has anointed us, by having sealed us and giving us the Spirit in our hearts as a first installment.

GOSPEL   Mark 2:1—12

When Jesus returned to Capernaum after some days, it was reported that he was at home. So many gathered around that there was no longer room for them, not even in front of the door; and he was speaking the word to them. Then some people came, bringing to him a paralyzed man, carried by four of them. And when they could not bring the man to Jesus because of the crowd, they removed the roof above him; and after having dug through it, they let down the mat on which the paralyzed man lay. When Jesus saw their faith, he said to the man, "My child, your sins are forgiven."

Now some of the scribes were sitting there, questioning in their hearts, "Why does this fellow speak in this way? It is blasphemy! Who can forgive sins but God alone?" At once Jesus perceived in his spirit that they were discussing these questions among themselves; and he said to them, "Why do you raise such questions in your hearts? Which is easier, to say to the paralyzed man, 'Your sins are forgiven,' or to say, 'Stand up and take your mat and walk'? But so that you may know that the Son-of-Man has authority on earth to forgive sins"—he said to the paralyzed man—"I say to you, stand up, take your mat and go to your home." And the man stood up, and immediately took the mat and went out before all of them; so that they were all amazed, and glorified God, saying, "We have never seen anything like this!"

Practice of Prayer

Psalm 41:2—3, 4—5, 13—14

Happy those who consider the poor and the weak.
The LORD will save them in the evil day,
will guard them, give them life,
   make them happy in the land
and will not give them up to the will of their foes.
The LORD will give them strength in their pain,
will bring them back from sickness to health.

As for me, I said: "LORD, have mercy on me,
heal my soul for I have sinned against you."

If you uphold me I shall be unharmed
and set in your presence for evermore.

Blessed be the LORD, the God of Israel
from age to age. Amen. Amen.

Practice of Justice

Grudges aren't good for us. Even the most "justified" reason for holding onto a hurt can drag us down, making us fearful, resentful and even hateful. When held corporately, past offenses can be used as an excuse to kill, plunder and wage war without end.

Today's first reading stands in sharp contrast to this. It urges letting go of the past and prompts a new way of seeing the world. God can do things as radical as creating lush pathways through dry and dusty deserts. God alone is capable of blotting out transgressions and forgetting sins. The prophet's dream is one that is inviting and reassuring. It envisions the harmony that is possible when we join our voices together instead of against one another.

Such an image is worthy of deeper reflection in these times. Starting here and now, what grudges can we relinquish in order to contribute to the greening of barren landscapes?

Scripture Insights

Jesus' first three healings dealt with diseases of body and mind. Today he grants forgiveness of sins. The scribes (interpreters of the law) are dismayed, for no one in the Old Testament claimed the power to forgive sins. Only God could blot out transgressions; only God could decide to forget one's sins. Isaiah's prophecy points to the importance of memory: If God remembers sin, it is punished; if God forgets sin, it is as though it never happened. For Mark, Jesus' forgiveness of sin is another manifestation of his authority. The use of the passive voice ("your sins are forgiven") is interesting and ambiguous. The scribes assume that Jesus is claiming for himself the power to forgive sins, but it could be read that he is announcing the fulfillment of Isaiah's prophecy in the first reading: God has forgiven the man's sins.

Mark explains that the scribes never spoke aloud. Their questions about Jesus' authority were silent, but Jesus knew them anyway. The man who understands forgiveness of sin can see into hearts as well. The riddle Jesus poses to them ("Which is easier . . . ?") seems obvious at first. At least it would seem that claiming to change a person's inner state would be easier than curing a physical disease. Jesus, however, forgives the sin first and then cures the paralysis as proof of his authority. His question even seems to equate the two actions, demonstrating his mastery of both inner and outer states. The excited murmur of the crowd indicates that this is certainly the "new thing" of Isaiah's prophecy.

The story ends with a significant detail. Jesus commands the paralytic not simply to stand—but to take up his mat and go home. The healing of soul and body restores the man to the community and family he had known. Restoration is one of Mark's signs that Jesus is the Son of God.

The contrast between the questions of the scribes and the faith of the friends is striking. What if both of these traits were in us? What are the questions we have? How does our faith respond to the questions?

March 2, 2003

EIGHTH SUNDAY IN ORDINARY TIME
OTHER CHURCHES: SEE PAGES 48—49

READING I *Hosea 2:16b, 17b, 21—22*

Thus says the LORD: I will bring her into the wilderness and speak tenderly to her. There she shall respond as in the days of her youth, as at the time when she came out of the land of Egypt. And I will take you for my wife forever; I will take you for my wife in righteousness and in justice, in steadfast love, and in mercy. I will take you for my wife in faithfulness; and you shall know the LORD.
[Verses are numbered slightly differently in the NRSV: 14b, 15b, 19—20]

READING II *2 Corinthians 3:1b—6*

Surely we do not need, as some do, letters of recommendation to you or from you, do we? You yourselves are our letter, written on our hearts, to be known and read by all; and you show that you are a letter of Christ, prepared by us, written not with ink but with the Spirit of the living God, not on tablets of stone but on tablets of human hearts. Such is the confidence that we have through Christ toward God. Not that we are competent of ourselves to claim anything as coming from us; our competence is from God, who has made us competent to be ministers of a new covenant, not of letter but of spirit; for the letter kills, but the Spirit gives life.

GOSPEL *Mark 2:18—22*

Now John's disciples and the Pharisees were fasting; and people came and said to Jesus, "Why do John's disciples and the disciples of the Pharisees fast, but your disciples do not fast?" Jesus said to them, "The wedding guests cannot fast while the bridegroom is with them, can they? As long as they have the bridegroom with them, they cannot fast. The days will come when the bridegroom is taken away from them, and then they will fast on that day.

"No one sews a piece of unshrunk cloth on an old cloak; otherwise, the patch pulls away from it, the new from the old, and a worse tear is made. And no one puts new wine into old wineskins; otherwise, the wine will burst the skins, and the wine is lost, and so are the skins; but one puts new wine into fresh wineskins."

Practice of Prayer

Psalm 103:1—2, 3—4, 8, 10, 12—13

My soul, give thanks to the LORD,
all my being, bless God's holy name.
My soul, give thanks to the LORD
and never forget all God's blessings.

It is God who forgives all your guilt,
who heals every one of your ills,
who redeems your life from the grave,
who crowns you with love and compassion,

The LORD is compassion and love,
slow to anger and rich in mercy.

God does not treat us according to our sins
nor repay us according to our faults.

As far as the east is from the west
so far does he remove our sins.

As parents have compassion on their children,
the LORD has pity on those who are God-fearing.

Practice of Temperance

Jesus was criticized for his habit of eating with tax collectors and sinners. These people were outcasts, and unlikely to be fastidious about following rules. In answering his critics, Jesus spoke of savoring the wedding feast while the bridegroom is still present. Was this a call to throw temperance to the wind?

Today's first reading lends fresh insight to the question. The prophet portrays God as sweet-tongued and inviting. Those being led are not brought to a site of pleasure and indulgence, however. Rather they are coaxed into the wilderness, a place free from frivolous distractions where faithfulness could flourish. The true value of temperance is not just refraining from something out of adherence to a rule. It leads us to simple places where we can better appreciate the presence of God in our midst.

Scripture Insights

Marriage symbolism dominates in the reading from the Old Testament and the gospel. Both the ancient Jews and the early Christians used marriage to talk about the relationship between God and God's people. In Hosea, God will take Israel back to the beginning of their relationship to remind Israel of the love they held for each other. After Israel left Egypt, the people learned to trust and love God who supplied their needs in the wilderness. Righteousness, justice, fidelity and mercy mark God's *hesed,* the Hebrew word for steadfast love. Our best response is to return the same faithful love to God.

Jesus answers a question about fasting by alluding to a wedding feast and the behavior of guests and bridegroom. For him, the relationship between God and community is characterized by deep joy. The time for fasting is when the bridegroom leaves, an allusion to his own death.

In the context of the wedding imagery, the two sayings Jesus quotes next are a profound statement about the transformation that takes place when God and humanity meet as marriage partners. In the presence of God's love—ever new and renewing—faith can be changed and must be changed if the marriage is to be permanent. The apostle Paul tells the Corinthians that ministers of a new covenant have the letter of Christ written in their hearts by the Holy Spirit. Marriage was often referred to as a covenant between partners. Paul's new covenant was a new relationship.

The two folk sayings also refer to the incompatibility of Jesus' new teaching and the old ways of observing the Law. As in successful businesses today, "thinking outside the box" was necessary to comprehend what Jesus was saying and to put it into action. John's disciples and the Pharisees and scribes had a hard time reconciling Jesus' new teaching with their old way of doing things. They would clash many more times.

Why do we fast today? What is valuable about that discipline?

March 2, 2003

READING I   2 Kings 2:1—12

Now when the LORD was about to take Elijah up to heaven by a whirlwind, Elijah and Elisha were on their way from Gilgal. Elijah said to Elisha, "Stay here; for the LORD has sent me as far as Bethel." But Elisha said, "As the LORD lives, and as you yourself live, I will not leave you." So they went down to Bethel. The company of prophets who were in Bethel came out to Elisha, and said to him, "Do you know that today the LORD will take your master away from you?" And he said, "Yes, I know; keep silent."

Elijah said to him, "Elisha, stay here; for the LORD has sent me to Jericho." But Elisha said, "As the LORD lives, and as you yourself live, I will not leave you." So they came to Jericho. The company of prophets who were at Jericho drew near to Elisha, and said to him, "Do you know that today the LORD will take your master away from you?" And he answered, "Yes, I know; be silent."

Then Elijah said to him, "Stay here; for the LORD has sent me to the Jordan." But Elisha said, "As the LORD lives, and as you yourself live, I will not leave you." So the two of them went on. Fifty men of the company of prophets also went, and stood at some distance from them, as they both were standing by the Jordan. Then Elijah took his mantle and rolled it up, and struck the water; the water was parted to the one side and to the other, until the two of them crossed on dry ground.

When they had crossed, Elijah said to Elisha, "Tell me what I may do for you, before I am taken from you." Elisha said, "Please let me inherit a double share of your spirit." He responded, "You have asked a hard thing; yet, if you see me as I am being taken from you, it will be granted you; if not, it will not." As they continued walking and talking, a chariot of fire and horses of fire separated the two of them, and Elijah ascended in a whirlwind into heaven. Elisha kept watching and crying out, "Father, father! The chariots of Israel and its drivers!" But when Elisha could no longer see Elijah, he grasped his own clothes and tore them in two pieces.

READING II   2 Corinthians 4:3—6

Even if our gospel is veiled, it is veiled to those who are perishing. In their case the god of this world has blinded the minds of the unbelievers, to keep them from seeing the light of the gospel of the glory of Christ, who is the image of God. For we do not proclaim ourselves; we proclaim Jesus Christ as Lord and ourselves as your slaves for Jesus' sake. For it is the God who said, "Let light shine out of darkness," who has shone in our hearts to give the light of the knowledge of the glory of God in the face of Jesus Christ.

GOSPEL   Mark 9:2—9

Six days later, Jesus took with him Peter and James and John, and led them up a high mountain apart, by themselves. And he was transfigured before them, and his clothes became dazzling white, such as no one on earth could bleach them. And there appeared to them Elijah with Moses, who were talking with Jesus. Then Peter said to Jesus, "Rabbi, it is good for us to be here; let us make three dwellings, one for you, one for Moses, and one for Elijah." He did not know what to say, for they were terrified. Then a cloud overshadowed them, and from the cloud there came a voice, "This is my Son, the Beloved; listen to him!" Suddenly when they looked around, they saw no one with them any more, but only Jesus.

As they were coming down the mountain, Jesus ordered them to tell no one about what they had seen, until after the Son-of-Man had risen from the dead.

Practice of Prayer

Psalm 50:1–6

The God of gods, the LORD,
has spoken and summoned the earth,
from the rising of the sun to its setting.
Out of Zion's perfect beauty God shines.

(Our God comes, and does not keep silence.)

Announced by devouring fire,
and surrounded by raging tempest,
God calls on the heavens and the earth
to witness the judgement of his people.

"Summon before me my people
who made covenant with me by sacrifice."
The heavens proclaim God's justice,
for God, indeed, is the judge.

Practice of Prudence

Peter had just witnessed an amazing sight. Jesus appeared before him shining like the sun and conversing with Moses and Elijah. Is it any wonder that Peter's first impulse was to stay where he was on the mountain?

It is not unusual for us to prefer mountaintop epiphanies over the plains of the mundane. When something wonderful happens it is only natural that we want to stay and savor the moment, to delay our return to the ordinary. Prudence has been described as sobriety and saneness, discretion and careful consideration of where we are headed. Prudence does not, however, mean timidity or fearfulness. Sometimes the most challenging paths are the ones that lead us right back to the same ordinary old places, opened anew to revelations, insights and opportunities that might be overshadowed by brighter, more dramatic experiences.

Scripture Insights

The Old Testament reading and the gospel describe two miraculous appearances. Elijah was, in legend and prophecy, the representative of all the prophets. He had multiplied food, raised children from the dead (1 Kings 17), called down miraculous manifestations of God (1 Kings 18) and had the famous encounter with the sheer silence of God after storm, fire and earthquake (1 Kings 19). His very name, which means "the Lord is my God," identified him as a holy man. Elijah had the great honor of being assumed into heaven in a flaming chariot and a whirlwind. Elisha asks for, and receives, a double portion of Elijah's spirit—the double portion a first-born son inherits from his father. He goes on to perform twice as many miracles as Elijah, but Elijah is the one remembered for his special relationship with God.

Peter, James and John ascend the mountain with Jesus and are treated to a heavenly manifestation. Elijah and Moses appear with Jesus; Elijah represents the prophets; Moses symbolizes the Law. Jesus fulfills both the law and the prophets. Moses is a friend of God; Elijah is the forerunner of the day of the Lord. Jesus is God's Son, identified here in the same way as at his baptism, and the Son enjoys a far more intimate relationship with God than either Moses or Elijah had.

In Mark's story, Peter has just identified Jesus as the Messiah (8:29) and Jesus has begun teaching that he must suffer and die. Mark interrupts Jesus' prediction of his suffering with this glorious manifestation of his sonship to remind disciples and readers that the Messiah in whom they believe is neither warrior-king nor Moses returned to life nor Elijah come down from heaven. He is a Son who is obedient to the Father—even to death.

Jesus continues to order that no one speak about what they have seen. This time he gives a time limit: "until after the Son of Man had risen from the dead." What difference would it make to wait until then?

Lent

FORTY·DAYS

Preparation for the Word

Loving God, in the waters of baptism
you clothed us with Christ,
but in these days of Lent
you clothe us also with the ashes:
Dust we are, to dust we shall return.
So marked we take on the forty days.

By our lenten discipline of fasting
may we grow hungry for your word
above all hunger for food or diversion.
By our lenten discipline of almsgiving
may we seek a paradise of justice long delayed.
God of mercy, make of this Lent a broad space
where the hungry church may assemble
and feed upon your word alone
and so prepare to come again to the waters
    of baptism,
one in Jesus who is Lord for ever and ever. Amen.

Thanksgiving for the Word

Creator God, you created us to live
not by bread alone, but by your words.
Exiles all, we have read these holy scriptures:
Your words are water from the desert rock
and manna to nourish us each day.
Your words are wine to warm our hearts
and turn us with good cheer
toward all our brothers and sisters
who are gathered at this world's hungry table.

Thus do we journey through Lent, merciful God,
and come little by little to the font and to the table.
Then exiles no longer,
we shall sing your praise
in Jesus who is Lord for ever and ever. Amen.

Weekday Readings

March 5: Ash Wednesday *Joel 2:12–18; 2 Corinthians 5:20–6:2; Matthew 6:1–6, 16–18*

March 6: *Deuteronomy 30:15–20; Luke 9:22–25*

March 7: *Isaiah 58:1–9a; Matthew 9:14–15*

March 8: *Isaiah 58:9b–14; Luke 5:27–32*

March 10: *Leviticus 19:1–2, 11–18; Matthew 25:31–46*

March 11: *Isaiah 55:10–11; Matthew 6:7–15*

March 12: *Jonah 3:1–10; Luke 11:29–32*

March 13:*Esther C:12, 14–16, 23–25; Matthew 7:7–12*

March 14: *Ezekiel 18:21–28; Matthew 5:20–26*

March 15: *Deuteronomy 26:16–19; Matthew 5:43–48*

March 17: *Daniel 9:4b–10; Luke 6:36–38*

March 18: *Isaiah 1:10, 16–20; Matthew 23:1–12*

March 19: Solemnity of Saint Joseph
2 Samuel 7:4–5a, 12–14a, 16; Romans 4:13, 16–18, 22; Matthew 1:16, 18–21, 24a

March 20: *Jeremiah 17:5–10; Luke 16:19–31*

March 21: *Genesis 37:3–4, 12–13a, 17b–28; Matthew 21: 33–43, 45–46*

March 22: *Micah 7:14–15, 18–20; Luke 15:1–3, 11–32*

March 24: *2 Kings 5:1–15a; Luke 4:24–30*

March 25: Solemnity of the Annunciation of the Lord
Isaiah 7:10–14; 8:10; Hebrews 10:4–10; Luke 1:26–38

March 26: *Deuteronomy 4:1, 5–9; Matthew 5:17–19*

March 27: *Jeremiah 7:23–28; Luke 11:14–23*

March 28: *Hosea 14:2–10; Mark 12:28b–34*

March 29: *Hosea 6:1–6; Luke 18:9–14*

March 31: *Isaiah 65:17–21; John 4:43–54*

April 1: *Ezekiel 47:1–9, 12; John 5:1–16*

April 2: *Isaiah 49:8–15; John 5:17–30*

April 3: *Exodus 32:7–14; John 5:31–47*

April 4: *Wisdom 2:1a, 12–22; John 7:1–2, 10, 25–30*

April 5: *Jeremiah 11:18–20; John 7:40–53*

April 7: *Deuteronomy 13:1–9, 15–17, 19–30, 33–62*

April 8: *Numbers 21:4–9; John 8:21–30*

April 9: *Deuteronomy 3:14–20, 91–92, 95; John 8:31–42*

April 10:*Genesis 17:3–9; John 8:51–59*

April 11: *Jeremiah 20:10–13; John 10:31–42*

April 12: *Ezekiel 37:21–28; John 11:45–56*

April 14: *Isaiah 42:1–7; John 12:1–11*

April 15: *Isaiah 49:1–6; John 13:21–33, 36–38*

April 16: *Isaiah 50:4–9a; Matthew 26:14–25*

March 9, 2003

READING I   Genesis 9:8—17

Roman Catholic: Genesis 9:9–15

God said to Noah and to his sons with him, "As for me, I am establishing my covenant with you and your descendants after you, and with every living creature that is with you, the birds, the domestic animals, and every animal of the earth with you, as many as came out of the ark. I establish my covenant with you, that never again shall all flesh be cut off by the waters of a flood, and never again shall there be a flood to destroy the earth." God said, "This is the sign of the covenant that I make between me and you and every living creature that is with you, for all future generations: I have set my bow in the clouds, and it shall be a sign of the covenant between me and the earth. When I bring clouds over the earth and the bow is seen in the clouds, I will remember my covenant that is between me and you and every living creature of all flesh; and the waters shall never again become a flood to destroy all flesh. When the bow is in the clouds, I will see it and remember the everlasting covenant between God and every living creature of all flesh that is on the earth." God said to Noah, "This is the sign of the covenant that I have established between me and all flesh that is on the earth."

READING II   1 Peter 3:18—22

Christ also suffered for sins once for all, the righteous for the unrighteous, in order to bring you to God. He was put to death in the flesh, but made alive in the spirit, in which also he went and made a proclamation to the spirits in prison, who in former times did not obey, when God waited patiently in the days of Noah, during the building of the ark, in which a few, that is, eight persons, were saved through water. And baptism, which this prefigured, now saves you—not as a removal of dirt from the body, but as an appeal to God for a good conscience, through the resurrection of Jesus Christ, who has gone into heaven and is at the right hand of God, with angels, authorities, and powers made subject to him.

GOSPEL   Mark 1:9—15

Roman Catholic: Mark 1:12–15

In those days Jesus came from Nazareth of Galilee and was baptized by John in the Jordan. And just as Jesus was coming up out of the water, he saw the heavens torn apart and the Spirit descending like a dove on him. And a voice came from heaven, "You are my Son, the Beloved; with you I am well pleased."

And the Spirit immediately drove Jesus out into the wilderness. He was in the wilderness forty days, tempted by Satan; and he was with the wild beasts; and the angels waited on him.

Now after John was arrested, Jesus came to Galilee, proclaiming the good news of God, and saying, "The time is fulfilled, and the dominion of God has come near; repent, and believe in the good news."

Practice of Prayer

Psalm 25:4—5, 6—7, 8—9

LORD, make me know your ways.
LORD, teach me your paths.
Make me walk in your truth, and teach me,
for you are God my savior.

Remember your mercy, LORD,
and the love you have shown from of old.
Do not remember the sins of my youth.
In your love remember me.

The LORD is good and upright,
showing the path to those who stray,
guiding the humble in the right path,
and teaching the way to the poor.

Practice of Fortitude

The wilderness has been a called a place of extremes. Certainly this theme is picked up in curious ways in today's gospel. It moves from Jesus' immersion in the river to his abandonment in the desert. The Spirit hovers over him in a protective, motherly way, and then drives him out into the wasteland. Angels, devils and beasts alternately comfort and torment him. Jesus withstands all of this and emerges from his desert experience fortified in his mission.

Life can be a wilderness when we are pulled in two opposing directions—between where we want to be and where we have to be, between protecting those in our care and challenging them to grow up, between desires for what's good and what's comfortable. Consider the contradictions creating tension in your own life. What is fortifying you as you face them?

Scripture Insights

The Genesis passage comes from the priestly writer, a post-exilic compiler with a special interest in worship and obedience to the law. This writer sees God as all-powerful, creative, transcendent, holy and orderly. Notice that perspective in the first creation story of Genesis 1:1—2:4a. God creates by the power of the word, creatures appear in orderly array, and God rests on the seventh day as if the sabbath were written into the very order of the cosmos.

For this writer, then, the flood represents a mighty tearing of the fabric of creation, which God had originally pronounced "very good" (Genesis 1:31). After sin causes the wrath of God to break forth, God forswears the violence of the flood by making a covenant. This seems to anticipate the unconditional covenant made with Abraham. God promises never to destroy creation and sets a sign of the covenant in the heavens: a rainbow. Alongside the dove, the rainbow becomes a sign of peace. So despite the terrors of war, the upheavals of nature, the catastrophes of human judgment, God's graciousness ensures stability "for all future generations." The re-establishment of God's orderly rule after the flood would have had a strong impact on the community hoping to regroup after the disaster of the exile.

Mark's gospel pictures Jesus being tempted in the wilderness following his baptism. But the most striking parallel today is between Jesus' proclamation of the gospel and God's good news of repudiating vengeance. The "good news of God" (1:13) is thus a message of reconciliation.

The first letter of Peter tells of Jesus going to make a proclamation to the spirits in prison who had disobeyed in the time of Noah. The precise meaning of this passage is hard to grasp, but the general sense seems clear: Christ's death is a powerful gospel for all times and people, admitting people into a new spiritual Noah's ark that saves them through the ritual flood of baptism.

How does Psalm 25 express the "good news of God"?

READING I   *Genesis 22:1—2, 9a, 10—13, 15—18*

Revised Common Lectionary: Genesis 17:1—7, 15—16

God tested Abraham and said to him, "Abraham!" And he said, "Here I am." God said, "Take your son, your only son Isaac, whom you love, and go to the land of Moriah, and offer him there as a burnt offering on one of the mountains that I shall show you."

When they came to the place that God had shown him, Abraham built an altar there and laid the wood in order. He bound his son Isaac, and laid him on the altar, on top of the wood. Then Abraham reached out his hand and took the knife to kill his son. But the angel of the LORD called to him from heaven, and said, "Abraham, Abraham!" And he said, "Here I am." The angel said, "Do not lay your hand on the boy or do anything to him; for now I know that you fear God, since you have not withheld your son, your only son, from me." And Abraham looked up and saw a ram, caught in a thicket by its horns. Abraham went and took the ram and offered it up as a burnt offering instead of his son.

The angel of the LORD called to Abraham a second time from heaven, and said, "By myself I have sworn, says the LORD: Because you have done this, and have not withheld your son, your only son, I will indeed bless you, and I will make your offspring as numerous as the stars of heaven and as the sand that is on the seashore. And your offspring shall possess the gate of their enemies, and by your offspring shall all the nations of the earth gain blessing for themselves, because you have obeyed my voice."

READING II   *Romans 8:31b—34*

Revised Common Lectionary: Romans 4:13—25

What then are we to say about these things? If God is for us, who is against us? The very Son of God was not withheld, but was given up for all of us; will God not along with the Son also give us everything else? Who will bring any charge against God's elect? It is God who justifies. Who is to condemn? It is Christ Jesus, who died, yes, who was raised, who is at the right hand of God, who indeed intercedes for us.

GOSPEL   *Mark 9:2—10*

Revised Common Lectionary: Mark 8:31—38

Six days later, Jesus took with him Peter and James and John, and led them up a high mountain apart, by themselves. And he was transfigured before them, and his clothes became dazzling white, such as no one on earth could bleach them. And there appeared to them Elijah with Moses, who were talking with Jesus. Then Peter said to Jesus, "Rabbi, it is good for us to be here; let us make three dwellings, one for you, one for Moses, and one for Elijah." He did not know what to say, for they were terrified. Then a cloud overshadowed them, and from the cloud there came a voice, "This is my Son, the Beloved; listen to him!" Suddenly when they looked around, they saw no one with them any more, but only Jesus. As they were coming down the mountain, he ordered them to tell no one about what they had seen, until after the Son of Man had risen from the dead. So they kept the matter to themselves, questioning what this rising from the dead could mean.

Practice of Prayer

Psalm 116:10, 15, 16—17, 18—19

I trusted, even when I said:
"I am sorely afflicted,"
O precious in the eyes of the Lord
is the death of the faithful.

Your servant, Lord, your servant am I;
you have loosened my bonds.
A thanksgiving sacrifice I make;
I will call on the Lord 's name.

My vows to the Lord I will fulfill
before all the people,
in the courts of the house of the Lord,
in your midst, O Jerusalem.

Practice of Temperance

Fasting is one of three lifelong disciplines that are given special attention during Lent. It puts the virtue of temperance into practice through the exercise of self-denial and self-control. This moderate and reflective way of feeding ourselves requires inner resolve.

The true value of fasting is that, in turning away from things we think we need, we discover resources much greater and more life-sustaining. Lenten austerity leads to a greater appreciation of Easter abundance. As we fast during the forty days before Easter, we feast during the fifty days that follow it.

How will you temper your physical nourishment in order to cultivate spiritual nourishment this Lent? Make some resolutions this week and try to stay alert to the new resources that are revealing themselves to you as a result of them.

Scripture Insights

God acts in mysterious ways in many places in the Hebrew Bible: rejecting Cain's sacrifice (Genesis 4:5), choosing Jacob over Esau (Genesis 25:23), sending Job's time of trial (Job 10:1–22), forcing Jeremiah to suffer (Jeremiah 20:7–18), using Babylon to judge Judah (Habakkuk 1:12–13). But the story of Abraham's sacrifice of Isaac renders God almost completely incomprehensible.

The entire story line about Abraham from Genesis 12 to this point has pointed to the birth of an heir to fulfill the astounding promise of descendants as countless as the sands of the seashore (Genesis 15:1–6). But God's frightening demand throws everything into jeopardy. The storyteller seems unconcerned about the picture of God that this episode draws: God putting God's own integrity at risk. Nor does the storyteller take into account the other parts of the Bible that repudiate child sacrifice. (See Jeremiah 7:31.)

If God is incomprehensible, Abraham's steadfast faith stands out more boldly than ever. Abraham bargained with God about destroying Sodom (Genesis 18:22–33), but not about this. Why? He became the father of the faithful not only by boldly believing in God's promise, but by boldly believing despite God's threat. He not only trusted, as Paul taught in his letters (Romans 4:16–22; Galatians 3:6–9), but *acted* on his trusting faith (James 2:18–24).

Put Isaac's sacrifice side by side with today's passage in Romans ("The very Son of God was not withheld," 8:32). In Jesus' death, God is not the one to demand the sacrifice, but the one to make the sacrifice. God offers up his Son not to himself, but to us. In the Jesus story, God is more like Abraham than like God in the Isaac story. So what made God believe in us? "God proves his love for us in that *while we still were sinners* Christ died for us" (Romans 5:8). God had no proof that this sacrifice would make any difference—but sacrificed his Son anyway. God made a sacrifice in faith and became the *Abba* of those who believe.

When have you been called to trust—and to act on your trust?

READING I   *Exodus 20:1—17*

God spoke all these words: I am the LORD your God, who brought you out of the land of Egypt, out of the house of slavery; you shall have no other gods before me.

You shall not make for yourself an idol, whether in the form of anything that is in heaven above, or that is on the earth beneath, or that is in the water under the earth. You shall not bow down to them or worship them; for I the LORD your God am a jealous God, punishing children for the iniquity of parents, to the third and the fourth generation of those who reject me, but showing steadfast love to the thousandth generation of those who love me and keep my commandments. You shall not make wrongful use of the name of the LORD your God, for the LORD will not acquit anyone who misuses the divine name.

Remember the sabbath day, and keep it holy. Six days you shall labor and do all your work. But the seventh day is a sabbath to the LORD your God; you shall not do any work—you, your son or your daughter, your male or female slave, your livestock, or the alien resident in your towns. For in six days the LORD made heaven and earth, the sea, and all that is in them, but rested the seventh day; therefore the LORD blessed the sabbath day and consecrated it.

Honor your father and your mother, so that your days may be long in the land that the LORD your God is giving you. You shall not murder. You shall not commit adultery. You shall not steal. You shall not bear false witness against your neighbor. You shall not covet your neighbor's house; you shall not covet your neighbor's wife, or male or female slave, or ox, or donkey, or anything that belongs to your neighbor.

READING II   *1 Corinthians 1:18—25*

Roman Catholic: 1 Corinthians 1:22—25

The message about the cross is foolishness to those who are perishing, but to us who are being saved it is the power of God. For it is written, "I will destroy the wisdom of the wise, and the discernment of the discerning I will thwart." Where is the one who is wise? Where is the scribe? Where is the debater of this age? Has not God made foolish the wisdom of the world?

For since, in the wisdom of God, the world did not know God through wisdom, God decided, through the foolishness of our proclamation, to save those who believe. For Jews demand signs and Greeks desire wisdom, but we proclaim Christ crucified, a stumbling block to Jews and foolishness to Gentiles, but to those who are the called, both Jews and Greeks, Christ the power of God and the wisdom of God. For God's foolishness is wiser than human wisdom, and God's weakness is stronger than human strength.

GOSPEL   *John 2:13—25*

Revised Common Lectionary: John 2:13—22

The Passover of the Jews was near, and Jesus went up to Jerusalem. In the temple he found people selling cattle, sheep, and doves, and the money changers seated at their tables. Making a whip of cords, he drove all of them out of the temple, both the sheep and the cattle. He also poured out the coins of the money changers and overturned their tables. He told those who were selling the doves, "Take these things out of here! Stop making my Father's house a marketplace!" His disciples remembered that it was written, "Zeal for your house will consume me." The Jews then said to him, "What sign can you show us for doing this?" Jesus answered them, "Destroy this temple, and in three days I will raise it up." The Jews then said, "This temple has been under construction for forty-six years, and will you raise it up in three days?" But he was speaking of the temple of his body. After he was raised from the dead, his disciples remembered that he had said this; and they believed the scripture and the word that Jesus had spoken. When he was in Jerusalem during the Passover festival, many believed in his name because they saw the signs that he was doing. But Jesus on his part would not entrust himself to them, because he knew all people and needed no one to testify about anyone; for he himself knew what was in everyone.

Practice of Prayer

Psalm 19:8, 9, 10, 11

The law of the LORD is perfect,
it revives the soul.
The rule of the LORD is to be trusted,
it gives wisdom to the simple.

The precepts of the LORD are right,
they gladden the heart.
The command of the LORD is clear,
it gives light to the eyes.

The fear of the LORD is holy,
abiding for ever.
The decrees of the LORD are truth
and all of them just.

They are more to be desired than gold,
than the purest of gold
and sweeter are they than honey,
than honey from the comb.

Practice of Prudence

"Don't go there." Throughout the gospels, his more pragmatic disciples caution Jesus about saying or doing anything that might offend. We can only imagine their horror, then, when they witnessed him charging into the Temple, tipping over tables and driving out the traders—a forceful and frightening scene.

Every day we are faced with choices about where to put our time and energy. Just when we are comfortable, Jesus is liable to come crashing into our lives, challenging us to get rid of anything that hinders our relationship with God. Taking stock of the stuff of our lives—our belongings, our activities, our priorities—can show us where we have imprudently strayed from our spiritual path. Having some of it thrown out may be just what we need.

Scripture Insights

We commonly learn, read and follow the Ten Commandments out of context. Whether in a catechism class or on a courtroom wall, they often stand alone like a timeless, universal statement of perfect morality. But the Bible places them firmly in their context within the story of Israel. In Exodus 3, God tells Moses that he is coming to deliver Israel from their oppressors. Exodus 4–11 narrates the struggle between Moses and the pharaoh before the deliverance. The first passover celebration comes in chapters 12–13. The spectacular rescue from the Egyptians and its aftermath appear in Exodus 14–15, and the events of the journey to Mount Sinai, including the first manna and the water from the rock, happen in chapters 16–18. Finally in Exodus 19, the people reach Sinai, where God tells them through Moses, "You have seen . . . how I bore you on eagles' wings and brought you to myself. Now therefore, if you obey my voice and keep my covenant, you shall be my treasured possession out of all the peoples. Indeed, the whole earth is mine, but you shall be for me a realm of priests and a holy nation" (19:4–6). Then follows in chapter 20 the text we read today.

The proper setting for understanding the Decalogue is the mighty act of salvation and the covenant that God established as its result. Its Ten Commandments presuppose that one is already participating in the covenant. People obey out of love, faithfulness and gratitude. The very first commandment emphasizes the context of salvation: "I am the LORD your God, *who brought you out of the land of Egypt* . . . you shall have no other gods before me" (Exodus 20:2).

Moses sealed the people's participation in the covenant by sprinkling them with the "blood of the covenant" (Exodus 24:8). Jesus renewed that as "my blood of the covenant which is poured out for many" (Mark 14:24). For Christians, the context for understanding and obeying is the paschal mystery of our Lord, who through the eucharist gives us the wisdom and power to obey.

The context for understanding and obeying is the Jewish Passover and the Christian Pasch. How are they similar?

READING I   *Exodus 17:3—7*

Revised Common Lectionary: Exodus 17:1–7

But the people thirsted there for water; and the people complained against Moses and said, "Why did you bring us out of Egypt, to kill us and our children and livestock with thirst?"

So Moses cried out to the LORD, "What shall I do with this people? They are almost ready to stone me." The LORD said to Moses, "Go on ahead of the people, and take some of the elders of Israel with you; take in your hand the staff with which you struck the Nile, and go. I will be standing there in front of you on the rock at Horeb. Strike the rock, and water will come out of it, so that the people may drink."

Moses did so, in the sight of the elders of Israel. He called the place Massah and Meribah, because the Israelites quarreled and tested the LORD, saying, "Is the LORD among us or not?"

READING II   *Romans 5:1—2, 5—8*

Revised Common Lectionary: Romans 5:1–11

Since we are justified by faith, we have peace with God through our Lord Jesus Christ, through whom we have obtained access to this grace in which we stand; and we boast in our hope of sharing the glory of God. And hope does not disappoint us, because God's love has been poured into our hearts through the Holy Spirit that has been given to us.

For while we were still weak, at the right time Christ died for the ungodly. Indeed, rarely will anyone die for a righteous person— though perhaps for a good person someone might actually dare to die. But it is proof of God's own love for us in that while we still were sinners Christ died for us.

Much more surely then, now that we have been justified by his blood, will we be saved through him from the wrath of God. For if while we were enemies, we were reconciled to God through the death of the Son of God, much more surely, having been reconciled, will we be saved by the life of the Son of God. But more than that, we even boast in God through our Lord Jesus Christ, through whom we have now received reconciliation.

GOSPEL   *John 4:5—15, 19b—26, 39a, 40—42*

Jesus came to a Samaritan city called Sychar, near the plot of ground that Jacob had given to his son Joseph. Jacob's well was there, and Jesus, tired out by his journey, was sitting by the well. It was about noon.

A Samaritan woman came to draw water, and Jesus said to her, "Give me a drink." (His disciples had gone to the city to buy food.) The Samaritan woman said to him, "How is it that you, a Jewish man, ask a drink of me, a woman of Samaria?" (Jewish people do not share things in common with Samaritans.) Jesus answered her, "If you knew the gift of God, and who it is that is saying to you, 'Give me a drink,' you would have asked him, and he would have given you living water." The woman said to him, "Sir, you have no bucket, and the well is deep. Where do you get that living water? Are you greater than our ancestor Jacob, who gave us the well, and with his children and his flocks drank from it?"

Jesus said to her, "Everyone who drinks of this water will be thirsty again, but those who drink of the water that I will give them will never be thirsty. The water that I will give will become in them a spring of water gushing up to eternal life." The woman said to Jesus, "Sir, give me this water, so that I may never be thirsty or have to keep coming here to draw water."

The woman said to Jesus, "Sir, I see that you are a prophet. Our ancestors worshiped on this mountain, but you say that the place where people must worship is in Jerusalem."

Jesus said to her, "Woman, believe me, the hour is coming when you will worship the Father neither on this mountain nor in Jerusalem. You worship what you do not know; we worship what we know, for salvation is from the Jewish people. But the hour is coming, and is now here, when the true worshipers will worship the Father in spirit and truth, for such worshipers the Father seeks. God is spirit, and those who worship God must worship in spirit and truth." The woman said to him, "I know that Messiah is coming" (who is called Christ). "When he comes, he will proclaim all things to us." Jesus said to her, "Here I am, the one who is speaking to you."

So when the Samaritans came to him, they asked him to stay with them; and Jesus stayed there two days. And many more believed because of his word. They said to the woman, "It is no longer because of what you said that we believe, for we have heard for ourselves, and we know that this is truly the Savior of the world."

Practice of Prayer

Psalm 95:8—9

"Harden not your hearts as at Meribah,
as on that day at Massah in the dessert
when your ancestors put me to the test;
when they tried me, though they saw my work."

Practice of Justice

Even for the most ardent critics of the death penalty, the 2001 execution of Timothy McVeigh was a hard one to oppose. His vicious attack on the federal building in Oklahoma City killed 168 people and maimed hundreds more, both physically and emotionally. For those who stand against the death sentence, justice is not served through the taking of someone else's life, no matter how hideous the crime.

On the day of the execution, McVeigh's lawyers stated that he was not just a criminal; he was also someone's son, someone's brother, someone's friend. It was a simple reminder of a great truth—we all count for something to somebody, and certainly to God. Pray today for guidance for all of us as we try to discern how to serve justice. Pray too for the outcasts in our society, especially those who are particularly difficult to love or to forgive.

Scripture Insights

Often in scripture, climactic spiritual moments are followed by times of doubt and testing. So the Israelites in the wilderness carp at God almost immediately after their stunning deliverance from Egypt. Later biblical tradition remembered Meribah and Massah ("resting" and "quarrel") as a scene of ungrateful hardness of heart after God had revealed his love in the Exodus (see Psalm 95; Hebrews 4:7–15).

But it was also remembered as a time when God showed endless patience and mercy to the people even while they continued to err. Our story in Exodus shows God's patient parental kindness providing water out of nowhere for the whining children on the road.

Jesus speaks to the woman of Samaria in a scene fraught with the tensions of history. Israel's defeat and exile in the late eighth century before Christ was due, according to the prophets, to its idolatrous worship of other gods (Jeremiah 3:1–10). The few who remained in the land intermarried with Assyrian colonists, followed a corrupted form of Yahwistic worship and antagonized the Jewish exiles returning from Babylon. These were the Samaritans; this is why the woman's conversation with Jesus the Jew turns to matters of worship. Some have thought that the reference to "five husbands" (verse 18, in the longer form of the reading) might allude to the five gods of their Canaanite worship. In any case, breaking with Jewish custom, Jesus accepted the Samaritan woman and her people (while maintaining nevertheless that "salvation is from the Jews"). The story portrays the merciful God extending compassion and wisdom far beyond the borders of Israel. In the synoptic gospels, Jesus says, "I come to call not the righteous, but sinners" (Matthew 9:13, Mark 2:17, Luke 5:32). It is a concrete illustration of the striking theology voiced by Paul that Christ gave his life not for holy people, but for "the ungodly . . . while we were still sinners."

What role does water play in these stories?

READING I   *2 Chronicles 36:14—16, 19—23*

Revised Common Lectionary: Numbers 21:4–9

All the leading priests and the people also were exceedingly unfaithful, following all the abominations of the nations; and they polluted the house of the LORD that he had consecrated in Jerusalem. The LORD, the God of their ancestors, sent persistently to them by his messengers, because he had compassion on his people and on his dwelling place; but they kept mocking the messengers of God, despising his words, and scoffing at his prophets, until the wrath of the LORD against his people became so great that there was no remedy. They burned the house of God, broke down the wall of Jerusalem, burned all its palaces with fire, and destroyed all its precious vessels. He took into exile in Babylon those who had escaped from the sword, and they became servants to him and to his sons until the establishment of the kingdom of Persia, to fulfill the word of the LORD by the mouth of Jeremiah, until the land had made up for its sabbaths. All the days that it lay desolate it kept sabbath, to fulfill seventy years. In the first year of King Cyrus of Persia, in fulfillment of the word of the LORD spoken by Jeremiah, the LORD stirred up the spirit of King Cyrus of Persia so that he sent a herald throughout all his kingdom and also declared in a written edict: "Thus says King Cyrus of Persia: The LORD, the God of heaven, has given me all the kingdoms of the earth, and he has charged me to build him a house at Jerusalem, which is in Judah. Whoever is among you of all his people, may the LORD his God be with him! Let him go up."

READING II   *Ephesians 2:1—10*

Roman Catholic: Ephesians 2:4–10

You were dead through the trespasses and sins in which you once lived, following the course of this world, following the ruler of the power of the air, the spirit that is now at work among those who are disobedient. All of us once lived among them in the passions of our flesh, following the desires of flesh and senses, and we were by nature children of wrath, like everyone else. But God, who is rich in mercy, out of the great love with which God loved us even when we were dead through our trespasses, made us alive together with Christ—by grace you have been saved. With Christ God raised us up and enthroned us in the heavenly places in Christ Jesus, so that in the ages to come might be shown the immeasurable riches of God's grace in kindness toward us in Christ Jesus. For by grace you have been saved through faith, and this is not your own doing; it is the gift of God—not the result of works, so that no one may boast. For we are what God has made us, created in Christ Jesus for good works, which God prepared beforehand to be our way of life.

GOSPEL   *John 3:14—21*

Jesus said: "Just as Moses lifted up the serpent in the wilderness, so must the Son-of-Man be lifted up, that whoever believes in him may have eternal life. For God loved the world in this way, that God gave the Son, the only begotten one, so that everyone who believes in him may not perish but may have eternal life.

"Indeed, God did not send the Son into the world to condemn the world, but in order that the world might be saved through him. Those who believe in him are not condemned; but those who do not believe are condemned already, because they have not believed in the name of the only Son of God. And this is the judgment, that the light has come into the world, and people loved darkness rather than light because their deeds were evil. For all who do evil hate the light and do not come to the light, so that their deeds may not be exposed. But those who do what is true come to the light, so that it may be clearly seen that their deeds have been done in God."

Practice of Prayer

Psalm 137:1— 2, 3, 4—5, 6

By the rivers of Babylon
there we sat and wept,
remembering Zion;
on the poplars that grew there
we hung up our harps.

For it was there that they asked us,
our captors, for songs,
our oppressors, for joy.
"Sing to us," they said,
"One of Zion's songs."

O how could we sing
the song of the LORD
on alien soil?
If I forget you, Jerusalem,
let my right hand wither!

O let my tongue
cleave to my mouth
if I remember you not,
if I prize not Jerusalem
above all my joys!

Practice of Prudence

Four weeks into the lenten journey we are surprised by the Solemnity of the Annunciation of the Lord on March 25. In the midst of penance we turn to contemplate the incarnation. This week's gospel reading helps to pull the two together as we hear Jesus explaining to Nicodemus why the Son came into the world. God sent him to save, not to condemn. Nevertheless we may condemn ourselves: "The light has come into the world, and people loved darkness rather than light because their deeds were evil." The Light taking human form in the Virgin's womb was sent to break through our darkness, but we must be willing to see our deeds exposed in it. Examined in Christ's light, our actions may look different than when we performed them in our own dimness. It is a work of prudence to present ourselves to that light, so painfully clarifying, yet saving.

Scripture Insights

Today's Chronicles reading tersely ends the sorrowful story of Judah's disobedience toward God. For this writer, the exile to Babylon was a natural outcome of grievous sin. He was heir to the viewpoint: "If you obey God's commandments, you will prosper. If not, you will perish." (See Deuteronomy 4:25–27; 8:19; 11:13–17; 13:22–28.) In this way the writers explained Israel and Judah's respective defeats by foreign powers as acts of divine justice that had been foretold. In today's text, we can hear the priests' concern that the rituals associated with the code of holiness could no longer be performed. This is reflected in the report of the fiery destruction of the Temple *and its vessels,* and the interpretation of the seventy years of exile as a *sabbath rest* for the land. But suddenly the divine sun shines through the storm clouds of the exile when Cyrus proclaims the release of the captives, the people are freed to return to their land, to rebuild their temple and to restore their spiritual fortunes. For the haggard exiles, the decree was an unimaginable grace, lavish and unexpected, an unparalleled act of divine mercy.

Imagining the beneficence of a new king and the state of the returning exiles gives us a perspective on the cornucopia of theological language of Ephesians. The gospel is the proclamation of favor issued by a powerful ruler and generous patron, "rich in mercy" (2:4), with "immeasurable riches of grace" (2:7) which are continually dispensed to the subjects. This generosity is beyond all measure, "far more than we can ask or imagine" (3:20), even when we were like the exiles, victims of our own disobedience, "dead through our trespasses and sins" (2:1, 5). This "kindness" is massively out of proportion to what we might have expected. Clearly, this situation is none of our doing but the result of God's unlimited favor. In Christian language, it is "grace," which excludes all boasting and spiritual preening.

Read in your Bible all of Psalm 137, which expresses the bitter experience of the exile, and contrast that with the experience of grace that came later. Does waiting for God's grace become easier when you know it will ultimately come?

READING I   *1 Samuel 16:1b, 6—7, 10—13a*

Revised Common Lectionary: 1 Samuel 16:1–13

The LORD said to Samuel, "Fill your horn with oil and set out; I will send you to Jesse the Bethlehemite, for I have provided for myself a king among his sons."

When they came, Samuel looked on Eliab and thought, "Surely the LORD's anointed is now before the LORD." But the LORD said to Samuel, "Do not look on his appearance or on the height of his stature, because I have rejected him; for the LORD does not see as mortals see; they look on the outward appearance, but the LORD looks on the heart." Jesse made seven of his sons pass before Samuel, and Samuel said to Jesse, "The LORD has not chosen any of these."

Samuel said to Jesse, "Are all your sons here?" And he said, "There remains yet the youngest, but he is keeping the sheep." And Samuel said to Jesse, "Send and bring him; for we will not sit down until he comes here." Jesse sent and brought him in. Now he was ruddy, and had beautiful eyes, and was handsome. The LORD said, "Rise and anoint him; for this is the one." Then Samuel took the horn of oil, and anointed him in the presence of his brothers; and the spirit of the LORD came mightily upon David from that day forward. Samuel then set out and went to Ramah.

READING II   *Ephesians 5:8—14*

Once you were darkness, but now in the Lord you are light. Live as children of light—for the fruit of the light is found in all that is good and right and true. Try to find out what is pleasing to the Lord. Take no part in the unfruitful works of darkness, but instead expose them. For it is shameful even to mention what such people do secretly; but everything exposed by the light becomes visible, for everything that becomes visible is light.

Therefore it says, "Sleeper, awake! Rise from the dead, and Christ will shine on you."

GOSPEL   *John 9:1—41*

As Jesus walked along, he saw a man blind from birth. His disciples asked him, "Rabbi, who sinned, this man or his parents, that he was born blind?" Jesus answered, "Neither this man nor his parents sinned; he was born blind so that God's works might be revealed in him. We must work the works of the one who sent me while it is day; night is coming when no one can work. As long as I am in the world, I am the light of the world."

When Jesus had said this, he spat on the ground and made mud with the saliva and spread the mud on the man's eyes, saying to him, "Go, wash in the pool of Siloam" (which means Sent). Then he went and washed and came back able to see.

The neighbors and those who had seen him before as a beggar began to ask, "Is this not the man who used to sit and beg?" Some were saying, "It is he." Others were saying, "No, but it is someone like him." He kept saying, "I am the man." But they kept asking him, "Then how were your eyes opened?" He answered, "The man called Jesus made mud, spread it on my eyes, and said to me, 'Go to Siloam and wash.' Then I went and washed and received my sight." They said to him, "Where is he?" He said, "I do not know."

They brought to the Pharisees the man who had formerly been blind. Now it was a sabbath day when Jesus made the mud and opened his eyes. Then the Pharisees also began to ask him how he had received his sight. He said to them, "He put mud on my eyes. Then I washed, and now I see." Some of the Pharisees said, "This man is not from God, for he does not observe the sabbath." But others said, "How can a man who is a sinner perform such signs?" And they were divided. So they said again to the blind man, "What do you say about him? It was your eyes he opened." He said, "He is a prophet."

The Judeans did not believe that he had been blind and had received his sight until they called the parents of the man who had received his sight and asked them, "Is this your son, who you say was born blind? How then does he now see?" His parents answered, "We know that this is our son, and that he was born blind; but we do not know how it is that now he sees, nor do we know who opened his eyes. Ask him; he is of age. He will speak for himself." His parents said this because they were afraid of the Judeans, who had already agreed that anyone who confessed Jesus to be the Messiah would be put out of the synagogue. Therefore his parents said, "He is of age; ask him."

So for the second time they called the man who had been blind, and they said to him, "Give glory to God! We know that this man is a sinner." He answered, "I do not know whether he is a sinner. One thing I do know, that though I was blind, now I see." They said to him, "What did he do to you? How did he open your eyes?" He answered them, "I have told you already, and you would not listen. Why do you want to hear it again? Do you also want to become his disciples?" Then they reviled him, saying, "You are his disciple, but we are disciples of Moses. We know that God has spoken to Moses, but as for this person, we do not know where he comes from." The man answered, "Here is an astonishing thing! You do not know where he comes from, and yet he opened my eyes. We know that God does not listen to sinners, but does listen to anyone who is devout and obeys God's will. Never since the world began has it been heard that anyone opened the eyes of someone born blind. If this person were not from God, he could do nothing." They answered him, "You were born entirely in sins, and are you trying to teach us?" And they drove him out.

Jesus heard that they had driven him out, and when he found him, he said, "Do you believe in the Son-of-Man?" He answered, "And who is he, sir? Tell me, so that I may believe in him." Jesus said to him, "You have seen him, and he is the one speaking with you." He said, "Lord, I believe." And he worshiped Jesus. Jesus said, "I came into this world for judgment so that those who do not see may see, and those who do see may become blind." Some of the Pharisees near Jesus heard this and said to him, "Surely we are not blind, are we?" Jesus said to them, "If you were blind, you would not have sin. But now that you say, 'We see,' your sin remains."

Scripture Insights

The texts enlarge on last week's instruction about looking past appearances to see to the spiritual heart of matters, as it were, with God's own eyes. Samuel was among the most powerful and celebrated figures of ancient Israel. He was born of his mother Hannah's prayer (1 Samuel 1:9–20), trained to discern the word of the Lord by the old priest Eli (3:1–10), and appointed Israel's prophet, judge and king-maker (3:19–20; 7:15; 8:22). But even Samuel needed instruction when he presumed that God's choice to succeed King Saul should be mature, handsome and tall. God says that mortals "look on the outward appearance, but the LORD looks on the heart" (16:7).

This theme recurs in John's gospel as Jesus advises succinctly, "Do not judge by appearances, but judge with right judgment" (John 7:24). The story of the man born blind is a case study in right judgment. When disciples come upon the man, they make him an occasion for philosophizing about sin and causality: "Who sinned . . . that he was born blind?" Jesus leads beyond their tired alternatives to a third possibility: His blindness is a special theater of God's glory.

The Pharisees' criteria for judgment seem calculated to avoid the obvious. First they say that the healing on the Sabbath violates the law, so the healer must not be from God; then they doubt it really happened; they bully the man's parents; they impugn both his character and Jesus'; they threaten excommunication. Their box of thought and argument remains tightly shut to any light but its own. The only place for them to see truly is outside the box, which not coincidentally is where Jesus is. It is also where the man ended up when they finally drove him out. When Jesus found him outside he gave the man the second, inward sight to see Jesus as he truly is (9:35–38).

Laying aside the most obvious images of what might be "works of darkness," read the Ephesians passage as if you had been given sight by Jesus, like the blind man of the gospel story. What new insights about your own inner work occur to you?

READING I   *Jeremiah 31:31—34*

The days are surely coming, says the LORD, when I will make a new covenant with the house of Israel and the house of Judah. It will not be like the covenant that I made with their ancestors when I took them by the hand to bring them out of the land of Egypt— a covenant that they broke, though I was married to them, says the LORD.

But this is the covenant that I will make with the house of Israel after those days, says the LORD: I will put my law within them, and I will write it on their hearts; and I will be their God, and they shall be my people. No longer shall they teach one another, or say to each other, "Know the LORD," for they shall all know me, from the least of them to the greatest, says the LORD; for I will forgive their iniquity, and remember their sin no more.

READING II   *Hebrews 5:5—10*

Roman Catholic: Hebrews 5:7–9

Christ did not glorify himself in becoming a high priest, but was appointed by the one who said to him, "You are my Son, today I have begotten you"; as God says also in another place, "You are a priest forever, according to the order of Melchizedek." In the days of his flesh, Jesus offered up prayers and supplications, with loud cries and tears, to the one who was able to save him from death, and he was heard because of his reverent submission. Although he was a Son, he learned obedience through what he suffered; and having been made perfect, he became the source of eternal salvation for all who obey him, having been designated by God a high priest according to the order of Melchizedek.

GOSPEL   *John 12:20—33*

Now among those who went up to worship at the festival were some Greeks. They came to Philip, who was from Bethsaida in Galilee, and said to him, "Sir, we wish to see Jesus." Philip went and told Andrew; then Andrew and Philip went and told Jesus. Jesus answered them, "The hour has come for the Son-of-Man to be glorified. Very truly, I tell you, unless a grain of wheat falls into the earth and dies, it remains just a single grain; but if it dies, it bears much fruit. Those who love their life lose it, and those who hate their life in this world will keep it for eternal life. Whoever serves me must follow me, and where I am, there will my servant be also. Whoever serves me, the Father will honor.

"Now my soul is troubled. And what should I say—'Father, save me from this hour'? No, it is for this reason that I have come to this hour. Father, glorify your name." Then a voice came from heaven, "I have glorified it, and I will glorify it again." The crowd standing there heard it and said that it was thunder. Others said, "An angel has spoken to him." Jesus answered, "This voice has come for your sake, not for mine. Now is the judgment of this world; now the ruler of this world will be driven out. And I, when I am lifted up from the earth, will draw all people to myself." Jesus said this to indicate the kind of death he was to die.

Practice of Prayer

Psalm 51:3—4, 12—13, 14—15

Have mercy on me, God, in your kindness.
In your compassion blot out my offense.
O wash me more and more from my guilt
and cleanse me from my sin.

A pure heart create for me, O God,
put a steadfast spirit within me.
Do not cast me away from your presence,
nor deprive me of your holy spirit.

Give me again the joy of your help;
with a spirit of fervor sustain me,
that I may teach transgressors your ways
and sinners may return to you.

Practice of the Fortitude

This week's readings from Hebrews and John show us Jesus in anguish preparing for his death. He wrestles with fears, recounts the principle guiding his destiny ("unless a grain of wheat . . . dies . . .) and steadily, clearly chooses what God has asked of him. Today, the week before the Sunday of the Lord's Passion, we share in his painful deliberations.

April 9, the anniversary of the death of Dietrich Bonhoeffer, a courageous and principled Lutheran theologian, is an opportunity to continue this meditation on self-sacrificing choices. Bonhoeffer's resistance to the Nazis in his native Germany put him in danger. Though he went to England for a time and was offered a teaching position in the United States where he would be safe, he decided to return to Germany in solidarity with those who were suffering there, and was eventually arrested and imprisoned. He wrote extensively in prison until he was sent to the concentration camps and finally hanged.

The fortitude of these fully conscious, fully human people—Jesus and his follower Dietrich Bonhoeffer—gives us much to ponder.

Scripture Insights

The short passage from the letter to the Hebrews casts unusual light on Jesus. The gospels tell us that Jesus prayed (Matthew 14:23; Mark 1:35; Luke 6:12), and what he prayed about (Mark 14:36; Luke 22:22); but here we read that Jesus prayed "with loud cries and tears." John's gospel tells us that Jesus was confident that God heard his prayers (John 11:41–42), perhaps because he was God's Son; here we read that Jesus "was heard because of his reverent submission." The gospels tell us that Jesus remained in constant communion with the will of God (Matthew 26:39; John 8:29); here we read that "he learned obedience through what he suffered." The gospels tell us that at Jesus' baptism he was already "my Son, the beloved" in whom God was "well pleased" (Luke 3:22); but here we read that Jesus was "made perfect."

The letter's frank statement that Jesus progressed toward perfection stands alongside a christology equal in majesty to any in the New Testament: This same human Jesus is the "heir of all things through whom God created the worlds," "the reflection of God's glory and the exact imprint of God's very being," the one who "sustains all things by his powerful word" (Hebrews 1:2–4).

This writer grasped what many views of Jesus lack: a clear understanding of Jesus' humanity. Human beings develop over time, feel doubt and pain, do not know their fate, aspire to achieve. Hebrews makes explicit what the gospels imply: Jesus progressed toward God by suffering.

The Jeremiah passage speaks of the new covenant where rule-keeping cannot pass for true devotion and God will write God's law "on their hearts." Jesus' moment-by-moment practice of obedience fulfilled that prophecy by engraving God's covenant into the human heart forever. He wrote this inner law on our hearts with the stylus of his passion.

In Psalm 51, what evidence do you see that the psalmist was praying about an obedience deep in the heart, not merely outward appearance?

April 6, 2003

READING I   *Ezekiel 37:12—14*

Revised Common Lectionary: Ezekiel 37:1–14

"Therefore prophesy, and say to them, Thus says the Lord GOD: I am going to open your graves, and bring you up from your graves, O my people; and I will bring you back to the land of Israel. And you shall know that I am the LORD, when I open your graves, and bring you up from your graves, O my people. I will put my spirit within you, and you shall live, and I will place you on your own soil; then you shall know that I, the LORD, have spoken and will act," says the LORD.

READING II   *Romans 8:8—11*

Revised Common Lectionary: Romans 8:6–11

Those who are in the flesh cannot please God. But you are not in the flesh; you are in the Spirit, since the Spirit of God dwells in you. Anyone who does not have the Spirit of Christ does not belong to Christ. But if Christ is in you, though the body is dead because of sin, the Spirit is life because of righteousness. If the Spirit of the one who raised Jesus from the dead dwells in you, the one who raised Christ from the dead will give life to your mortal bodies also through this Spirit dwelling in you.

GOSPEL   *John 11:3—7, 17, 20—27, 33b—45*

So the sisters sent a message to Jesus, "Lord, he whom you love is ill." But when Jesus heard it, he said, "This illness does not lead to death; rather it is for God's glory, so that the Son of God may be glorified through it." Accordingly, though Jesus loved Martha and her sister and Lazarus, after having heard that Lazarus was ill, he stayed two days longer in the place where he was.

Then after this he said to the disciples, "Let us go to Judea again."

When Jesus arrived, he found that Lazarus had already been in the tomb four days. When Martha heard that Jesus was coming, she went and met him, while Mary stayed at home. Martha said to Jesus, "Lord, if you had been here, my brother would not have died. But even now I know that whatever you ask from God, God will give you." Jesus said to her, "Your brother will rise again." Martha said to him, "I know that he will rise again in the resurrection on the last day." Jesus said to her, "I am the resurrection and the life. Those who believe in me, even though they die, will live, and everyone who lives and believes in me will never die. Do you believe this?" She said to him, "Yes, Lord, I believe that you are the Messiah, the Son of God, the one coming into the world."

Jesus was greatly disturbed in spirit and deeply moved. He said, "Where have you laid him?" They said to him, "Lord, come and see." Jesus began to weep. So the Judeans said, "See how he loved him!" But some of them said, "Could not the one who opened the eyes of the blind man have kept this man from dying?"

Then Jesus, again greatly disturbed, came to the tomb. It was a cave, and a stone was lying against it. Jesus said, "Take away the stone." Martha, the sister of the dead man, said to him, "Lord, already there is a stench because he has been dead four days." Jesus said to her, "Did I not tell you that if you believed, you would see the glory of God?"

So they took away the stone. And Jesus looked upward and said, "Father, I thank you for having heard me. I knew that you always hear me, but I have said this for the sake of the crowd standing here, so that they may believe that you sent me." When Jesus had said this, he cried with a loud voice, "Lazarus, come out!" The dead man came out, his hands and feet bound with strips of cloth, and his face wrapped in a cloth. Jesus said to them, "Unbind him, and let him go."

Many of the Judeans therefore, who had come with Mary and had seen what Jesus did, believed in him.

Practice of Prayer

Psalm 130:1—2, 3—4, 5—6, 7—8

Out of the depths I cry to you, O LORD,
LORD, hear my voice!
O let your ears be attentive
to the voice of my pleading.

If you, O LORD, should mark our guilt,
LORD, who would survive?
But with you is found forgiveness:
for this we revere you.

My soul is waiting for the LORD.
I count on God's word.
My soul is longing for the LORD
more than those who watch for daybreak.

Because with the LORD there is mercy
and fullness of redemption,
Israel indeed God will redeem
from all its iniquity.

Practice of Justice

Ezekiel's description of God opening the graves and bringing the people up from their depths is always riveting. Earlier in that chapter the scene was vividly set: God brings the prophet into a valley full of dry bones and demonstrates how the bones will be brought together, enfleshed and filled with breath.

Those who have seen news photos of the aftermath of recent conflicts can't help but picture the discovered bones of Holocaust dead, the victims of the Khmer Rouge, the uncovered mass graves of Bosnians or of those massacred in Rwanda. Scenes of carnage are always painful to behold, and even more painful to hold in the heart, though hold them we do—in solidarity with the victims. Ezekiel's image gives us the perfect companion image to place alongside these as we work for the conditions of justice that must precede peace.

Scripture Insights

Today's texts emphasize the mystery, certainty and glory of God's power of resurrection. We might be content with their encouragement and leave it at that. But the placement of these texts in the depths of Lent rather than during the Easter season suggests another dimension—the presence of life in the midst of death.

The prophecy of Ezekiel appeared in the midst of the national calamity of Judah's exile in Babylon. With the land overrun, the Temple destroyed, its sacrifices halted and the king in chains, Ezekiel might well envision the glory of the Lord departing the land (10:1–21). Well might the people mourn, "Our bones are dried up, and our hope is lost; we are cut off completely" (Ezekiel 37:11). But into this scene of death and despair comes the prophet, commanded by the Lord to "breathe upon these slain" his words of hope "that they may live" (Ezekiel 37:9). The resurrection spoken of in this text engenders the corporate soul of the people of Judah and the historical resuscitation of their national identity and their relationship to God. Ezekiel's message of life gets its impact from its timing, when the people's hope of a future is dead.

Paradoxically, Jesus' raising of Lazarus is not primarily about resurrection. Lazarus's new life was, after all, the old life brought back again. Rather it is a provocative metaphor showing how believing in Jesus brings about the beginning of that new life in the present. Jesus says, "I am the resurrection and the life." To emphasize the continuous life remaining in the midst of death, he adds, "those who believe in me, even though they die [physically], will live [spiritually], and everyone who lives [spiritually] and believes in me will never die [spiritually]." The power of resurrection life is available now within our lenten "valley of tears," and not only at the future resurrection.

As you lead this double life, "in the flesh" and "in the spirit," how do you keep Christ's resurrection active in your awareness?

67

READING I   Isaiah 50:4—9a

Roman Catholic: Isaiah 50:4—7

The Lord GOD has given me
  the tongue of a teacher,
that I may know how to sustain
  the weary with a word.
Morning by morning the Lord GOD wakens—
  wakens my ear
  to listen as those who are taught.
The Lord GOD has opened my ear,
  and I was not rebellious,
  I did not turn backward.
I gave my back to those who struck me,
  and my cheeks to those
    who pulled out the beard;
I did not hide my face
  from insult and spitting.

The Lord GOD helps me;
  therefore I have not been disgraced;
therefore I have set my face like flint,
  and I know that I shall not be put to shame;
  the one who vindicates me is near.
Who will contend with me?
  Let us stand up together.
Who are my adversaries?
  Let them confront me.
It is the Lord GOD who helps me;
  who will declare me guilty?

READING II   Philippians 2:5—11

Roman Catholic: Philippians 2:6—11

Let the same mind be in you that was in Christ Jesus, who, although being in the form of God, did not regard equality with God as something to be exploited, but relinquished it all, taking the form of a slave, being born in human likeness. And being found in human form, he humbled himself and became obedient to the point of death—even death on a cross.

Therefore God also highly exalted him and gave him the name that is above every name, so that at the name of Jesus every knee should bend, in heaven and on earth and under the earth, and every tongue should confess that Jesus Christ is Lord, to the glory of God, the Father.

GOSPEL   Mark 14:1—15:47

It was two days before the Passover and the festival of Unleavened Bread. The chief priests and the scribes were looking for a way to arrest Jesus by stealth and kill him; for they said, "Not during the festival, or there may be a riot among the people."

While Jesus was at Bethany in the house of Simon the leper, as he sat at the table, a woman came with an alabaster jar of very costly ointment of nard, and she broke open the jar and poured the ointment on his head. But some were there who said to one another in anger, "Why was the ointment wasted in this way? For this ointment could have been sold for more than three hundred denarii, and the money given to the poor." And they scolded her. But Jesus said, "Let her alone; why do you trouble her? She has performed a good service for me. For you always have the poor with you, and you can show kindness to them whenever you wish; but you will not always have me. She has done what she could; she has anointed my body beforehand for its burial. Truly I tell you, wherever the good news is proclaimed in the whole world, what she has done will be told in remembrance of her."

Then Judas Iscariot, who was one of the twelve, went to the chief priests in order to betray Jesus to them. When they heard it, they were greatly pleased, and promised to give Judas money. So he began to look for an opportunity to betray Jesus.

On the first day of Unleavened Bread, when the Passover lamb is sacrificed, his disciples said to him, "Where do you want us to go and make the preparations for you to eat the Passover?" So Jesus sent two of his disciples, saying to them, "Go into the city, and a man carrying a jar of water will meet you; follow him, and wherever he enters, say to the owner of the house, 'The Teacher asks, Where is my guest room where I may eat the Passover with my disciples?' The owner will show you a large room upstairs, furnished and ready. Make preparations for us there." So the disciples set out and went to the city, and found everything as Jesus had told them; and they prepared the Passover meal.

When it was evening, Jesus came with the twelve. And when they had taken their places and were eating, Jesus said, "Truly I tell you, one of you will betray me, one who is eating with me." They began to be distressed and to say to him one after another, "Surely, not I?" He said to them, "It is one of the twelve, one who is dipping bread into the bowl with me. For the Son-of-Man goes as it is written of him, but woe to that one by whom the Son-of-Man is betrayed! It would have been better for that one not to have been born."

While they were eating, Jesus took a loaf of bread, and after blessing it he broke it, gave it to them, and said, "Take; this is my body." Then he took a cup, and after giving thanks he gave it to them, and all of them drank from it. He said to them, "This is my blood of the covenant, which is poured out for many. Truly I tell you, I will never again drink of the fruit of the vine until that day when I drink it new in the dominion of God."

When they had sung the hymn, they went out to the Mount of Olives. And Jesus said to them, "You will all become deserters; for it is written,

'I will strike the shepherd,
and the sheep will be scattered.'

But after I am raised up, I will go before you to Galilee." Peter said to him, "Even though all become deserters, I will not." Jesus said to him, "Truly I tell you, this day, this very night, before the cock crows twice, you will deny me three times." But Peter said vehemently, "Even though I must die with you, I will not deny you." And all of them said the same.

They went to a place called Gethsemane; and Jesus said to his disciples, "Sit here while I pray." He took with him Peter and James and John, and began to be distressed and agitated. And he said to them, "I am deeply grieved, even to death; remain here, and keep awake." And going a little farther, Jesus threw himself on the ground and prayed that, if it were possible, the hour might pass from him. He said, "Abba, Father, for you all things are possible; remove this cup from me; yet, not what I want, but what you want." Jesus came and found them sleeping; and he said to Peter,

"Simon, are you asleep? Could you not keep awake one hour? Keep awake and pray that you may not come into the time of trial; the spirit indeed is willing, but the flesh is weak." And again Jesus went away and prayed, saying the same words. And once more he came and found them sleeping, for their eyes were very heavy; and they did not know what to say to him. He came a third time and said to them, "Are you still sleeping and taking your rest? Enough! The hour has come; the Son-of-Man is betrayed into the hands of sinners. Get up, let us be going. See, my betrayer is at hand."

Immediately, while Jesus was still speaking, Judas, one of the twelve, arrived; and with him there was a crowd with swords and clubs, from the chief priests, the scribes, and the elders. Now the betrayer had given them a sign, saying, "The one I will kiss is the man; arrest him and lead him away under guard." So when Judas came, he went up to Jesus at once and said, "Rabbi!" and kissed him. Then they laid hands on Jesus and arrested him. But one of those who stood near drew his sword and struck the slave of the high priest, cutting off his ear. Then Jesus said to them, "Have you come out with swords and clubs to arrest me as though I were a bandit? Day after day I was with you in the temple teaching, and you did not arrest me. But let the scriptures be fulfilled." All of them deserted him and fled.

A certain youth was following him, wearing nothing but a linen cloth. They caught hold of him, but he left the linen cloth and ran off naked.

They took Jesus to the high priest; and all the chief priests, the elders, and the scribes were assembled. Peter had followed him at a distance, right into the courtyard of the high priest; and he was sitting with the guards, warming himself at the fire. Now the chief priests and the whole council were looking for testimony against Jesus to put him to death; but they found none. For many gave false testimony against Jesus, and their testimony did not agree. Some stood up and gave false testimony against him, saying, "We heard him say, 'I will destroy this temple that is made with hands, and in three days I will build another, not made with hands.'" But even on this point their testimony did not agree. Then the high priest stood up before them and asked Jesus, "Have you no answer? What is it that they testify against you?" But Jesus was silent and did not answer. Again the high priest asked him, "Are you the Messiah, the Son of the Blessed One?" Jesus said, "I am; and

'you will see the Son-of-Man
seated at the right hand of the Power,'
and 'coming with the clouds of heaven.'"

Then the high priest tore his clothes and said, "Why do we still need witnesses? You have heard his blasphemy! What is your decision?" All of them condemned him as deserving death. Some began to spit on him, to blindfold him, and to strike him, saying to him, "Prophesy!" The guards also took him over and beat him.

While Peter was below in the courtyard, one of the servants of the high priest came by. When she saw Peter warming himself, she stared at him and said, "You also were with Jesus, the man from Nazareth." But he denied it, saying, "I do not know or understand what you are talking about." And he went out into the forecourt. Then the cock crowed. And the servant, on seeing him, began again to say to the bystanders, "This man is one of them." But again he denied it. Then after a little while the bystanders again said to Peter, "Certainly you are one of them; for you are a Galilean." But he began to curse, and he swore an oath, "I do not know this man you are talking about." At that moment the cock crowed for the second time. Then Peter remembered that Jesus had said to him, "Before the cock crows twice, you will deny me three times." And he broke down and wept. As soon as it was morning, the chief priests held a consultation with the elders and scribes and the whole council. They bound Jesus, led him away, and handed him over to Pilate. Pilate asked him, "Are you the King of the Jews?" Jesus answered him, "You say so." Then the chief priests accused him of many things. Pilate asked him again, "Have you no answer? See how many charges they bring against you." But Jesus made no further reply, so that Pilate was amazed.

Now at the festival Pilate used to release a prisoner for them, anyone for whom they asked. Now a man called Barabbas was in prison with the rebels who had committed murder during the insurrection. So the crowd came and began to ask Pilate to do for them according to his custom. Then he answered them, "Do you want me to release for you the King of the Jews?" For he realized that it was out of jealousy that the chief priests had handed him over. But the chief priests stirred up the crowd to have Pilate release Barabbas for them instead. Pilate spoke to them again, "Then what do you wish me to do with the man you call the King of the Jews?" They shouted back, "Crucify him!" Pilate asked them, "Why, what evil has he done?" But they shouted all the more, "Crucify him!" So Pilate, wishing to satisfy the crowd, released Barabbas for them; and after flogging Jesus, he handed him over to be crucified.

Then the soldiers led Jesus into the courtyard of the palace (that is, the governor's headquarters); and they called together the whole cohort. And they clothed him in a purple cloak; and after twisting some thorns into a crown, they put it on him. And they began saluting him, "Hail, King of the Jews!" They struck his head with a reed, spat upon him, and knelt down in homage to him. After mocking him, they stripped him of the purple cloak and put his own clothes on him. Then they led him out to crucify him.

They compelled a passer-by, who was coming in from the country, to carry his cross; it was Simon of Cyrene, the father of Alexander and Rufus. Then they brought Jesus to the place called Golgotha (which means the place of a skull). And they offered him wine mixed with myrrh; but he did not take it. And they crucified him, and divided his clothes among them, casting lots to decide what each should take.

It was nine o'clock in the morning when they crucified him. The inscription of the charge against him read, "The King of the Jews." And with him they crucified two bandits, one on his right and one on his left. Those who passed by derided Jesus, shaking their heads and saying, "Aha! You who would destroy the temple and build it in three days, save yourself, and come down from the cross!" In the same way the chief priests, along with the scribes, were also mocking him among themselves and saying, "He saved others; he cannot save himself. Let the Messiah, the King of Israel, come down from the cross now, so that we may see and believe." Those who were crucified with him also taunted him.

When it was noon, darkness came over the whole land until three in the afternoon. At three o'clock Jesus cried out with a loud voice, "Eloi, Eloi, lema sabachthani?" which means, "My God, my God, why have you forsaken me?" When some of the bystanders heard it, they said, "Listen, he is calling for Elijah." And someone ran, filled a sponge with sour wine, put it on a stick, and gave it to him to drink, saying, "Wait, let us see whether Elijah will come to take him down." Then Jesus gave a loud cry and breathed his last. And the curtain of the temple was torn in two, from top to bottom. Now when the centurion, who stood facing him, saw that in this way Jesus breathed his last, he said, "Truly this man was God's Son!"

There were also women looking on from a distance; among them were Mary Magdalene, and Mary the mother of James the younger and of Joses, and Salome. These used to follow him and provided for Jesus when he was in Galilee; and there were many other women who had come up with him to Jerusalem.

When evening had come, and since it was the day of Preparation, that is, the day before the sabbath, Joseph of Arimathea, a respected member of the council, who was also himself waiting expectantly for the dominion of God, went boldly to Pilate and asked for the body of Jesus. Then Pilate wondered if Jesus were already dead; and summoning the centurion, he asked him whether he had been dead for some time. When Pilate learned from the centurion that Jesus was dead, he granted the body to Joseph. Then Joseph bought a linen cloth, and taking down the body, wrapped it in the linen cloth, and laid it in a tomb that had been hewn out of the rock. Joseph then rolled a stone against the door of the tomb. Mary Magdalene and Mary the mother of Joses saw where the body was laid.

Despite his apparently dispassionate reporting style, Mark gives an intensely theological portrayal of Jesus, inspired by the figure of the suffering servant, who came "not to be served, but to serve, and to give his life as a ransom for many" (Mark 10:45). The focus of Mark's passion story is the crowning of the King. Because Jesus' coronation takes place through suffering, the story is unrelentingly ironic. Jesus' subjects flee (14:50); his court repudiates him (14:64); the state condemns him (15:15); soldiers pay mock homage with crown and cloak (15:16–20); his royal title sits atop the instrument of execution (15:26); his enthronement as Son of God occurs only at the moment of his death (15:39).

Paul's letter to the Philippians contains an early Christian hymn, already widely used in Paul's time, only thirty years after Jesus' crucifixion. Its theology of the passion unfolds in a sequence: (1) Christ begins in glory, equal with God, referring either to his divinity or perhaps to his perfect humanity in God's image; (2) he descends to a humiliating slave's death on the cross; (3) then, because he "humbled himself," God lifts him up again to unimaginable glory.

The prophet's ancient words poetically convey the inner experience of the suffering servant, personifying the narrative of Mark and the theological structure of Paul. The anonymous writer composed four "servant songs" (Isaiah 42:1–4; 49:1–6; 50:4–7; 52:13—53:12), perhaps based on the life of Jeremiah; this is a portion of the third song. The servant speaks in the first person, reflecting on the certainty of his mission and the strength he receives from the Lord. Jesus quoted and alluded to many Old Testament themes and figures to interpret his mission. But he especially adopted and fulfilled the persona of the suffering servant as a key to his passion. In this mysterious figure, we come close to Jesus' inner life and the meaning that he gave to his work.

How might the words of the servant strengthen you in a crisis?

Holy Thursday brings the end to the Forty Days of Lent, which make up the season of anticipation of the great Three Days. Composed of prayer, alms-giving, fasting and the preparation of the catechumens for baptism, the season of Lent is now brought to a close and the Three Days begin as we approach the liturgy of Holy Thursday evening. As those to be initiated into the church have prepared themselves for their entrance into the fullness of life, so have we been awakening in our hearts, minds and bodies our own entrances into the life of Christ, experienced in the life of the church.

The Three Days, this Easter Triduum (Latin for "three days"), is the center, the core, of the entire year for Christians. These days mark the mystery around which our entire lives are played out. Adults in the community are invited to plan ahead so that the whole time from Thursday night until Easter Sunday is free of social engagements, free of entertainment and free of meals except for the simplest nourishment. We measure these days—indeed, our very salvation in the life of God—in step with the catechumens themselves; our own rebirths are revitalized as we participate in their initiation rites and as we have supported them along the way.

We are asked to fast on Good Friday and to continue fasting, if possible, all through Holy Saturday as strictly as we can so that we come to the Easter Vigil hungry and full of excitement, parched and longing to feel the sacred water of the font on our skin. Good Friday and Holy Saturday are days of paring down distractions so that we may be free for prayer and anticipation, for reflection, preparation and silence. The church is getting ready for the Great Night of the Easter Vigil.

As one who has been initiated into the church, as one whose life has been wedded to this community gathered at the table, you should anticipate the Triduum with concentration and vigor. With you, the whole church knows that our presence for the liturgies of the Triduum is not just an invitation. Everyone is needed. We "pull out all the stops" for these days. As human persons, wedded to humanity by the joys and travails of life and grafted onto the body of the church by the sanctifying waters of baptism, we lead the new members into new life in this community of faith.

To this end, the Three Days are seen not as three liturgies distinct from one another but as one movement. These days have been connected intimately and liturgically from the early days of the Christian church. As a member of this community, you should be personally committed to preparing for and anticipating the Triduum and its culmination in the Vigil of the Great Night, Holy Saturday.

The church proclaims the direction of the Triduum by the opening antiphon of Holy Thursday, which comes from Paul's Letter to the Galatians (6:14). With this verse the church sets a spiritual environment into which we as committed Christians enter the Triduum:

> We should glory in the cross of our Lord Jesus Christ, for he is our salvation, our life and resurrection; through him we are saved and made free.

HOLY THURSDAY

On Thursday evening we enter into this Triduum together. Whether presider, baker, lector, preacher, wine maker, greeter, altar server, minister of the eucharist, decorator or person in the remote corner in the last pew of the church, we begin, as always, by hearkening to the word of God. These are the scriptures for the liturgy of Holy Thursday:

Exodus 12:1–8, 11–14
Ancient instructions for the meal of the Passover.

1 Corinthians 11:23–26
Eat the bread and drink the cup until the return of the Lord.

John 13:1–15
Jesus washes the feet of the disciples.

Then we, like Jesus, do something strange: We wash feet. Jesus gave us this image of what the church is supposed to look like, feel like, act like. Our position—whether as washer or washed, servant or served—is a difficult one for us to take. Yet we learn from the discomfort, from the awkwardness.

Then we celebrate the eucharist. Because it is connected to the other liturgies of the Triduum on Good Friday and Holy Saturday night, the evening liturgy of Holy Thursday has no ending. Whether we stay to pray awhile or leave, we are now in the quiet, peace and glory of the Triduum.

GOOD FRIDAY

We gather quietly in community on Friday and again listen to the Word of God:

Isaiah 52:13—53:12
The servant of the Lord was crushed for our sins.

Hebrews 4:14–16; 5:7–9
The Son of God learned obedience through his suffering.

John 18:1—19:42
The passion of Jesus Christ.

After the sermon, we pray at length for all the world's needs: for the church; for the pope, the clergy and all the baptized; for those preparing for initiation; for the unity of Christians; for Jews; for non-Christians; for atheists; for all in public office; and for those in special need.

Then there is another once-a-year event: The holy cross is held up in our midst and we come forward one by one to do reverence with a kiss, bow or genuflection. This communal reverence of an instrument of torture recalls the painful price, in the past and today, of salvation, the way in which our redemption is wrought, the stripes and humiliation of Jesus Christ that bring direction and life back to a humanity that is lost and dead. During the veneration of the cross, we sing not only of the sorrow but of the glory of the cross by which we have been saved.

Again, we bring to mind the words of Paul: "The cross of Jesus Christ . . . our salvation, our life and resurrection; through him we are saved and made free."

We continue in fasting and prayer and vigil, in rest and quiet, through Saturday. This Saturday for us is God's rest at the end of creation. It is Christ's repose in the tomb. It is Christ's visit with the dead.

EASTER VIGIL

Hungry now, pared down to basics, lightheaded from vigilance and full of excitement, we committed members of the church, the already baptized, gather in darkness and light a new fire. From this blaze we light a great candle that will make this night bright for us and will burn throughout the Easter season.

We hearken again to the Word of God with some of the most powerful narratives and proclamations of our tradition:

Genesis 1:1—2:2
Creation of the world.

Genesis 22:1–18
The sacrifice of Isaac.

Exodus 14:15—15:1
The crossing of the Red Sea.

Isaiah 54:5–14
You will not be afraid.

Isaiah 55:1–11
Come, come to the water.

Baruch 3:9–15, 32—4:4
The shining light.

Ezekiel 36:16–28
The Lord says: I will sprinkle water.

Romans 6:3–11
United with him in death.

Mark 16:1–7
Jesus has been raised up.

After the readings, we pray to all our saints to stand with us as we go to the font and bless the waters. The chosen of all times and all places attend to what is about to take place. The catechumens renounce evil, profess the faith of the church and are baptized and anointed.

All of us renew our baptism. For us these are the moments when death and life meet, when we reject evil and give our promises to God. All of this is in the communion of the church. So together we go to the table and celebrate the Easter eucharist.

DO·NOT·BE ALARMED

Preparation for the Word

Mighty God,
like the two making their way to the town
    of Emmaus
we do not know what to make
    of all that has happened.
Draw near us now in the stranger
    who is your child,
Jesus the risen Lord.
Through Easter's fifty days, saving God,
may Jesus walk with us
and open the scriptures to us
so that our hearts are on fire.
Then we shall run in excitement
and shall sing our alleluia to you
high and low, morning and night,
    for ever and ever. Amen.

Thanksgiving for the Word

Through all the days of Easter, holy God,
we seek in scripture what was said long ago:
"Your promises are sweet to taste,
sweeter than honey."
Feed us with this honey,
so that we not only hear your word,
but taste it,
not only taste it,
but inhale its gentle fragrance.

So may we ourselves become like this word
    of yours:
the fragrance of Christ to all who meet us,
the sweet taste of Christ to all
    with whom we share the earth.
May this be so for we pray in Jesus' name
who is Lord for ever and ever. Amen.

Weekday Readings

April 21: Solemnity of Monday in the Octave of Easter
Acts 2:14, 22–23; Matthew 28:8–15
April 22: Solemnity of Tuesday in the Octave of Easter
Acts 2:36–41; John 20:11–18
April 23: Solemnity of Wednesday in the Octave of Easter
Acts 3:1–10; Luke 24:13–35
April 24: Solemnity of Thursday in the Octave of Easter
Acts 3:11–26; Luke 24:35–48
April 25: Solemnity of Friday in the Octave of Easter
Acts 4:1–12; John 21:1–14
April 26: Solemnity of Saturday in the Octave of Easter
Acts 4:13–21; Mark 16:9–15

April 28: *Acts 4:23–31; John 3:1–8*
April 29: *Acts 4:32–37; John 3:7b–15*
April 30: *Acts 5:17–26; John 3:16–21*
May 1: *Acts 5:27–33; John 3:31–36*
May 2: *Acts 5:34–42; John 6:1–15*
May 3: Feast of Saints Philip and James
1 Corinthians 15:1–8; John 14:6–14

May 5: *Acts 6:8–15; John 6:22–29*
May 6: *Acts 7:51–8:1a; John 6:30–35*
May 7: *Acts 8:1b–8; John 6:35–40*
May 8: *Acts 8:26–40; John 6:44–51*
May 9: *Acts 9:1–20; John 6:52–59*
May 10: *Acts 9:31–42; John 6:60–69*

May 12: *Acts 11:1–18; John 10:1–10*
May 13: *Acts 11:19–26; John 10:22–30*
May 14: Feast of Saint Matthias
Acts 1:15–17, 20–26; John 15:9–17
May 15: *Acts 13:13–25; John 13:16–20*
May 16: *Acts 13:26–33; John 14:1–6*
May 17: *Acts 13:44–52; John 14:7–14*

May 19: *Acts 14:5–18; John 14:21–26*
May 20: *Acts 14:19–28; John 14:27–31a*
May 21: *Acts 15:1–6; John 15:1–8*
May 22: *Acts 15:7–21; John 15:9–11*
May 23: *Acts 15:22–31; John 15:12–17*
May 24: *Acts 16:1–10; John 15:18–21*

May 26: *Acts 16:11–15; John 15:26–16:4a*
May 27: *Acts 16:22–34; John 16:5–11*
May 28: *Acts 17: 15, 22–18:1; John 16:12–15*
May 29: Solemnity of the Ascension of the Lord
Acts 1:1–11; Ephesians 1:17–23; Mark 16:15–20
May 30: *Acts 18:9–18; John 16:20–23a*
May 31: Feast of the Visitation of the Blessed Virgin Mary
Zephaniah 3:14–18; Luke 1:39–56

June 2: *Acts 19:1–8; John 16:29–33*
June 3: *Acts 20:17–27; John 17:1–11a*
June 4: *Acts 20:28–38; John 17:11b–19*
June 5: *Acts 22:30; 23:6–11; John 17:20–26*
June 6: *Acts 25:13b–21; John 21:15–19*
June 7 morning: *Acts 28:16–20, 30–31; John 21:20–25*

READING I   Acts 10:34—43

Roman Catholic: Acts 10:34a; 37–43

Peter began to speak to the people: "I truly understand that God shows no partiality, but in every nation anyone who is God-fearing and does what is right is acceptable to God.

"You know the message God sent to the people of Israel, preaching peace by Jesus Christ—who is Lord of all. That message spread throughout Judea, beginning in Galilee after the baptism that John announced: how God anointed Jesus of Nazareth with the Holy Spirit and with power; how Jesus went about doing good and healing all who were oppressed by the devil, for God was with him. We are witnesses to all that he did both in Judea and in Jerusalem. They put him to death by hanging him on a tree; but God raised him on the third day and allowed him to appear, not to all the people but to us who were chosen by God as witnesses, and who ate and drank with him after he rose from the dead.

"Jesus commanded us to preach to the people and to testify that he is the one ordained by God as judge of the living and the dead. All the prophets testify about him that everyone who believes in him receives forgiveness of sins through his name."

READING II   Colossians 3:1—4

Revised Common Lectionary: 1 Corinthians 15:1–11

If you have been raised with Christ, seek the things that are above, where Christ is, seated at the right hand of God. Set your minds on things that are above, not on things that are on earth, for you have died, and your life is hidden with Christ in God. When Christ who is your life is revealed, then you also will be revealed with him in glory.

GOSPEL   John 20:1—18

Roman Catholic: John 20:1–9

Early on the first day of the week, while it was still dark, Mary Magdalene came to the tomb and saw that the stone had been removed from the tomb. So she ran and went to Simon Peter and the other disciple, the one whom Jesus loved, and said to them, "They have taken the Lord out of the tomb, and we do not know where they have laid him."

Then Peter and the other disciple set out and went toward the tomb. The two were running together, but the other disciple outran Peter and reached the tomb first. He bent down to look in and saw the linen wrappings lying there, but he did not go in. Then Simon Peter came, following him, and went into the tomb. He saw the linen wrappings lying there, and the cloth that had been on Jesus' head, not lying with the linen wrappings but rolled up in a place by itself. Then the other disciple, who reached the tomb first, also went in, and he saw and believed; for as yet they did not understand the scripture, that Jesus must rise from the dead. Then the disciples returned to their homes.

But Mary stood weeping outside the tomb. As she wept, she bent over to look into the tomb; and she saw two angels in white, sitting where the body of Jesus had been lying, one at the head and the other at the feet. They said to her, "Woman, why are you weeping?" She said to them, "They have taken away my Lord, and I do not know where they have laid him." When she had said this, she turned around and saw Jesus standing there, but she did not know that it was Jesus. Jesus said to her, "Woman, why are you weeping? Whom are you looking for?" Supposing him to be the gardener, she said to him, "Sir, if you have carried him away, tell me where you have laid him, and I will take him away." Jesus said to her, "Mary!" She turned and said to him in Hebrew, "Rabbouni!" (which means Teacher). Jesus said to her, "Do not hold on to me, because I have not yet ascended to the Father. But go to my brothers and say to them, 'I am ascending to my Father and your Father, to my God and your God.'"

Mary Magdalene went and announced to the disciples, "I have seen the Lord"; and she told them that Jesus had said these things to her.

Practice of Prayer

Psalm 118:1—2, 16—17, 22—23

Alleluia!
Give thanks to the LORD who is good,
for God's love endures for ever.
Let the family of Israel say:
"God's love endures for ever."

God's right hand raised me.
The LORD's right hand has triumphed;
I shall not die, I shall live
and recount God's deeds.

The stone which the builders rejected
has become the corner stone.
This is the work of the LORD,
a marvel in our eyes.

Practice of Prudence

As she peeks into the empty tomb, Mary Magdalene is challenged by an angel who asks why she looks for the living among the dead. She turns toward the garden and sees someone there. Her recognition of Jesus comes slowly, but it is riveting and joyous. Her immediate impulse is to share this great news with others.

It often takes time and attention to recognize what is truly life-giving, and sometimes we miss the revelation that is standing in front of us. But prudence can assure us that life is waiting for us to recognize it, and encourages us to expand our expectations beyond the concern of the moment. Easter is the classic example of such an event, and a little prudence can be a good way to prepare.

Scripture Insights

The resurrection was too much for the disciples to take in. They were disoriented by terror, by wonder and by joy. What could be the same if even death itself is unreliable? Mary thinks Jesus is the gardener, but when he speaks her name she melts. "The sheep know his voice" (John 10:4). Like the lover of the Song of Songs, her joy soon shivers into uncertainty when she moves to embrace him and he is changed. "Do not hold on to me," he says. What? Jesus asks Mary to adopt new ways of seeing and touching him, to know him in a new way, in spirit. But we learn the ways of spirit clumsily; like learning to write with the opposite hand, it means unlearning the old way. This bizarre experience of knowing but not knowing emerges in an odd line from the later story of the lakeshore breakfast: "None of the disciples dared to ask him, 'Who are you?' because they knew it was the Lord" (21:12).

Resurrection is more than a new phase of the old life. Jesus invites followers to rise with him into a strange, upside-down world where apparent irreversibles are reversed: life defeats death, love trumps evil, weakness means power, humility wins out, last come first, and "nothing will be impossible with God" (Luke 1:37).

Keeping this in focus demands an attitude of prayerful concentration like contemplation. So the letter to the Colossians urges believers to "set your minds on things that are above." The Greek word translated "set your minds" *(phroneo)* means not just having an idea, but practicing habitual patterns of thinking. The marvelous news of resurrection announces itself only to those who return repeatedly to question, ponder and insist on understanding such statements as "you have died," "your life is hidden with Christ in God" and "you also will be revealed with him in glory." Members of the Christian community who listen intently and often to this message of Jesus' life gradually learn to live the resurrection as a fact of life.

Colossians 3:1—4 also is meant as a guide for community life. Each "you" is plural. Reread 3:1—4 from the plural perspective. What might "things above" and "things upon earth" mean for life in a community of faith?

April 27, 2003

READING I   Acts 4:32–35

Now the whole group of those who believed were of one heart and soul, and no one claimed private ownership of any possessions, but everything they owned was held in common. With great power the apostles gave their testimony to the resurrection of the Lord Jesus, and great grace was upon them all. There was not a needy person among them, for as many as owned lands or houses sold them and brought the proceeds of what was sold. They laid it at the apostles' feet, and it was distributed to each as any had need.

READING II   1 John 5:1–6

Revised Common Lectionary: 1 John 1:1–2:2

Everyone who believes that Jesus is the Christ has been born of God, and everyone who loves the parent loves the child. By this we know that we love the children of God, when we love God and obey God's commandments. For the love of God is this, that we obey the commandments, which are not burdensome, for whatever is born of God conquers the world. And this is the victory that conquers the world, our faith. Who is it that conquers the world but the one who believes that Jesus is the Son of God?

This is the one who came by water and blood, Jesus Christ, not with the water only but with the water and the blood. And the Spirit is the one that testifies, for the Spirit is the truth.

GOSPEL   John 20:19–31

When it was evening on that day, the first day of the week, and the doors of the house where the disciples had met were locked for fear of the Judeans, Jesus came and stood among them and said, "Peace be with you." After he said this, he showed them his hands and his side. Then the disciples rejoiced when they saw the Lord. Jesus said to them again, "Peace be with you. As the Father has sent me, so I send you." When he had said this, he breathed on them and said to them, "Receive the Holy Spirit. If you forgive the sins of any, they are forgiven them; if you retain the sins of any, they are retained."

But Thomas (who was called the Twin), one of the twelve, was not with them when Jesus came. So the other disciples told him, "We have seen the Lord." But he said to them, "Unless I see the mark of the nails in his hands, and put my finger in the mark of the nails and my hand in his side, I will not believe."

A week later his disciples were again in the house, and Thomas was with them. Although the doors were shut, Jesus came and stood among them and said, "Peace be with you." Then he said to Thomas, "Put your finger here and see my hands. Reach out your hand and put it in my side. Do not doubt but believe." Thomas said to Jesus, "My Lord and my God!" Jesus said to him, "Have you believed because you have seen me? Blessed are those who have not seen and yet have come to believe."

Now Jesus did many other signs in the presence of his disciples, which are not written in this book. But these are written so that you may come to believe that Jesus is the Messiah, the Son of God, and that through believing you may have life in his name.

Practice of Prayer

Psalm 118:2—4, 13—15, 22—24

Let the family of Israel say:
"God's love endures for ever."
Let the family of Aaron say:
"God's love endures for ever."
Let those who fear the LORD say:
"God's love endures for ever."

I was thrust down, thrust down and falling,
but the LORD was my helper.
The LORD is my strength and my song;
and has been my savior.
There are shouts of joy and victory
in the tents of the just.

The stone which the builders rejected
has become the corner stone.
This is the work of the LORD,
a marvel in our eyes.
This day was made by the LORD;
we rejoice and are glad.

Practice of Justice

There is something very compassionate about Jesus' invitation to Thomas to place a hand within his wounded side. Instead of judging Thomas for what he lacks (unswerving faith), Jesus provides the doubting disciple with what he needs to grow stronger in faith. The invitation also offers Thomas some much-needed reassurance when he must have felt frightened, confused and disillusioned. This is indeed a compassionate justice!

All of us, at one time or another, need reassurance and compassion. For some, that may take a tangible form; providing food or housing may lend them the strength they need. Others have needs that are harder to discern but no less crucial. Fears and doubts, heartaches and worries have left them feeling adrift and alone. Follow the example of Jesus and offer someone some reassurance this week.

Scripture Insights

John 20:31 says the gospel was written to nurture the act of committing oneself to the Son of God. For this act, John constantly uses the verb "believe" (*pisteuo*, 98 times). It takes time and prayer to learn the spiritually powerful meaning of the word "believe" in John's gospel. Believing does not mean merely acting as if something is real. Believing means developing the spiritual faculty to perceive the invisible reality at the heart of all things, analogous to the ability to see and hear the physical world. Two levels of seeing operate in John. Physical seeing leads to an embryonic form of faith (see 6:30, "What sign are you going to give us then?") which remains tied to earthly forms of existence (3:6). But true believing enables one to see beyond physical sight (6:40; 9:35—39).

For the early Christian communities, apostles were those who had had the honor of being an eyewitness to the risen Jesus (Acts 1:22, 10:40—41; 1 Corinthians 15:3—8). The community of the beloved disciple that produced John's gospel accepted that tradition. "What we have seen with our eyes . . . and touched with our hands . . . we declare to you" (1 John 1:1—4). But in a crucial sense, the gospel subordinates apostleship to the task of ordinary Christians to *believe*. For John, believing in Jesus is the important step. Apostles might see Jesus risen, but they too must learn to believe. Thomas moves in one instant from earthly to spiritual believing. Jesus teaches that anyone who knows him through believing is equal to the apostles, who know him by sight.

The power of believing in Jesus to transform human existence is evident in Luke's vignettes of the early Jerusalem community. "Those who believed" throbbed with paschal life, conquered deeply rooted human habits, and became "one heart and soul."

In Mark's gospel, Jesus has a strong concern for physical touch. (Mark 1:21—31, 40—45; 5:21—43; 7:31—35; 8:22—26; 10:13—16; 14:3—9.) Why is that so important—to him, as well as to Mark who includes it in his story?

May 4, 2003

THIRD SUNDAY OF EASTER

READING I Acts 3:12–19

Roman Catholic: Acts 3:13–15, 17–19

Peter addressed the people, "You Israelites, why do you wonder at this, or why do you stare at us, as though by our own power or piety we had made this man walk? The God of Abraham, Isaac, and Jacob, the God of our ancestors has glorified Jesus, the servant of God, whom you handed over and rejected in the presence of Pilate, though Pilate had decided to release him. But you rejected the Holy and Righteous One and asked to have a murderer given to you, and you killed the Author of life, whom God raised from the dead. To this we are witnesses. And by faith in the name of Jesus, his name itself has made this man strong, whom you see and know; and the faith that is through Jesus has given him this perfect health in the presence of all of you.

"And now, friends, I know that you acted in ignorance, as did also your rulers. In this way God fulfilled what had been foretold through all the prophets, that the Messiah of God would suffer. Repent therefore, and turn to God so that your sins may be wiped out."

READING II 1 John 2:1–5a

Revised Common Lectionary: 1 John 3:1–7

My little children, I am writing these things to you so that you may not sin. But if anyone does sin, we have an advocate with the Father, Jesus Christ the righteous; and he is the atoning sacrifice for our sins, and not for ours only but also for the sins of the whole world. Now by this we may be sure that we know him, if we obey his commandments. Whoever says, "I have come to know him," but does not obey his commandments, is a liar, and in such a person the truth does not exist; but whoever obeys his word, truly in this person the love of God has reached perfection.

GOSPEL Luke 24:35–48

Revised Common Lectionary: Luke 24:36b–48

Then they told what had happened on the road, and how Jesus had been made known to them in the breaking of the bread.

While they were talking about this, Jesus himself stood among them and said to them, "Peace be with you." They were startled and terrified, and thought that they were seeing a ghost. He said to them, "Why are you frightened, and why do doubts arise in your hearts? Look at my hands and my feet; see that it is I myself. Touch me and see; for a ghost does not have flesh and bones as you see that I have." And when he had said this, he showed them his hands and his feet. While in their joy they were disbelieving and still wondering, he said to them, "Have you anything here to eat?" They gave him a piece of broiled fish, and he took it and ate in their presence.

Then Jesus said to them, "These are my words that I spoke to you while I was still with you—that everything written about me in the law of Moses, the prophets, and the psalms must be fulfilled." Then he opened their minds to understand the scriptures, and said to them, "Thus it is written, that the Messiah is to suffer and to rise from the dead on the third day, and that repentance and forgiveness of sins is to be proclaimed in his name to all nations, beginning from Jerusalem. You are witnesses of these things."

Practice of Prayer

Psalm 4:2, 4, 7—8, 9

When I call, answer me, O God of justice;
from anguish you released me,
   have mercy and hear me!

It is the LORD who grants favors to those
   who are merciful;
the LORD hears me whenever I call.

"What can bring us happiness?" many say.
Lift up the light of your face on us, O LORD.

You have put into my heart a greater joy
than they have from abundance of corn
   and new wine.

I will lie down in peace and sleep comes at once
for you alone, LORD, make me dwell in safety.

Practice of Justice

Julia Ward Howe is best known for writing "The Battle Hymn of the Republic." She was a social activist who worked to establish Mother's Day. Its original intent was not to honor mothers. It was an international call for peace. In an eloquent statement, Julia appealed to "all women who have hearts." Women of one country, she wrote, would be "too tender of those of another country to allow our sons to injure theirs" (*Reminiscences*, Julia Ward Howe, Houghton Mifflin Co., 1899).

Julia's vision of a mother-to-mother, person-to-person connection still has great potential for realizing the dream of global peace. What can you do to actively work for peace in your home, neighborhood, workplace or parish?

Scripture Insights

Knowing something of the Holocaust, we are troubled by the way Peter accuses the Jews of crucifying Jesus: "this Jesus whom *you* handed over" (3:13–15). Are these and similar words in Acts 2:23, 36; 4:10–11; 5:30; 7:52 not unjust and implicitly anti-Jewish? The important search for the sense intended by Luke (who composed Peter's speech as a way of summarizing his essential message) should take into account these things.

1. Peter carefully restricts his accusation to those Jews who were actually involved in the Lord's death. Later Christian preachers in Acts do not accuse Jews of other times and places.

2. Significantly, Peter implicitly groups himself with those he accuses. He says the Jews had "handed over" and "rejected" Jesus. These are exactly the same Greek words that Luke's gospel uses not only to describe Judas's betrayal (22:48), but also Peter's own denial (22:57). Peter for this reason considers himself no different than the people he is accusing.

3. Peter immediately attaches an offer of forgiveness (Acts 2:38; 3:19; 5:31). Undeniably, the crucifixion was a malicious act; but God has reversed that evil in the resurrection, and so shows the cross to be the very means of salvation.

4. Peter readily offers pardon because "I know that you acted in ignorance" (Acts 3:17). Is this why the Lord forgave him? It certainly evokes Jesus' prayer of forgiveness for his crucifiers, "for they do not know what they are doing" (Luke 23:34). The deep irony of Christian anti-Judaism through the centuries is that Christ explicitly forbade it even as he suffered on the cross.

Far from stirring up Christian hatred for Jews, Peter maps a path to mercy for both. Jesus forgave both Peter and his crucifiers. Against this backdrop, the assurance of 1 John 2:1 is dramatic and solid: "If anyone does sin, we have an advocate with the Father, Jesus Christ the righteous."

Create a profile of Peter from the major passages about him in Mark's gospel: 1:16–20, 29–31; 8:27–33; 9:2–8; 14:26–42, 66–72; 16:7.

READING I   Acts 4:5—12

Roman Catholic: Acts 4:8—12

The next day their rulers, elders, and scribes assembled in Jerusalem, with Annas the high priest, Caiaphas, John, and Alexander, and all who were of the high-priestly family. When they had made the prisoners Peter and John stand in their midst, they inquired, "By what power or by what name did you do this?" Then Peter, filled with the Holy Spirit, said to them, "Rulers of the people and elders, if we are questioned today because of a good deed done to someone who was sick and are asked how this man has been healed, let it be known to all of you, and to all the people of Israel, that this man is standing before you in good health by the name of Jesus Christ of Nazareth, whom you crucified, whom God raised from the dead. This Jesus is

> 'the stone that was rejected by you, the builders;
> it has become the cornerstone.'

There is salvation in no one else, for there is no other name under heaven given among mortals by which we must be saved."

READING II   1 John 3:1—2

Revised Common Lectionary: 1 John 3:16—24

See what love the Father has given us, that we should be called children of God; and that is what we are. The reason the world does not know us is that it did not know God. Beloved, we are God's children now; what we will be has not yet been revealed. What we do know is this: when it is revealed, we will be like God, for we will see God as God is.

GOSPEL   John 10:11—18

"I am the good shepherd. The good shepherd lays down his life for the sheep. The hired hand, who is not the shepherd and does not own the sheep, sees the wolf coming and leaves the sheep and runs away—and the wolf snatches them and scatters them. The hired hand runs away because a hired hand does not care for the sheep. I am the good shepherd. I know my own and my own know me, just as the Father knows me and I know the Father. And I lay down my life for the sheep. I have other sheep that do not belong to this fold. I must bring them also, and they will listen to my voice. So there will be one flock, one shepherd. For this reason the Father loves me, because I lay down my life in order to take it up again. No one takes it from me, but I lay it down of my own accord. I have power to lay it down, and I have power to take it up again. I have received this command from my Father."

Practice of Prayer

Psalm 118:1, 8—9, 21—23, 26, 28, 29

Alleluia!

Give thanks to the LORD who is good,
for God's love endures for ever.

It is better to take refuge in the LORD
than to trust in mortals;
it is better to take refuge in the LORD
than to trust in rulers.

I will thank you for you have answered
and you are my savior.

The stone which the builders rejected
has become the corner stone.
This is the work of the LORD,
a marvel in our eyes.

Blessed in the name of the LORD
is he who comes.
We bless you from the house of the LORD;

You are my God, I thank you.
My God, I praise you.
Give thanks to the LORD who is good;
for God's love endures for ever.

Practice of Prudence

Shepherds have great affection as well as responsibility for their sheep. When a sheep strays from the flock or becomes tangled in a thorny thicket, the shepherd is there to guide and rescue.

Parents, teachers, coaches and guardians are examples of modern-day shepherds. Their role demands great prudence: to provide direction without autocracy, and to protect without smothering those within their care. Such a process helps their "sheep" to grow more observant about their choices, their direction and their place within a larger community. Shepherding takes skill and vigilance.

This week offer a word of encouragement to someone you know who is responsible for the care, upbringing or education of a child or adolescent. Remember them in your prayers to the One who shepherds us all.

Scripture Insights

Christianity's focus on Jesus as the source and center of salvation is hard to miss and impossible to overstate. The New Testament slowly and lovingly turns Jesus before the eye of faith like a diamond in the sun. Its language seeks to reflect every glorious ray of this "bright morning star" (Revelation 22:16) through whom "all things came into being" (John 1:4) and who "sustains all things by his powerful word" (Hebrews 1:3). But he is also gentle and lowly of heart, inviting disciples to "Come to me" (Matthew 11:28) as he asks tenderly "Do you love me?" (John 21:15).

Clearly these are not just doctrinal assertions, mere brain badges; they are terms of adoration. Last week's reading called Jesus "the Author of life" (Acts 3:15) and "the Holy and Righteous one" (3:14), and identified him with the suffering just one of Psalm 31. Luke says Jesus prayed this same psalm on the cross: "Father, into your hands I commend my spirit" (Luke 23:46; Psalm 31:5). Peter also called him God's "servant" (Acts 3:13), recalling the mysterious "suffering servant" of Isaiah 53:11: "The righteous one, my servant, shall make many righteous, and he shall bear their iniquities." He is also the "prophet like Moses" whom the great lawgiver foretold in Deuteronomy 18:15 (Acts 3:22). He is the long-awaited "Messiah" (Acts 4:10), "the stone that was rejected by you, the builders" (Acts 4:11). This quote from Psalm 118:22 was a favorite among the first Christians for understanding Jesus: See Matthew 21:42; Mark 12:10; Luke 20:17.

The very name of Jesus means "Savior" (Matthew 1:21). It takes nothing away from the majestic wisdom of the world's religions to note Christianity's fundamental difference: Other teachers point to a way of salvation, but Christianity alone embraces its Founder as the source of the salvation he proclaims. Peter was justified in saying, "There is no other name under heaven . . . by which we must be saved" (Acts 4:12).

In Mark, Jesus is a divine figure who also has deep human feelings. His compassion for the crowds "like sheep without a shepherd" (6:34) gives a glimpse into his Sacred Heart. What other indications of Jesus' humanity can you find in Mark?

READING I   Acts 9:26—31

Revised Common Lectionary: Acts 8:26—40

When he had come to Jerusalem, he attempted to join the disciples; and they were all afraid of him, for they did not believe that he was a disciple. But Barnabas took him, brought him to the apostles, and described for them how on the road he had seen the Lord, who had spoken to him, and how in Damascus he had spoken boldly in the name of Jesus. So he went in and out among them in Jerusalem, speaking boldly in the name of the Lord. He spoke and argued with the Hellenists; but they were attempting to kill him. When the believers learned of it, they brought him down to Caesarea and sent him off to Tarsus. Meanwhile the church throughout Judea, Galilee, and Samaria had peace and was built up. Living in the fear of the Lord and in the comfort of the Holy Spirit, it increased in numbers.

READING II   1 John 3:18—24

Revised Common Lectionary: 1 John 4:7—21

Little children, let us love, not in word or speech, but in truth and action. And by this we will know that we are from the truth and will reassure our hearts before God whenever our hearts condemn us; for God is greater than our hearts, and God knows everything. Beloved, if our hearts do not condemn us, we have boldness before God; and we receive from God whatever we ask, because we obey the commandments and do what pleases God.

And this is God's commandment, that we should believe in the name of Jesus Christ, the Son of God, and love one another, just as Jesus has commanded us. All who obey God's commandments abide in God, and God abides in them. And by this we know that God abides in us, by the Spirit that God has given us.

GOSPEL   John 15:1—8

Jesus said: "I am the true vine, and my Father is the vinegrower. My Father removes every branch in me that bears no fruit. Every branch that bears fruit my Father prunes to make it bear more fruit. You have already been cleansed by the word that I have spoken to you. Abide in me as I abide in you. Just as the branch cannot bear fruit by itself unless it abides in the vine, neither can you unless you abide in me. I am the vine, you are the branches. Those who abide in me and I in them bear much fruit, because apart from me you can do nothing. Whoever does not abide in me is thrown away like a branch and withers; such branches are gathered, thrown into the fire, and burned.

"If you abide in me, and my words abide in you, ask for whatever you wish, and it will be done for you. My Father is glorified by this, that you bear much fruit and become my disciples."

Practice of Prayer

Psalm 22:26—27, 28, 30, 31—32

You are my praise in the great assembly.
My vows I will pay before those who fear God.
The poor shall eat and shall have their fill.
Those who seek the Lord shall praise the Lord.
May their hearts live for ever and ever!

All the earth shall remember and return
    to the Lord,
all families of the nations shall bow down in awe;

They shall bow down in awe, all the mighty
    of the earth,
all who must die and go down to the dust.

My soul shall live for God and my children too
    shall serve.
They shall tell of the Lord to generations
    yet to come;
declare to those unborn, the faithfulness of God,
"These things the Lord has done."

Practice of Fortitude

Overbearing evangelizers can be hard to take. Boldly challenging other people's faith, they often drive them away. Sharing faith and imposing it are two different things. Those who are wise enough to know the difference make great evangelizers. Saul is one of them.

The first reading describes Saul's boldness in speaking about Jesus. The other believers are understandably leery of him. After all, his zeal had been turned against them not so long ago. But thanks to the testimony of Barnabas, they accept his conversion as genuine and send him on his apostolic travels.

It takes courage to go public with one's faith. For some, it means taking on a very visible role; for others, faith is more subtly exhibited through daily actions and attitudes. No matter what style we choose, it is important to support and encourage one another in the manner of the earliest disciples.

Scripture Insights

When he brought Saul to the apostles, Barnabas told the story of how in Damascus Saul "had spoken boldly in the name of Jesus." The phrase "spoken boldly" uses a form of the Greek *parrhesia*, often translated in the New Testament as "boldness." It combines the words for "everything" *(pan)* and "speaking" *(rhesis)*. Words spoken with *parrhesia* say everything there is to be said. *Parrhesia* suggests the act of communicating ideas directly, bluntly, without elaborate logic and vague metaphors—plain speaking.

Parrhesia suggests not so much a talent for speaking as a habit of speaking candidly, born of honesty and simplicity. So the word also came to be used for the inner attitude of confidence that lay behind this practice of plain speaking. Intimate friends and family normally speak with *parrhesia* because they can speak without shame or fear of embarrassment or recrimination.

Preaching the gospel with *parrhesia* was prized in the early church as strong evidence that the Holy Spirit had certified one's authenticity as a disciple. This is what Barnabas saw in Paul. It is also something Luke himself saw and admired in the apostle, as we can see in his stories of Paul's courageous speaking in the latter half of Acts. Paul himself once described the effect of this gift of boldness. When he found himself poised to receive a Roman sentence of death, he wrote confidently: "by my speaking with all *parrhesia*, Christ will be exalted in my body . . . whether by life or by death" (Philippians 1:20).

These uses of *parrhesia* help illumine the theme of confidence in prayer in today's other texts. John's letter says that Christians who act in love receive new assurance of God's love that swallows up self-condemnation. Freedom from self-condemnation in turn nurtures courageous boldness—John uses the word *parrhesia*—in prayer to God. This creates the confidence that we have received whatever we ask for from God. The passage from John's gospel grounds this confident prayer in the indwelling life of Jesus (John 15:7).

How might Jesus' teaching on prayer in Mark 11:23–25 be understood in terms of *parrhesia*?

85

May 25, 2003

READING I Acts 10:25—26, 34—35, 44—48

Revised Common Lectionary: Acts 17:22–31

On Peter's arrival Cornelius met him, and falling at his feet, worshiped him. But Peter made him get up, saying, "Stand up; I am only a mortal." Then Peter began to speak to them: "I truly understand that God shows no partiality, but in every nation anyone who fears him and does what is right is acceptable to him. While Peter was still speaking, the Holy Spirit fell upon all who heard the word. The circumcised believers who had come with Peter were astounded that the gift of the Holy Spirit had been poured out even on the Gentiles, for they heard them speaking in tongues and extolling God. Then Peter said, "Can anyone withhold the water for baptizing these people who have received the Holy Spirit just as we have?" So he ordered them to be baptized in the name of Jesus Christ. Then they invited him to stay for several days.

READING II 1 John 4:7—10

Revised Common Lectionary: 1 Peter 3:13–22

Beloved, let us love one another, because love is from God; everyone who loves is born of God and knows God. Whoever does not love does not know God, for God is love. God's love was revealed among us in this way: God sent into the world God's only Son so that we might live through him. In this is love, not that we loved God but that God loved us and sent the Son to be the atoning sacrifice for our sins.

GOSPEL John 15:9—17

Jesus said: "As the Father has loved me, so I have loved you; abide in my love. If you keep my commandments, you will abide in my love, just as I have kept my Father's commandments and abide in my Father's love. I have said these things to you so that my joy may be in you, and that your joy may be complete.

"This is my commandment, that you love one another as I have loved you. No one has greater love than this, to lay down one's life for one's friends. You are my friends if you do what I command you. I do not call you servants any longer, because the servant does not know what the master is doing; but I have called you friends, because I have made known to you everything that I have heard from my Father. You did not choose me but I chose you. And I appointed you to go and bear fruit, fruit that will last, so that the Father will give you whatever you ask in my name. I am giving you these commands so that you may love one another."

Practice of Prayer

Psalm 98:1, 2—3, 3—4

Sing a new song to the Lord
who has worked wonders;
whose right hand and holy arm
have brought salvation.

The Lord has made known salvation;
has shown justice to the nations;
has remembered truth and love
for the house of Israel.

All the ends of the earth have seen
the salvation of our God.
Shout to the Lord, all the earth,
ring out your joy.

Practice of Temperance

May 7 is the birthday of the Russian composer Peter Ilyich Tschaikovsky, composer of music for the ballets "Swan Lake" and "The Nutcracker," and many other beautiful and beloved pieces of music. Tschaikovsky found "The Nutcracker," the last of his three great ballets, difficult to complete. The challenge grew so great that he almost gave up composing altogether. The ballet's Russian premiere was an unqualified flop. It was forty years before it was produced for Western audiences, and even longer before it achieved widespread appreciation. Now, of course, it is a standard.

This story offers an insightful look at the human tendency to self-doubt and the need for trust in the eventual fruitfulness of our talent. Listen to some beautiful music this week and let it remind you to temper any thoughts of dismissing the gifts you have been given to share.

Scripture Insights

The lectionary's snippets often drop us into the middle of a story, like latecomers to a movie. Today, we are in the midst of the Acts of the Apostles. From a human point of view, this haphazard, surprising sequence of events in Acts leaves two impressions about the infant church: its vulnerability and its energetic joy. The larger spiritual view sees the steady hand of providence as God gradually unveils a master plan of salvation.

These surprises culminate in the greatest shock of all, as Luke explains in today's passage: the dramatic shift to include the Gentiles among the people of God. Since the second century, the church has been almost exclusively made up of Gentiles—non-Jews—a situation that none of the apostles or New Testament writers could have imagined. In turn, it is hard for us to imagine how wrenching this change was for them. Israel had always expected the Gentile nations to come to their God (see Isaiah 2:1—4), but thought they would do so by way of Judaism.

Peter's remark in verse 28 supplies context: "God has shown me that I should not call anyone profane." It dawned on him and the young church that God was going to save the Gentiles not as Jews but as Gentiles. Note their astonishment in 10:34. The Greek phrase calls to mind something like an overpowering idea suddenly taking hold. Gentiles were no longer dogs under the Jewish table begging for the children's bread (see Matthew 15:27), but full partners and joint heirs with the ancient people of the covenant.

This shift signals a major new theme in Acts. Jesus says in our gospel today, "I do not call you servants any longer . . . [but] friends." The reason for this is the unconditional and total love with which the Father loves the Son: "As the Father has loved me, so I have loved you" (15:9). This in turn requires the same surrender to each other: Now "love one another as I have loved you" (15:12).

What can you tell about the gospel Jesus preached among the Jews from passages like Mark 2:1—3:6; 3:22–27; 7:1–23; 8:11–13; 10:2–9; 11:27—12:40?

READING I   Acts 1:1—11

Luke writes: In the first book, Theophilus, I wrote about all that Jesus did and taught from the beginning until the day when he was taken up to heaven, after giving instructions through the Holy Spirit to the apostles whom he had chosen. After his suffering Jesus presented himself alive to them by many convincing proofs, appearing to them during forty days and speaking about the dominion of God. While staying with them, Jesus ordered them not to leave Jerusalem, but to wait there for the promise of the Father. "This," he said, "is what you have heard from me; for John baptized with water, but you will be baptized with the Holy Spirit not many days from now."

So when they had come together, they asked him, "Lord, is this the time when you will restore dominion to Israel?" He replied, "It is not for you to know the times or periods that the Father has set by divine authority. But you will receive power when the Holy Spirit has come upon you; and you will be my witnesses in Jerusalem, in all Judea and Samaria, and to the ends of the earth." When Jesus had said this, as they were watching, he was lifted up, and a cloud took him out of their sight.

While he was going and they were gazing up toward heaven, suddenly two men in white robes stood by them. They said, "You Galileans, why do you stand looking up toward heaven? This Jesus, who has been taken up from you into heaven, will come in the same way as you saw him go into heaven."

READING II   Ephesians 4:1—13

Revised Common Lectionary: Ephesians 1:15–23

I therefore, the prisoner in the Lord, beg you to lead a life worthy of the calling to which you have been called, with all humility and gentleness, with patience, bearing with one another in love, making every effort to maintain the unity of the Spirit in the bond of peace. There is one body and one Spirit, just as you were called to the one hope of your calling, one Lord, one faith, one baptism, one God and Father of all, who is above all and through all and in all.

But each of us was given grace according to the measure of Christ's gift. Therefore it is said,

> "When he ascended on high he made captivity
>   itself a captive;
> he gave gifts to his people."

(When it says, "He ascended," what does it mean but that he had also descended into the lower parts of the earth? He who descended is the same one who ascended far above all the heavens, so that he might fill all things.) The gifts Christ gave were that some would be apostles, some prophets, some evangelists, some pastors and teachers, to equip the saints for the work of ministry, for building up the body of Christ, until all of us come to the unity of the faith and of the knowledge of the Son of God, to maturity, to the measure of the full stature of Christ.

GOSPEL   Mark 16:15—20

Revised Common Lectionary: Luke 24:44–53

And he said to them, "Go into all the world and proclaim the good news to the whole creation. The one who believes and is baptized will be saved; but the one who does not believe will be condemned. And these signs will accompany those who believe: by using my name they will cast out demons; they will speak in new tongues; they will pick up snakes in their hands, and if they drink any deadly thing, it will not hurt them; they will lay their hands on the sick, and they will recover." So then the Lord Jesus, after he had spoken to them, was taken up into heaven and sat down at the right hand of God. And they went out and proclaimed the good news everywhere, while the Lord worked with them and confirmed the message by the signs that accompanied it."

Practice of Prayer

Psalm 47:2—3, 6—7, 8—9

All peoples, clap your hands,
cry to God with shouts of joy!
For the LORD, the Most High, we must fear,
great king over all the earth.

God goes up with shouts of joy;
the LORD goes up with trumpet blast.
Sing praise for God, sing praise,
sing praise to our king, sing praise.

God is king of all the earth,
sing praise with all your skill.
God is king over the nations;
God reigns enthroned in holiness.

Practice of Prudence

When the Soviet Union sent its first man into space, it is said that one of the cosmonauts reported seeing no sign of Jesus. Supposedly this was a Communist way of denying the Ascension. Even as fiction, this story goes beyond the ridiculous. Yet in our own way perhaps we look for Jesus in the wrong places. In today's first reading, two angelic figures ask the disciples why they are staring at the sky. Move along, they seem to imply, there is work to be done elsewhere. The gospel reaffirms this in Jesus' final instruction to his disciples. "Go into all the world and proclaim the good news to the whole creation" (Mark 16:15). We can look for Jesus in outer space, but we're much more likely to find him in those around us right here on earth.

Scripture Insights

Luke constructs a bridge between the gospel and Acts when Jesus and the two mysterious men of the resurrection story in Luke 24 reprise their roles at the Ascension in Acts 1. Curiously, Jesus ascends on the evening of Easter Day in Luke 24, while in Acts 1 he ascends after forty days. This is a reminder that we can't read Bible narratives as though they were news reports. The scripture texts deal with real events that were well known in the Christian community of their day, but Luke and the other evangelists reserved the freedom to shape the stories to bring out their deepest meanings. We need to let go of our modern expectations for literal facts and to learn the biblical writers' symbolic approach. Take Luke's use of the forty days between Easter and the Ascension. The number deliberately evokes related events in the Bible.

The disciples themselves at first tended to see matters in the literal terms of the old life. When Jesus promises the outpouring of the Spirit, they rightly remember that as a signal that the final days are coming. A little too eagerly, they ask about finally getting their share in Israel's enthronement. (This recalls the remarkable inattention of Christian literalists in every age who plot the date of the Lord's return.) But Jesus says, basically, "None of your business." He tells the disciples to take their faith to another level as his witnesses to the ends of the earth. Verse 8 in fact outlines Acts' progression from Jerusalem in chapter 1 to Rome in chapter 28.

Jesus then vanishes from sight, literally "taken from their eyes." His ascending body takes their worldly hopes and self-interested ideas away. In the same vein, the writer to the Ephesians calls everyone to "the work of ministry . . . until all of us come . . . to the measure of the full stature of Christ." This cultivation of unity and spiritual maturity is both the theme of Acts and the never-ending task of the Christian disciple.

Mark 16:19 alludes to Jesus at God's "right hand," a phrase found in our Creed. Check Psalm 110:1; Acts 2:33; Romans 8:34; Hebrews 1:3; 1 Peter 3:22. What does it seem to mean?

June 1, 2003

READING I *Acts 1:15—17, 20a, 20c—26*

Revised Common Lectionary: Acts 1:15–17, 21–26

In those days Peter stood up among the believers (together the crowd numbered about one hundred twenty persons) and said, "Friends, the scripture had to be fulfilled, which the Holy Spirit through David foretold concerning Judas, who became a guide for those who arrested Jesus—for he was numbered among us and was allotted his share in this ministry. For it is written in the book of Psalms: 'Let another take his position of overseer.' So one of the men who have accompanied us during all the time that the Lord Jesus went in and out among us, beginning from the baptism of John until the day when Jesus was taken up from us—one of these must become a witness with us to his resurrection." So they proposed two, Joseph called Barsabbas, who was also known as Justus, and Matthias. Then they prayed and said, "Lord, you know everyone's heart. Show us which one of these two you have chosen to take the place in this ministry and apostleship from which Judas turned aside to go to his own place." And they cast lots for them, and the lot fell on Matthias; and he was added to the eleven apostles.

READING II *1 John 4:11—16*

Revised Common Lectionary: 1 John 5:9–13

Beloved, since God loved us so much, we also ought to love one another. No one has ever seen God; if we love one another, God lives in us, and God's love is perfected in us.

By this we know that we abide in God and God in us, because we have been given of God's own Spirit. And we have seen and do testify that the Father has sent the Son as the Savior of the world. God abides in those who confess that Jesus is the Son of God, and they abide in God. So we have known and believe the love that God has for us.

GOSPEL *John 17:6—19*

Roman Catholic: John 17:11b–19

Jesus prayed:"I have made your name known to those whom you gave me from the world. They were yours, and you gave them to me, and they have kept your word. Now they know that everything you have given me is from you; for the words that you gave to me I have given to them, and they have received them and know in truth that I came from you; and they have believed that you sent me. I am asking on their behalf; I am not asking on behalf of the world, but on behalf of those whom you gave me, because they are yours. All mine are yours, and yours are mine; and I have been glorified in them. And now I am no longer in the world, but they are in the world, and I am coming to you.

"Holy Father, protect them in your name that you have given me, so that they may be one, as we are one. While I was with them, I protected them in your name that you have given me. I guarded them, and not one of them was lost except the one destined to be lost, so that the scripture might be fulfilled. But now I am coming to you, and I speak these things in the world so that they may have my joy made complete in themselves. I have given them your word, and the world has hated them because they do not belong to the world, just as I do not belong to the world. I am not asking you to take them out of the world, but I ask you to protect them from the evil one. They do not belong to the world, just as I do not belong to the world. Sanctify them in the truth; your word is truth. As you have sent me into the world, so I have sent them into the world. And for their sakes I sanctify myself, so that they also may be sanctified in truth."

Practice of Prayer

Psalm 103:1—2, 11—12, 19—20

My soul, give thanks to the LORD,
all my being, bless God's holy name.
My soul, give thanks to the LORD
and never forget all God's blessings.

For as the heavens are high above the earth
so strong is God's love for the God-fearing;
As far as the east is from the west
so far does he remove our sins.

The LORD has set his throne in heaven
and his kingdom rules over all.
Give thanks to the LORD, all you angels,
mighty in power, fulfilling God's word,
who heed the voice of that word.

Practice of Prudence

June is a month to celebrate graduations. Parents, teachers, friends and relatives watch with pride as young people make the transition toward greater independence. It takes trust to nudge a loved one out into the world and to believe that he or she has been sufficiently prepared to face what lies ahead.

Jesus' prayer in today's gospel is filled with affection for his disciples. He asks not that they be kept isolated from the rest of the world, but that they be protected from evil. It echoes the sentiments a parent has for a child, a teacher for a student. Jesus' words contain a balance between love for his disciples and a recognition that they now must be off on their own. As you offer congratulations to graduates this year, incorporate the sprit of this prayer into your best wishes.

Scripture Insights

In this Acts passage, Luke is shifting the focus from Jesus to the disciples. Followers in other traditions simply carry out the vision of their teacher, but here the disciples are important in their own right. We know their ideas and writings, even their weaknesses, failures and arguments.

More remarkable still, Luke places the story of the church in Acts on the same level of importance as the story of Jesus in the gospel. Note the strong sense of destiny that flows through our passage: Peter twice uses the strong phrase "it had to be" (*dei:* 16, 21), the same word Jesus used in speaking about his coming suffering (see Mark 8:31). Events that were not of their own making or choosing were happening all around them. A sense of the Lord's hidden, guiding hand pervades the atmosphere of Acts 1.

But more was at work than a sense of destiny; the apostles fulfilled unique roles in the salvation story. Their symbolic number "twelve" recalls the twelve tribes of Israel. Despite the emphasis on choosing a replacement for Judas, Matthias disappears from scripture after his election; so when the apostle James was killed (Acts 12:2), no one replaced him. The twelve performed a symbolic role that was unrepeatable.

Jesus' prayer in John shows how he continues to pray for the church even now. Here the symbolic number is "one": "that they may be one, as we are one." Jesus prays that the community may not be subverted by treachery like that of Judas, or by the hatred of the world. The oneness of the disciples is the basis of their mission in the world. Laying the passages from Acts and John side by side on a spiritual plane, one surmises that although the disciples draw straws, it is really Jesus' prayer for the church's protection and unity that guides its destiny.

Take a look at a few of the following passages and consider how Mark views Jesus' disciples: See Mark 1:16—20; 3:13—19; 3:31—35; 4:35—41; 6:45—52; 8:14—21; 9:14—29; 9:33—37; 10:35—45; 14:26—50.

READING I   Acts 2:1–21

Roman Catholic: Acts 2:1–11

When the day of Pentecost had come, they were all together in one place. And suddenly from heaven there came a sound like the rush of a violent wind, and it filled the entire house where they were sitting. Divided tongues, as of fire, appeared among them, and a tongue rested on each of them. All of them were filled with the Holy Spirit and began to speak in other languages, as the Spirit gave them ability.

Now there were devout Jews from every nation under heaven living in Jerusalem. And at this sound the crowd gathered and was bewildered, because each one heard them speaking in the native language of each. Amazed and astonished, they asked, "Are not all these who are speaking Galileans? And how is it that we hear, each of us, in our own native language? Parthians, Medes, Elamites, and residents of Mesopotamia, Judea and Cappadocia, Pontus and Asia, Phrygia and Pamphylia, Egypt and the parts of Libya belonging to Cyrene, and visitors from Rome, both Jewish-born and proselytes, Cretans and Arabs— in our own languages we hear them speaking about God's deeds of power."

All were amazed and perplexed, saying to one another, "What does this mean?" But others sneered and said, "They are filled with new wine."

But Peter, standing with the eleven, raised his voice and addressed them, "You Judeans and all who live in Jerusalem, let this be known to you, and listen to what I say. Indeed, these are not drunk, as you suppose, for it is only nine o'clock in the morning. No, this is what was spoken through the prophet Joel:

'In the last days it will be, God declares,
  that I will pour out my Spirit upon all flesh,
    and your sons and your daughters shall
      prophesy,
  and your youth shall see visions,
    and your elders shall dream dreams.
Even upon my slaves, both men and women,
  in those days I will pour out my Spirit;
    and they shall prophesy.

And I will show portents in the heaven above
  and signs on the earth below,
    blood, and fire, and smoky mist.
The sun shall be turned to darkness
  and the moon to blood,
    before the coming of the Lord's great
      and glorious day.
Then everyone who calls on the name
  of the Lord shall be saved.'"

READING II   Galatians 5:16–25

Revised Common Lectionary: Romans 8:22–27

Live by the Spirit, I say, and do not gratify the desires of the flesh. For what the flesh desires is opposed to the Spirit, and what the Spirit desires is opposed to the flesh; for these are opposed to each other, to prevent you from doing what you want. But if you are led by the Spirit, you are not subject to the law. Now the works of the flesh are obvious: fornication, impurity, licentiousness, idolatry, sorcery, enmities, strife, jealousy, anger, quarrels, dissensions, factions, envy, drunkenness, carousing, and things like these. I am warning you, as I warned you before: those who do such things will not inherit the dominion of God.

By contrast, the fruit of the Spirit is love, joy, peace, patience, kindness, generosity, faithfulness, gentleness, and self-control. There is no law against such things. And those who belong to Christ Jesus have crucified the flesh with its passions and desires. If we live by the Spirit, let us also be guided by the Spirit.

GOSPEL   John 15:26–27; 16:12–15

Jesus said, "When the Advocate comes, whom I will send to you from the Father, the Spirit of truth who comes from the Father, the Advocate will testify on my behalf. You also are to testify because you have been with me from the beginning.

"I still have many things to say to you, but you cannot bear them now. When the Spirit of truth comes, you will be guided into all the truth; for the Spirit will not speak out of the Spirit's own authority, but will speak whatever the Spirit hears, and will declare to you the things that are to come.

The Spirit will glorify me, taking what is mine and declaring it to you. All that the Father has is mine. For this reason I said that the Spirit will take what is mine and declare it to you."

Practice of Prayer

Psalm 104:1, 24, 29–30, 31, 34

Bless the LORD, my soul!
LORD God, how great you are.

How many are your works, O LORD!
In wisdom you have made them all.
The earth is full of your riches.

You hide your face, they are dismayed;
you take back your spirit, they die,
returning to the dust from which they came.
You send forth your spirit, they are created;
and you renew the face of the earth.

May the glory of the LORD last for ever!
May the LORD rejoice in creation!

May my thoughts be pleasing to God.
I find my joy in the LORD.

Practice of Temperance

In her book *Women of the Word*, author Mary Lou Sleevi combines art and prose to create portraits of various female figures in the Bible. Her portrayal of the Blessed Mother on Pentecost shows a smiling woman with gray hair and wrinkled face; her eyes hold the expression of one who has known both joy and sorrow in deep measure. In the accompanying story, Sleevi writes about Mary's ability to overcome any anger toward the disciples who abandoned her son in the hours before his death. What an important task this was at the moment when the Christian community was taking its shape from the Spirit's outpouring!

Working through anger is especially hard when someone dear to us has suffered. Ask Mary for her prayers this Pentecost to help you temper any anger, resentment or vengeance, and to put that energy into community building.

Scripture Insights

The texts invite us to consider the Spirit's vast activity in both an outer, geographical sense and an inner, spiritual sense. Jesus apparently lived his life within a tiny territory, but the outpouring of his Spirit at Pentecost sent his disciples to the ends of the earth. The same Spirit pressed them deep within themselves to explore the truth about Jesus.

Outwardly, Luke's list is not a roll call of people who literally heard Peter's Pentecost sermon, but of people who had heard the gospel by Luke's time in the late first century. The places named can be found on a good Bible map. They form a circle around Jerusalem, always the spiritual starting point for Luke. In Luke's gospel, the devil showed Jesus "all the dominions of the world" because they were his to give (Luke 4:5–6); Acts shows us the kingdoms that became Christ's by the power of the Holy Spirit.

The list symbolizes the scope of God's grace and the Spirit's power. It also previews the rest of Acts. The apostles would experience many successes and much rejoicing, but also many conflicts and reversals. "It is through many persecutions that we must enter the kingdom of God" (Acts 14:22). The Spirit's relentless energy constantly stirred and pushed the disciples beyond themselves. Their story became part of the story of "God's deeds of power" (2:11).

Inwardly, the Spirit comes from Jesus to guide the disciples to all the truth about him. In the context of John's gospel, this means penetrating to the awesome mystery of Jesus' divine being, the Word made flesh who in the beginning was with God, and is himself God (John 1:1, 14).

Galatians says that by grace the Spirit instructs Christians about life by uniting them with Jesus' crucifixion. For those who understand, Christ's death powerfully centers the inner life of individuals and communities in the fruit of the Spirit.

The Spirit is mentioned rarely but momentously in Mark's gospel (1:8, 10, 12; 3:29; 12:36; 13:11). If you had only these statements, what would you know about the Spirit?

Summer Ordinary Time

EPHPHATHA!

Preparation for the Word

Take away our hurry and our haste,
    ever-patient God,
so we may savor these summer scriptures.
Give us wisdom to balance our busy days
and cultivate a leisure of the heart,
to pore over these words, lines and pages.
Help us to throw off the tyranny of the clock
and come here fresh-minded,
that you may press us to question and ponder.

Lord of the long summer days,
teach us how to contemplate, how to ruminate,
how to chew these words over;
that even the most expected phrases
will trouble and puzzle us.
And so may our reading be to your glory
and our salvation in Jesus who is Lord
for ever and ever. Amen.

Thanksgiving for the Word

Blessed are you, Lord, God of all creation,
in the sun's long summer path,
in the earth's warmth
and the glories of dawn and dusk.
Blessed are you in the rain
and in all the goodness of grain and fruit.
When we open and ponder our scripture, O God,
let your word be these wonders for us.

So may your word be light for our path.
May it be rain that cleanses our thought
and makes fruitful and fresh our spirit.
May this word be warmth for our whole being.
Then may we, who have received your Holy Spirit,
in that Spirit renew the face of the earth.
We pray in Jesus' name who is Lord
    for ever and ever.
Amen.

Weekday Readings

June 9: *2 Corinthians 1:1–7; Matthew 5:1–12*
June 10: *2 Corinthians 1:18–22; Matthew 5:13–16*
June 11: *Acts 11:21b–26; 13:1–3; Matthew 5:17–19*
June 12: *2 Corinthians 3:15–4:1, 3–6; Matthew 5:20–26*
June 13: *2 Corinthians 4:7–15; Matthew 5:27–32*
June 14: *2 Corinthians 5:14–21; Matthew 5:33–37*

June 16: *2 Corinthians 6:1–10; Matthew 5:38–42*
June 17: *2 Corinthians 8:1–9; Matthew 5:43–48*
June 18: *2 Corinthians 9:6–11; Matthew 6:1–6; 16–18*
June 19: *2 Corinthians 11:1–11; Matthew 6:7–15*
June 20: *2 Corinthians 11:18, 21b-30; Matthew 6:19–23*
June 21: *2 Corinthians 12:1–10; Matthew 6:24–34*

June 23: *Genesis 12:1–9; Matthew 7:1–5*
June 24: Solemnity of the Nativity of John the Baptist
   Isaiah 49:1–6; Acts 13:22–26; Luke 1:57–66, 80
June 25: *Genesis 15:1–12, 17–18; Matthew 7:15–20*
June 26: *Genesis 16:1–12, 15–16; Matthew 7:21–29*
June 27: Solemnity of the Most Sacred Heart of Jesus
   Hosea 11:1, 3–4, 8c–9; Ephesians 3:8–12, 14–19;
   John 19:31–37
June 28: *Genesis 18:1–15; Matthew 8:5–17*

June 30: *Genesis 18:16–33; Matthew 8:18–22*
July 1: *Genesis 19:15–29; Matthew 8:23–27*
July 2: *Genesis 21:5, 8–20; Matthew 8:28–34*
July 3: Feast of Saint Thomas
   Ephesians 2:19–22; John 20:24–29
July 4: *Genesis 23:1–4, 19; 24:1–8, 62–67; Matthew 9:9–13*
July 5: *Genesis 27:1–5, 15–29; Matthew 9:14–17*

July 7: *Genesis 28:10–22a; Matthew 9:18–26*
July 8: *Gensis 32:23–33; Matthew 9:32–38*
July 9: *Genesis 41:55–57; 42:5–7a, 17–24a; Matthew 10:1–7*
July 10: *Genesis 44:18–21, 23b–29; 45:1–5; Matthew 10:7–15*
July 11: *Genesis 46:1–7, 28–30; Matthew 10:16–23*
July 12: *Genesis 49:29–32; 50:15–26a; Matthew 10:24–33*

July 14: *Exodus 1:8–14, 22; Matthew 10:34–11:1*
July 15: *Exodus 2:1–15a; Matthew 11:20–24*
July 16: *Exodus 3:1–6, 9–12; Matthew 11:25–27*
July 17: *Exodus 3:13–20; Matthew 11:28–30*
July 18: *Exodus 11:10–12:14; Matthew 12:1–8*
July 19: *Exodus 12:37–42; Matthew 12:14–21*

July 21: *Exodus 14:5–18; Matthew 12:38–42*
July 22: *Exodus 14:21–15:1; John 20:1–2, 11–18*
July 23: *Exodus 16:1–5, 9–15; Matthew 13:1–9*
July 24: *Exodus 19:1–2, 9–11, 16–20b; Matthew 13:10–17*
July 25: Feast of Saint James
   2 Corinthians 4:7–15; Matthew 20:20–28
July 26: *Exodus 24:3–8; Matthew 13:24–30*

July 28: *Exodus 32:15–24, 30–34; Matthew 13:31–35*
July 29: *Exodus 33:7–11; 34:5b–9, 28; John 11:19–27*
July 30: *Exodus 34:29–35; Matthew 13:44–46*
July 31: *Exodus 40:16–21, 34–38; Matthew 13:47–53*

August 1: *Leviticus 23:1, 4–11, 15–16, 27, 34b-37;*
   Matthew 13:54–58
August 2: *Leviticus 25:1, 8–17; Matthew 14:1–12*

August 4: *Numbers 11:4b–15; Matthew 14:13–21*
August 5: *Numbers 12:1–13; Matthew 14:22–36*
August 6: Feast of the Transfiguration of the Lord
   Deuteronomy 7:9–10, 13–14; 2 Peter 1:16–19;
   Mark 9:2–10
August 7: *Numbers 20:1–13; Matthew 16:13–23*
August 8: *Deuteronomy 4:32–40; Matthew 16:24–28*
August 9: *Deuteronomy 6:4–13; Matthew 17:14–20*

August 11: *Deuteronomy 10:12–22; Matthew 17:22–27*
August 12: *Deuteronomy 31:1–8; Matthew 18:1–5, 10, 12–14*
August 13: *Deuteronomy 34:1–12; Matthew 18:15–20*
August 14: *Joshua 3:7–10a, 11, 13–17; Matthew 18:21–19:1*
August 15: Solemnity of the Assumption of the Blessed
   Virgin Mary   Revelation 11:19a; 12:1–6a, 10ab;
   1 Corinthians 15:20–27; Luke 1:39–56
August 16: *Joshua 24:14–29; Matthew 19:13–15*

August 18: *Judges 2:11–19; Matthew 19:16–22*
August 19: *Judges 6:11–24a; Matthew 19:23–30*
August 20: *Judges 9:6–15; Matthew 20:1–16a*
August 21: *Judges 11:29–39a; Matthew 22:1–14*
August 22: *Ruth 1:1, 3–6, 14b–16, 22; Matthew 22:34–40*
August 23: *Ruth 2:1–3, 8–11; 4:13–17; Matthew 23:1–12*

August 25: *1 Thessalonians 1:1–5, 8b-10; Matthew 23:13–22*
August 26: *1 Thessalonians 2:1–8; Matthew 23:23–26*
August 27: *1 Thessalonians 2:9–13; Matthew 23:27–32*
August 28: *1 Thessalonians 3:7–13; Matthew 24:42–51*
August 29: *1 Thessalonians 4:1–8; Mark 6:17–29*
August 30: *1 Thessalonians 4:9–11; Matthew 25:14–30*

September 1: *1 Thessalonians 4:13–18; Luke 4:16–30*
September 2: *1 Thessalonians 5:1–6, 9–11; Luke 4:31–37*
September 3: *Colossians 1:1–8; Luke 4:38–44*
September 4: *Colossians 1:9–14; Luke 5:1–11*
September 5: *Colossians 1:15–20; Luke 5:33–39*
September 6: *Colossians 1:21–23; Luke 6:1–5*

September 8: Feast of the Birth of the Blessed Virgin Mary
   Micah 5:1–4a; Matthew 1:1–16, 18–23
September 9: *Colossians 2:6–15; Luke 6:12–19*
September 10: *Colossians 3:1–11; Luke 6:20–26*
September 11: *Colossians 3:12–17; Luke 6:27–38*
September 12: *1 Timothy 1:1–2, 12–14; Luke 6:39–42*
September 13: *1 Timothy 1:15–17; Luke 6:43–49*

September 15: *1 Timothy 2:1–8; John 19:25–27*
September 16: *1 Timothy 3:1–13; Luke 7:11–17*
September 17: *1 Timothy 3:14–16; Luke 7:31–35*
September 18: *1 Timothy 4:12–16; Luke 7:36–50*
September 19: *1 Timothy 6:2c-12; Luke 8:1–3*
September 20: *1 Timothy 6:13–16; Luke 8:4–15*

June 15, 2003

THE MOST HOLY TRINITY
OTHER CHURCHES: SEE PAGES 98—99

READING I *Deuteronomy 4:32—34, 39—40*

For ask now about former ages, long before your own, ever since the day that God created human beings on the earth; ask from one end of heaven to the other: has anything so great as this ever happened or has its like ever been heard of? Has any people ever heard the voice of a god speaking out of a fire, as you have heard, and lived? Or has any god ever attempted to go and take a nation for himself from the midst of another nation, by trials, by signs and wonders, by war, by a mighty hand and an outstretched arm, and by terrifying displays of power, as the LORD your God did for you in Egypt before your very eyes? So acknowledge today and take to heart that the LORD is God in heaven above and on the earth beneath; there is no other. Keep his statues and his commandments, which I am commanding you today for your own well-being and that of your descendants after you, so that you may long remain in the land that the LORD your God is giving you for all time.

READING II *Romans 8:14—17*

For all who are led by the Spirit of God are children of God. For you did not receive a spirit of slavery to fall back into fear, but you have received a spirit of adoption. When we cry, "Abba! Father!" it is that very Spirit bearing witness with our spirit that we are children of God, and if children, then heirs, heirs of God and joint heirs with Christ—if, in fact, we suffer with Christ so that we may also be glorified with Christ.

GOSPEL *Matthew 28:16—20*

Now the eleven disciples went to Galilee, to the mountain to which Jesus had directed them. When they saw Jesus, they worshiped him; but some doubted.

And Jesus came and said to them, "All authority in heaven and on earth has been given to me. Go therefore and make disciples of all nations, baptizing them in the name of the Father and of the Son and of the Holy Spirit, and teaching them to obey everything that I have commanded you. And remember, I am with you always, to the end of the age."

Practice of Prayer

Psalm 33:4—5, 6, 9, 18—19, 20, 22

For the word of the LORD is faithful
and all his works done in truth.
The LORD loves justice and right
and fills the earth with love.

By God's word the heavens were made,
by the breath of his mouth all the stars.
For God spoke; it came to be.
God commanded; it sprang into being.

The LORD looks on those who fear him,
on those who hope in his love,
to rescue their souls from death,
to keep them alive in famine.

Our soul is waiting for the LORD.
The Lord is our help and our shield.

May your love be upon us, O LORD,
as we place all our hope in you.

Practice of Justice

Today there are many missionaries who proclaim the gospel by their preaching and teaching and also by their service and genuine friendship. They bring comfort, aid and education to the poor and oppressed of the world. Their efforts to end human misery and bring justice witness to a vital aspect of Christ's gospel and, coupled with their teaching, respond to that long-ago command of Jesus to make disciples of all nations.

To learn more about the missions, you could start at the website of the Society for the Propagation of the Faith: www.propfaith.org. Then find out what efforts your diocese or parish sponsors. Do you feel called to help in their work?

Scripture Insights

Scripture contains no philosophically mature doctrine of the Trinity; the word itself never appears. But its reality lies deeply embedded in the New Testament and emerged over time. Painstakingly, the church discerned and taught from scripture the only doctrine adequate to the witness of both Testaments: That the one God of biblical Israel at the heart of creation and redemption is a Reality of three persons. It is the mind of the church interpreting scripture, and not scripture alone, that leads us to the truth of salvation.

Still, the best way to begin to learn about the Trinity is to go to scripture. Who God *is* in heaven above (the deep mystery of God's being) can always be seen in what God *does* on earth below (God's relentless divine activity in the world for the sake of salvation).

In this week's Romans passage, Paul seems to presume three separate, self-aware divine persons in the Holy: Father-God, Christ-Son, and Spirit of God. Those who are led by God's Spirit are God's children, having lost servile fear of God when the Spirit bestows the consciousness of being God's beloved child. This "spirit of adoption" puts our relationship with God on an intimate basis; the Spirit inscribes its reality in our hearts. Paul also suggests that the Spirit's work infuses in us Jesus' own beloved-child relationship to God.

Passages that interrelate the three divine persons can be found in Matthew 28:19 (today's gospel); John 14:26; 15:26; 16:13—15; Acts 2:33—36; Romans 8:9—11; 1 Corinthians 2:6—16; 2 Corinthians 13:13; Ephesians 1:3—14; 1 Peter 1:2; Revelation 1:4—5. Even if scripture contains no explicit trinitarian formula, this threefold description of God's work is used strikingly often by otherwise very different New Testament writers. It is even more striking that these writers were devout monotheistic Jews.

Look up the New Testament passages listed above. What do they teach you about the Trinity?

June 15, 2003

READING I   Isaiah 6:1—8

In the year that King Uzziah died, I saw the LORD sitting on a throne, high and lofty; and the hem of the LORD's robe filled the temple. Seraphs were in attendance above the LORD; each had six wings: with two they covered their faces, and with two they covered their feet, and with two they flew. And one called to another and said: "Holy, holy, holy is the LORD of hosts; the whole earth is full of the glory of the LORD. The pivots on the thresholds shook at the voices of those who called, and the house filled with smoke. And I said: "Woe is me! I am lost, for I am a man of unclean lips, and I live among a people of unclean lips; yet my eyes have seen the Sovereign, the LORD of hosts!"

Then one of the seraphs flew to me, holding a live coal that had been taken from the altar with a pair of tongs. The seraph touched my mouth with it and said: "Now that this has touched your lips, your guilt has departed and your sin is blotted out." Then I heard the voice of the LORD saying, "Whom shall I send, and who will go for us?" And I said, "Here am I; send me!"

READING II   Romans 8:12—17

Brothers and sisters, we are debtors, not to the flesh, to live according to the flesh—for if you live according to the flesh, you will die; but if by the Spirit you put to death the deeds of the body, you will live. For all who are led by the Spirit of God are children of God. For you did not receive a spirit of slavery to fall back into fear, but you have received a spirit of adoption. When we cry, "Abba! Father!" it is that very Spirit bearing witness with our spirit that we are children of God, and if children, then heirs, heirs of God and joint heirs with Christ—if, in fact, we suffer with Christ so that we may also be glorified with Christ.

GOSPEL   John 3:1—17

Now there was a Pharisee named Nicodemus, a leader of the Jewish people. He came to Jesus by night and said to him, "Rabbi, we know that you are a teacher who has come from God; for no one can do these signs that you do apart from the presence of God." Jesus answered him, "Very truly, I tell you, no one can see the dominion of God without being born from above."

Nicodemus said to Jesus, "How can anyone be born after having grown old? Can one enter a second time into the mother's womb and be born?" Jesus answered, "Very truly, I tell you, no one can enter the dominion of God without being born of water and Spirit. What is born of the flesh is flesh, and what is born of the Spirit is spirit. Do not be astonished that I said to you, 'You must be born from above.' The wind blows where it chooses, and you hear the sound of it, but you do not know where it comes from or where it goes. So it is with everyone who is born of the Spirit."

Nicodemus said to Jesus, "How can these things be?" Jesus answered him, "Are you a teacher of Israel, and yet you do not understand these things? Very truly, I tell you, we speak of what we know and testify to what we have seen; yet you do not receive our testimony. If I have told you about earthly things and you do not believe, how can you believe if I tell you about heavenly things?

"No one has ascended into heaven except the one who descended from heaven, the Son-of-Man. And just as Moses lifted up the serpent in the wilderness, so must the Son-of-Man be lifted up, that whoever believes in him may have eternal life.

"For God loved the world in this way, that God gave the Son, the only begotten one, so that everyone who believes in him may not perish but may have eternal life. Indeed, God did not send the Son into the world to condemn the world, but in order that the world might be saved through him."

Practice of Prayer

Psalm 29:1— 6, 8—9, 11

O give the LORD you children of God,
give the LORD glory and power;
give the LORD the glory of his name.
Adore the LORD, resplendent and holy.

The LORD's voice resounding on the waters,
the LORD on the immensity of waters;
the voice of the LORD, full of power,
the voice of the LORD, full of splendor.

The LORD's voice shattering the cedars,
the LORD shatters the cedars of Lebanon,
makes Lebanon leap like a calf
and Sirion like a young wild ox.

The LORD's voice shaking the wilderness,
the LORD shakes the wilderness of Kadesh;
the LORD's voice rending the oak tree
and stripping the forest bare.

The LORD will give strength to his people,
the LORD will bless his people with peace.

Practice of Temperance

"God grant me the serenity to accept the things I cannot change, the courage to change the things I can, and the wisdom to know the difference."

The serenity prayer has become a standard part of the recovery process used by Alcoholics Anonymous and other self-help organizations. In very simple terms, it encourages those struggling with addiction to strike a balance between effecting change and recognizing their limitations. This is not an easy process. It means being able to admit our own weaknesses and to humbly acknowledge our need for the support, wisdom and encouragement of others.

June 21st is the birthday of Reinhold Niebuhr, author of an earlier form of the serenity prayer. Use the day to offer support and encouragement to anyone you know who is fighting any form of addiction.

Scripture Insights

Jesus's discussion with Nicodemus concerns the organ of spiritual perception and knowing, the spiritual eye. Jesus declares that no one may "see" God's dominion ("the kingdom of God") without being born "from above." Here Jesus reveals his ways of working and the ways of knowing necessary for following him. Flesh and spirit are ordered in a stair-step relationship that begins on the level of the flesh and moves to the realm of the spirit. In the first part of John's gospel, often called "The Book of Signs," Jesus acts upon or speaks of some external reality as a way of drawing people into the deeper, spiritual reality. So it was with the water become wine in chapter 2, the Samaritan woman's water in chapter 4, the feeding of the 5000 in chapter 6, the blind man's healing in chapter 9, and the raising of Lazarus in chapter 11: Each points beyond itself to deeper realities of the Spirit.

We make the transition from flesh to spirit by means of God's gift of Jesus' sacrifice. This was foreshadowed by the striking story of Moses lifting up the serpent in the wilderness. Wandering Israel was chastised by a plague of serpents for wanting to return to their old life in Egypt. God instructed Moses to raise a serpent's image on a pole, and everyone bitten by serpents who looked at the image recovered. Jesus compared his coming to God's gift of the serpent raised on the pole that restored people's lives after sin. But Jesus also gave them eternal life.

In John, Jesus' "lifting up" refers to his crucifixion (John 8:28, 12:32—33). It was by his death that he would be "glorified" (12:23—26; 13:31—32). Jesus' glorification by death gives a very distinctive shape to the meaning of the word "glory" that should be taken into account in reading John's gospel. When the evangelist says, "the Word became flesh . . . and we saw his glory" (1:14), he is referring not only to the incarnation but also to the Lord's paschal mystery.

Isaiah witnesses the Lord enthroned in glory. How does spiritual perception function in his vision?

READING I   *Exodus 24:3—8*

Moses came and told the people all the words of the LORD and all the ordinances; and all the people answered with one voice, and said, "All the words that the LORD has spoken we will do." And Moses wrote down all the words of the LORD. He rose early in the morning, and built an altar at the foot of the mountain, and set up twelve pillars, corresponding to the twelve tribes of Israel. He sent young men of the people of Israel, who offered burnt offerings and sacrificed oxen as offerings of well-being to the LORD. Moses took half of the blood and put it in basins, and half of the blood he dashed against the altar. Then he took the book of the covenant, and read it in the hearing of the people; and they said, "All that the LORD has spoken we will do, and we will be obedient." Moses took the blood and dashed it on the people, and said, "See the blood of the covenant that the LORD has made with you in accordance with all these words."

READING II   *Hebrews 9:11—15*

When Christ came as a high priest of the good things that have come, then through the greater and perfect tent (not made with hands, that is, not of this creation), he entered once for all into the Holy Place, not with the blood of goats and calves, but with his own blood, thus obtaining eternal redemption.

For if the blood of goats and bulls, with the sprinkling of the ashes of a heifer, sanctifies those who have been defiled so that their flesh is purified, how much more will the blood of Christ, who through the eternal Spirit offered himself without blemish to God, purify our conscience from dead works to worship the living God!

For this reason Christ is the mediator of a new covenant, so that those who are called may receive the promised eternal inheritance, because a death has occurred that redeems them from the transgressions under the first covenant.

GOSPEL   *Mark 14:12—16, 22—26*

On the first day of Unleavened Bread, when the Passover lamb is sacrificed, his disciples said to him, "Where do you want us to go and make the preparations for you to eat the Passover?" So he sent two of his disciples, saying to them, "Go into the city, and a man carrying a jar of water will meet you; follow him, and wherever he enters, say to the owner of the house, 'The Teacher asks, Where is my guest room where I may eat the Passover with my disciples?' He will show you a large room upstairs, furnished and ready. Make preparations for us there." So the disciples set out and went to the city, and found everything as he had told them; and they prepared the Passover meal. While they were eating, he took a loaf of bread, and after blessing it he broke it, gave it to them, and said, "Take; this is my body." Then he took a cup, and after giving thanks he gave it to them, and all of them drank from it. He said to them, "This is my blood of the covenant, which is poured out for many. Truly I tell you, I will never again drink of the fruit of the vine until that day when I drink it new in the kingdom of God." When they had sung the hymn, they went out to the Mount of Olives.

Practice of Prayer

Psalm 116:12—13, 15—16, 17—18

How can I repay the LORD
for his goodness to me?
The cup of salvation I will raise;
I will call on the LORD's name.

O precious in the eyes of the LORD
is the death of the faithful.
Your servant, LORD, your servant am I;
you have loosened my bonds.
A thanksgiving sacrifice I make;
I will call on the LORD's name.

My vows to the LORD I will fulfill
before all the people.

Practice of Temperance

How much is too much? Restaurants offer super-sized meals. Frozen dinners come in "hungry man" size. The capacity of everything from dinner plates to soup bowls has increased. We are a nation of overfed people. The burgeoning diet industry attests to the problems that result from such trends.

Since the Middle Ages, the feast of the Body and Blood of Christ has been a day to celebrate the eucharist. It is a gift of Jesus meant to fill us, not bloat us. There is a certain satisfaction that comes from holding back, from resisting the urge to overindulge. Feasting is not the same as gluttony. A real feast leaves us with appreciation of what is placed before us, to savor our food as gift. It helps us appreciate that "just enough" is what we really need to be satisfied.

Scripture Insights

Blood is life. The people of ancient Israel knew that. They enacted laws against the spilling of blood (Deuteronomy 19; 21; Leviticus 17) and used blood in rituals to sanctify altars, consecrate priests (Exodus 29) and seal covenants between God and the people. It is fitting, then, that Jesus talks about his blood as the blood of the covenant. To drink his blood is to sprinkle it on one's heart, just as Moses dashed blood on the people as a sign of their relationship with God.

The epistle to the Hebrews contrasts the blood of Jesus with the blood of the sacrifice for atonement in Leviticus 16. Aaron was forbidden to enter the Holy Place until he had sacrificed a bull to atone for his sins and a goat to atone for the sins of the people. Jesus comes before God by way of his own blood. The blood of the old covenant, says the letter to the Hebrews, sanctified the body; the blood of the new covenant sanctifies the mind and heart forever.

In the story of the Exodus, Moses sprinkled the blood of a lamb on the doorposts of the Israelites so that the angel of death who came to destroy the firstborn children of Egypt would pass over their houses. In his first letter to the Corinthians, Paul states: "For our paschal lamb, Christ, has been sacrificed" (I Corinthians 6:7). In Paul's theology, Christ becomes the means by which we escape the death caused by sin. It is the living sign of Christ's blood that transforms our lives with grace.

We remember the last supper at every liturgy during the eucharistic prayer. We tell the full story of the last supper during the reading of the Passion on Palm Sunday and in Paul's letter to the Corinthians on Holy Thursday. In the readings for the feast of Body and Blood of Jesus, we ponder the power and depth of Jesus' sacrifice for us. His blood ratifies and sanctifies out relationship with God, atones for our sin and protects us from "soul death." When we remember the last supper, Jesus' selfless act of love becomes present to us once again so that we can be transformed.

The word *covenant* means agreement. What is the new covenant about which Paul speaks and which is ratified by Christ's blood?

June 22, 2003

ROMAN CATHOLIC: SEE PAGES 100—101
SECOND SUNDAY AFTER PENTECOST

READING I   Job 38:1—11

The LORD answered Job out of the whirlwind: "Who is this that darkens counsel by words without knowledge? Brace yourself like a warrior; I will question you, and you shall declare to me.

"Where were you when I laid the foundation of the earth? Tell me, if you have understanding. Who determined its measurements—surely you know! Or who stretched the line upon it? On what were its bases sunk, or who laid its cornerstone when the morning stars sang together and all the heavenly beings shouted for joy?

"Or who shut in the sea with doors when it burst out from the womb?—when I made the clouds its garment, and thick darkness its swaddling band, and prescribed bounds for it, and set bars and doors, and said, 'Thus far shall you come, and no farther, and here shall your proud waves be stopped'?"

READING II   2 Corinthians 6:1—13

As we work together with God, we urge you also not to accept the grace of God in vain. For God says, "At an acceptable time I have listened to you, and on a day of salvation I have helped you." See, now is the acceptable time; see, now is the day of salvation! We are putting no obstacle in anyone's way, so that no fault may be found with our ministry, but as servants of God we have commended ourselves in every way: through great endurance, in afflictions, hardships, calamities, beatings, imprisonments, riots, labors, sleepless nights, hunger; by purity, knowledge, patience, kindness, holiness of spirit, genuine love, truthful speech, and the power of God; with the weapons of righteousness for the right hand and for the left; in honor and dishonor, in ill repute and good repute. We are treated as impostors, and yet are true; as unknown, and yet are well known; as dying, and see—we are alive; as punished, and yet not killed; as sorrowful, yet always rejoicing; as poor, yet making many rich; as having nothing, and yet possessing everything. We have spoken frankly to you Corinthians; our heart is wide open to you. There is no restriction in our affections, but only in yours. In return—I speak as to children—open wide your hearts also.

GOSPEL   Mark 4:35—41

When evening had come, Jesus said to the disciples, "Let us go across to the other side." And leaving the crowd behind, they took him with them in the boat, just as he was. Other boats were with him.

A great windstorm arose, and the waves beat into the boat, so that the boat was already being swamped. But Jesus was in the stern, asleep on the cushion; and they woke him up and said to him, "Teacher, do you not care that we are perishing?" Jesus woke up and rebuked the wind, and said to the sea, "Peace! Be still!" Then the wind ceased, and there was a dead calm. He said to them, "Why are you afraid? Have you still no faith?"

And they were filled with great awe and said to one another, "Who then is this, that even the wind and the sea obey him?"

Practice of Prayer

Psalm 107:1—3, 23—26, 29—30

"O give thanks to the LORD who is good;
whose love endures for ever."

Let them say this, the LORD's redeemed,
those redeemed from the hand of the foe
and gathered from far-off lands,
from east and west, north and south.

Some sailed to the sea in ships
to trade on the mighty waters.
They saw the deeds of the LORD,
the wonders he does in the deep.

For God spoke and summoned the gale,
tossing the waves of the sea
up to heaven and back into the deep;
their souls melted away in distress.

God stilled the storm to a whisper;
all the waves of the sea were hushed.
They rejoiced because of the calm
and God led them to the haven they desired.

Practice of Fortitude

"Why are you afraid? Have you still no faith?" Imagine it: terror in the midst of a storm, bewilderment and exasperation that the teacher could sleep through the tumult, amazement at the instant calm Jesus could command, and then these questions. Mark tells us that the disciples were "filled with great awe" as they pondered what manner of person their teacher might be. And surely they were also perplexed and disheartened at Jesus' chiding. Again they'd come up short.

It takes great fortitude to be a faithful disciple on the spiritual path—to continue trying to understand inscrutable lessons when our human assumptions are challenged at every turn. Sometimes we have to be content to simply feel the spiritual power of the teacher in the boat with us while we wait for the next glimmer of understanding. What fortifies your discipleship when you're waiting for a breakthrough?

Scripture Insights

In God's words to Job, the series of rhetorical questions is designed to force Job and the reader to admit that God is Lord of all and knows all. God's speech to Job is compelling. It leaves us the understanding that God's power and creative force are far greater than we can imagine.

Paul, in the letter to the Corinthians, and Mark, in his gospel, also speak of God's power, but evoke it in different ways. Paul points to proof of God's enduring care, power and grace in the dedication that he and his companion Timothy feel for their work. By their example he hopes to persuade the Corinthians to be equally generous in affection and service (2 Corinthians 6:13).

Mark, on the other hand, provides a graphic illustration of the power of the Son of God over the forces of nature. The wind and the sea obey him as readily as the demon he had ordered out of the man in the synagogue (Mark 1:23). Mark uses the same word, "rebuke," to describe what Jesus does to both. The word suggests an authoritative scolding that only God can give.

Jesus' question to the disciples (and to us), "Have you still no faith?" pushes them to remember everything they have learned or believed about God, including God's acts of power over Egypt and the words of God in the mouths of the prophets, calling them to faith and faithfulness. Ultimately, though, the best explanations may lie in God's speech to Job. God's power is beyond comprehension and Jesus, this holy man of God, shares in it.

Under what circumstances would we use a series of rhetorical questions as God does with Job? What do such questions teach us?

Mark tells us that Jesus was asleep in the boat when the storm arose. Why might Mark have found this detail important?

June 29, 2003

SAINTS PETER AND PAUL, APOSTLES
OTHER CHURCHES: SEE PAGES 106—107

READING I   Acts 12:1—11

About that time King Herod laid violent hands upon some who belonged to the church. He had James, the brother of John, killed with the sword. After he saw that it pleased the Jews, he proceeded to arrest Peter also. (This was during the festival of Unleavened Bread.) When he had seized him, he put him in prison and handed him over to four squads of soldiers to guard him, intending to bring him out to the people after the Passover. While Peter was kept in prison, the church prayed fervently to God for him. The very night before Herod was going to bring him out, Peter, bound with two chains, was sleeping between two soldiers, while guards in front of the door were keeping watch over the prison. Suddenly an angel of the Lord appeared and a light shone in the cell. He tapped Peter on the side and woke him, saying, "Get up quickly." And the chains fell of his wrists. The angel said to him, "Fasten your belt and put on your sandals." He did so. Then he said to him, "Wrap your cloak around you and follow me." Peter went out and followed him; he did not realize that what was happening with the angel's help was real; he though he was seeing a vision. After they had passed the first and the second guard, they came before the iron gate leading into the city. It opened for them of its own accord, and they went out side and walked along a lane, when suddenly the angel left him. Then Peter came to himself and said, "Now I am sure that the Lord has sent his angel and rescued me from the hands of Herod and from all that the Jewish people were expecting.

READING II   2 Timothy 4:6—8, 17—18

As for me, I am already being poured out as a libation, and the time of my departure has come. I have fought the good fight, I have finished the race, I have kept the faith. From now on there is reserved for me the crown of righteousness, which the Lord, the righteous judge, will give me on that day, and not only to me but also to all who have longed for the Lord's appearing. But the Lord stood by me and gave me strength, so that through me the message might be fully proclaimed and all the Gentiles might hear it. So I was rescued from the lion's mouth. The Lord will rescue me from every evil attack and save me for the dominion of heaven. To the Lord be the glory forever and ever. Amen.

GOSPEL   Matthew 16:13—19

Now when Jesus came into the district of Caesarea Philippi, he asked his disciples, "Who do people say that the Son-of-Man is?" And they said, "Some say John the Baptist, but others Elijah, and still others Jeremiah or one of the prophets." Jesus said to them, "But who do you say that I am?" Simon Peter answered, "You are the Messiah, the Son of the living God."

And Jesus answered him, "Blessed are you, Simon son of Jonah! For flesh and blood has not revealed this to you, but my Father in heaven. And I tell you, you are Peter, and on this rock I will build my church, and the gates of Hades will not prevail against it. I will give you the keys of the dominion of heaven, and whatever you bind on earth will be bound in heaven, and whatever you loose on earth will be loosed in heaven."

Practice of Prayer

Psalm 34:2—3, 4—5, 6—7, 8—9

I will bless the LORD at all times,
God's praise always on my lips;
in the LORD my soul shall make its boast.
The humble shall hear and be glad.

Glorify the LORD with me.
Together let us praise God's name.
I sought the LORD and was heard;
from all my terrors set free.

Look towards God and be radiant;
let your faces not be abashed.
When the poor cry out the LORD hears them
and rescues them from all their distress.

The angel of the LORD is encamped
around those who fear God, to rescue them.
Taste and see that the LORD is good.
They are happy who seek refuge in God.

Practice of Temperance

Several years ago a made-for-TV movie about these two great apostles had actor Anthony Hopkins playing the role of Paul, and he threw himself into the part with an intensity that seemed to fit Paul perfectly. When a group of Greeks laughed out loud at his explanation of the resurrection, he reacted as one who would find imprisonment preferable to ridicule.

Paul seems the very picture of an intemperate man, one obsessed with his new-found faith. Nevertheless, he had to learn to wait upon God's timing and to abide by the wisdom of the community. He knew he was simply an instrument and, as such, had to keep his own interests in check.

Paul's passion for bringing the gospel to others resulted in widespread conversion and helped give birth to the church. Great drama—and inspiration.

Scripture Insights

The gospels of Matthew and Mark both contain a story of Peter identifying Jesus as the Messiah (see Mark 8:27–30). Matthew uses two titles to make clear who Jesus is: Son of Man and Messiah. "Who do people say that the Son-of-Man is?" Jesus asks. The idiomatic Hebrew expression "son of . . . " signifies membership in a family. Later in the passage, Jesus calls Peter "Simon son of Jonah," to indicate he belongs to the family of Jonah. "Son of man" appears in the Old Testament, meaning simply human being, although it picks up a more exalted connotation in Daniel 7:13, an apocalyptic vision in which one "like a son of man" is given eternal dominion by God. This aspect of the title developed further into New Testament times, suggesting a semi-divine being who would come to judge the wicked and establish the reign of God. When Jesus asks that question about the Son of Man, he is being ambiguous. Is he referring to himself or to another? The answers he gets indicate that many consider the Son of Man, whether Jesus or someone else, to be a prophet who will announce the coming reign or the new covenant of God.

Having heard what people are saying, Jesus now asks the disciples: "But who do you say that I am?" Here, Jesus refers only to himself. Peter brings in a different title: "You are the Messiah, the Son of the living God." Peter's bold proclamation draws together identities expressed more evocatively in the Old Testament. There the title Messiah (anointed one) is associated with only two figures: the foreign King Cyrus, who freed the Jews from exile, and David, the anointed one of God, who is also referred to as God's son (Psalm 2:45). Matthew underscores the connection between Messiah and Son of God, giving the reader a fuller understanding of the nature of Jesus' mission and his close relationship with God. For this, Peter earns the blessing of Jesus, because he sees beyond what is merely expected to everything that can be hoped for.

The Messiah of Israel was supposed to be a great warrior or king who would save Israel from oppression. How does Jesus subvert and transform those expectations? How did he live up to them?

READING I   Lamentations 3:22—33

The steadfast love of the LORD never ceases, the mercies of God never come to an end; they are new every morning; great is your faithfulness. "The LORD is my portion," says my soul, "therefore in the LORD I will hope."

The LORD is good to those who are patient, to the soul that seeks after God. It is good that a warrior should wait quietly for the salvation of the LORD. It is good for a warrior to bear the yoke in youth, to sit alone in silence when the LORD has imposed it, to put his mouth to the dust (there may yet be hope), to give his cheek to the smiter, and be filled with insults.

For the LORD will not reject forever. Although causing grief, the LORD will have compassion out of an abundance of steadfast love; for the LORD does not willingly afflict or grieve anyone.

READING II   2 Corinthians 8:7—15

Now as you excel in everything—in faith, in speech, in knowledge, in utmost eagerness, and in our love for you—so we want you to excel also in this generous undertaking.

I do not say this as a command, but I am testing the genuineness of your love against the earnestness of others. For you know the generous act of our Lord Jesus Christ, that though he was rich, yet for your sakes he became poor, so that by his poverty you might become rich. And in this matter I am giving my advice: it is appropriate for you who began last year not only to do something but even to desire to do something—now finish doing it, so that your eagerness may be matched by completing it according to your means. For if the eagerness is there, the gift is acceptable according to what one has—not according to what one does not have. I do not mean that there should be relief for others and pressure on you, but it is a question of a fair balance between your present abundance and their need, so that their abundance may be for your need, in order that there may be a fair balance. As it is written, "The one who had much did not have too much, and the one who had little did not have too little."

GOSPEL   Mark 5:21— 43

When Jesus had crossed again in the boat to the other side, a great crowd gathered around him; and he was by the sea. Then one of the leaders of the synagogue named Jairus came and, when he saw Jesus, fell at his feet and begged him repeatedly, "My little daughter is at the point of death. Come and lay your hands on her, so that she may be made well, and live." So Jesus went with him.

And a large crowd followed him and pressed in on him. Now there was a woman who had been suffering from hemorrhages for twelve years. She had endured much under many physicians, and had spent all that she had; and she was no better, but rather grew worse. She had heard about Jesus, and came up behind him in the crowd and touched his cloak, for she said, "If I but touch his clothes, I will be made well." Immediately her hemorrhage stopped; and she felt in her body that she was healed of her disease. Immediately aware that power had gone forth from him, Jesus turned about in the crowd and said, "Who touched my clothes?" And his disciples said to him, "You see the crowd pressing in on you; how can you say, 'Who touched me?' " Jesus looked all around to see who had done it. But the woman, knowing what had happened to her, came in fear and trembling, fell down before him, and told him the whole truth. He said to her, "Daughter, your faith has made you well; go in peace, and be healed of your disease."

While he was still speaking, some people came from the leader's house to say, "Your daughter is dead. Why trouble the teacher any further?" But overhearing what they said, Jesus said to the leader of the synagogue, "Do not fear, only believe." Jesus allowed no one to follow him except Peter, James, and John, the brother of James.

When they came to the house of the leader of the synagogue, Jesus saw a commotion, people weeping and wailing loudly. When he had entered, he said to them, "Why do you make a commotion and weep? The child is not dead but sleeping." And they laughed at him. Then he put them all outside, and took the child's father and mother and those who were with him, and went in where the child was. Jesus took her by the hand and said to her, "Talitha cum," which means, "Little girl, get up!" And immediately the girl got up and began to walk about (she was twelve years of age). At this they were overcome with amazement. Jesus strictly ordered them that no one should know this, and told them to give her something to eat.

Practice of Prayer

Psalm 30:2—6

I will praise you, LORD, you have rescued me
and have not let my enemies rejoice over me.

O LORD, I cried to you for help
and you, my God, have healed me.
O LORD, you have raised my soul from the dead,
restored me to life from those who sink into
    the grave.

Sing psalms to the LORD you faithful ones,
give thanks to his holy name.
God's anger lasts a moment; God's favor all
    through life.
At night there are tears, but joy comes with dawn.

Practice of Prudence

Needs often spur actions. Jairus is downright persistent in his supplication, begging Jesus repeatedly to come and save his dying child. The woman with the hemorrhage pushed her way through a crowd of people in order to touch Jesus' cloak. If either felt intimidated by Jesus, his disciples or the crowd, it didn't matter. Their needs were simply too great.

Prudence is sometimes mistaken for timidity or extreme caution. Thomas Aquinas defined it as "right reason in action." Simply put, a prudent person knows at heart what needs to be done and does it. The actions of the two gospel figures resulted in healing and restoration of life. What heartfelt needs are prodding you to act with the persistence of Jairus and the tenacity of the healed woman?

Scripture Insights

Mark's story within a story expands the picture of Jesus' healing work, showing the boundaries that must be crossed so that Jesus can bring life. The woman Jesus encounters in the story today is dying, and the flow of blood that has afflicted her for years makes her unclean. Later, in spite of the unbelieving crowd, Jesus touches a child who is dead and brings her back to life.

Mark offers significant details in the ways that people approach Jesus to be healed. Jairus brings Jesus to his daughter, and the woman with the hemorrhage touches Jesus as he goes by, almost secretly. As Jesus' ministry grows, he moves out among the people. He goes to them. The healing power in him is so abundant that it overflows whenever he is confronted by suffering and death. Thus he knows when the woman touches him and sends her away in peace.

Other details link today's stories. The woman has been dying for as long as the child has been alive. Twelve years is a long time to suffer from a disease; it is a short time for a child to live. The woman touches Jesus, making him ritually unclean; Jesus takes the child by the hand, again making himself unclean. As in other instances (Mark 2; 3), Jesus is far less concerned about the finer points of the law than he is about helping those in need. Finally, the disciples are unaware of the healing of the woman, but three are eyewitnesses to the resurrection of the child. With each detail, Mark paints a picture of Jesus as a miraculous healer and teacher, unlike the prophets before him. Many of those prophets healed others; some even raised children from the dead (2 Kings 4:8—36). Jesus is the first to have power drawn out of him by someone else's touch. He is the first to have shown his authority so consistently over demons, illness and death. He is the first, as Paul says, to become poor so that we might be made rich in love and grace.

Jesus uses the same gesture with the little girl as he does with Peter's mother-in-law (Mark 1). He takes both by the hand. What might be significant about Jesus' use of touch in these healing stories? What might we learn from it?

READING I *Ezekiel 2:1—5*

Roman Catholic: Ezekiel 2:2–5

A voice said to me: O mortal, stand up on your feet, and I will speak with you. And when the LORD spoke to me, a spirit entered into me and set me on my feet; and I heard the LORD speaking to me, saying, Mortal, I am sending you to the people of Israel, to a nation of rebels who have rebelled against me; they and their ancestors have transgressed against me to this very day. The descendants are impudent and stubborn. I am sending you to them, and you shall say to them, "Thus says the Lord GOD." Whether they hear or refuse to hear (for they are a rebellious house), they shall know that there has been a prophet among them.

READING II *2 Corinthians 12:2—10*

I know a person in Christ who fourteen years ago was caught up to the third heaven—whether in the body or out of the body I do not know; God knows. And I know that such a person—whether in the body or out of the body I do not know; God knows—was caught up into Paradise and heard things that are not to be told, that no mortal is permitted to repeat. On behalf of such a one I will boast, but on my own behalf I will not boast, except of my weaknesses. But if I wish to boast, I will not be a fool, for I will be speaking the truth. But I refrain from it, so that no one may think better of me than what is seen in me or heard from me, even considering the exceptional character of the revelations.

Therefore, to keep me from being too elated, a thorn was given me in the flesh, a messenger of Satan to torment me, to keep me from being too elated. Three times I appealed to the Lord about this, that it would leave me, but the Lord said to me, "My grace is sufficient for you, for power is made perfect in weakness." So, I will boast all the more gladly of my weaknesses, so that the power of Christ may dwell in me. Therefore I am content with weaknesses, insults, hardships, persecutions, and calamities for the sake of Christ; for whenever I am weak, then I am strong.

GOSPEL *Mark 6:1—13*

Roman Catholic: Mark 6:1–6

Jesus came to his hometown, and his disciples followed him. On the sabbath he began to teach in the synagogue, and many who heard him were astounded. They said, "Where did this man get all this? What is this wisdom that has been given to him? What deeds of power are being done by his hands! Is not this the carpenter, the son of Mary and brother of James and Joses and Judas and Simon, and are not his sisters here with us?" And they took offense at him.

Then Jesus said to them, "Prophets are not without honor, except in their hometown, and among their own kin, and in their own house." And Jesus could do no deed of power there, except that he laid his hands on a few sick people and cured them. And he was amazed at their unbelief.

Then Jesus went about among the villages teaching. He called the twelve and began to send them out two by two, and gave them authority over the unclean spirits. He ordered them to take nothing for their journey except a staff; no bread, no bag, no money in their belts; but to wear sandals and not to put on two tunics. Jesus said to them, "Wherever you enter a house, stay there until you leave the place. If any place will not welcome you and they refuse to hear you, as you leave, shake off the dust that is on your feet as a testimony against them." So they went out and proclaimed that all should repent. They cast out many demons, and anointed with oil many who were sick and cured them.

Practice of Prayer

To you have I lifted up my eyes,
you who dwell in the heavens;
my eyes, like the eyes of slaves
on the hand of their lords.

Like the eyes of a servant
on the hand of her mistress,
so our eyes are on the LORD our God
till we are shown mercy.

Have mercy on us, LORD, have mercy.
We are filled with contempt.

Practice of Justice

What does it take to set us on our feet? A burst of gunfire in a school hallway? The news of a child dead as a result of abuse? The smell of a noxious brown cloud of pollution? The voice of a prophet, one who speaks for God, can come forth from even the mildest of us. Sometimes we have to let it out—the outrage, alarm or indignation is too great. Other times it is the voice of another that rouses us to action, alerting us to injustices that we would otherwise have missed. Sitting it out would be impossible.

Is there anything stirring in you these days, urging you to stand up and speak out? What's keeping you quiet, distracting you, holding you back from acting on the promptings of the spirit within you?

Scripture Insights

Ezekiel is the last of the major prophets, preaching in the period of the exile in Babylon (approximately 597 to 537 BCE). In fact, he had already been taken captive to Babylon when he received his call. Ezekiel's prophesies stand out from those of the other prophets. The visions he reports are especially vivid and surreal: the wheel within the wheel (1:15) and the four living creatures with faces like an ox, a lion, an eagle and a human being (1:10). (These would later be associated with the four gospel writers, Mark, Matthew, John and Luke, respectively.) Finally, Ezekiel speaks in the first person, as though he is relating his conversation with God as it happens, whereas most other prophets repeat what God has told them: "Thus says the Lord . . . "

We do not hear the subject of his preaching in this passage. In general, he prophesied the further destruction of Jerusalem by the Babylonians, an unpopular topic. When the Temple was destroyed in 587 BCE, Ezekiel's prophecy was fulfilled. The subject of his preaching, however, is not as important as the outcome. The Lord tells Ezekiel to preach so that "They shall know that there has been a prophet among them." Later in the prophecy, God tells Ezekiel: "They shall know that I, the Lord their God, am with them." In the similarity of phrases, the reader can sense the close relationship between God and God's prophet.

In his hometown, Jesus faces similar issues. He must preach the good news whether people listen or not. Unlike Ezekiel, who expected a stubborn and rebellious people, Jesus is amazed and perplexed when people do not believe him. We readers, who have been following Mark's story as Jesus touches and heals every kind of separation that people experience, from sin to illness to death, are also surprised. And yet, in spite of firm disbelief, Jesus is able to effect some healing for those who sought it. It is enough. He continues teaching in every town that will have him.

Why does the crowd discuss Jesus' background and family? What does that have to do with their lack of belief?

July 13, 2003

READING I   Amos 7:7–15

Roman Catholic: Amos 7:12–15

This is what the LORD God showed me: the LORD was standing beside a wall built with a plumb line, holding a plumb line. And the LORD said to me, "Amos, what do you see?" And I said, "A plumb line." Then the LORD said, "See, I am setting a plumb line in the midst of my people Israel; I will never again pass them by; the high places of Isaac shall be made desolate, and the sanctuaries of Israel shall be laid waste, and I will rise against the house of Jeroboam with the sword."

Then Amaziah, the priest of Bethel, sent to King Jeroboam of Israel, saying, "Amos has conspired against you in the very center of the house of Israel; the land is not able to bear all his words. For thus Amos has said, 'Jeroboam shall die by the sword, and Israel must go into exile away from its land.'" And Amaziah said to Amos, "O seer, go, flee away to the land of Judah, earn your bread there, and prophesy there; but never again prophesy at Bethel, for it is the king's sanctuary, and it is a temple of the kingdom."

Then Amos answered Amaziah, "I am no prophet, nor a prophet's son; but I am a shepherd, and a dresser of sycamore trees, and the LORD took me from following the flock, and the LORD said to me, 'Go, prophesy to my people Israel.'"

READING II   Ephesians 1:3–14

Blessed be the God and Father of our Lord Jesus Christ, who has blessed us in Christ with every spiritual blessing in the heavenly places, just as God chose us in Christ before the foundation of the world that before God we should be holy and blameless in love. God destined us for adoption as children through Jesus Christ; this was God's good pleasure and will, to the praise of God's glorious grace freely bestowed on us in the Beloved.

In Christ we have redemption through his blood, the forgiveness of our trespasses, according to the riches of God's grace lavished on us.

With all wisdom and insight God has made known to us the mystery of the divine will, according to God's good pleasure set forth in Christ, as a plan for the fullness of time, to gather up all things in Christ, things in heaven and things on earth. In Christ we have also obtained an inheritance, having been destined according to the purpose of the one who accomplishes all things according to the divine counsel and will, so that we, who were the first to set our hope on Christ, might live for the praise of God's glory. In Christ you also, when you had heard the word of truth, the gospel of your salvation, and had believed in him, were marked with the seal of the promised Holy Spirit; this is the pledge of our inheritance toward redemption as God's own people, to the praise of God's glory.

GOSPEL   Mark 6:7–13

Revised Common Lectionary: Mark 6:14–29

He called the twelve and began to send them out two by two, and gave them authority over the unclean spirits. He ordered them to take nothing for their journey except a staff; no bread, no bag, no money in their belts; but to wear sandals and not to put on two tunics. Jesus said to them, "Wherever you enter a house, stay there until you leave the place. If any place will not welcome you and they refuse to hear you, as you leave, shake off the dust that is on your feet as a testimony against them." So they went out and proclaimed that all should repent. They cast out many demons, and anointed with oil many who were sick and cured them.

Practice of Prayer

Psalm 85:9—10, 11—12, 13—14

I will hear what the LORD has to say,
a voice that speaks of peace,
peace for his people and friends
and those who turn to God in their hearts.
Salvation is near for the God-fearing,
and his glory will dwell in our land.

Mercy and faithfulness have met;
justice and peace have embraced.
Faithfulness shall spring from the earth
and justice look down from heaven.

The LORD will make us prosper
and our earth shall yield its fruit.
Justice shall march in the forefront,
and peace shall follow the way.

Practice of Fortitude

It's not easy to be rejected, ignored or discounted. The disciples must have been relieved to hear Jesus' instructions about what to do if they found themselves unwelcome on their mission. "Shake off the dust that is on your feet as a testimony against them" (Mark 6:11).

When we feel slighted, it can be deliciously satisfying to stamp away in a huff of righteous indignation. This is not what Jesus intended. "Shaking off the dust" can be an invitation to act with dignity and grace. It can help us shake off indifference, rudeness or hard-heartedness, and continue on, undeterred. It is no accident that Jesus sent the disciples off in pairs. The support and encouragement of another is no small part of keeping going no matter what we find along the road.

Scripture Insights

After Jesus' unfortunate experience in his hometown (Mark 6:1–6), he sends his disciples out to preach repentance, cast out demons and anoint and heal the sick. Jesus' injunction to travel light appears to serve several purposes. The apostles need to move easily and quickly from place to place. The directions to carry a staff and wear sandals are reminiscent of the instructions Moses gave for the Passover meal. "This is how you shall eat it: with your loins girded, your sandals on your feet, and your staff in your hand; and you shall eat hurriedly" (Exodus 12:11). Going out without food, baggage or money forces the apostles to depend on the hospitality of strangers and, ultimately, on God. It was a lesson the Jews learned in the wilderness, even though they carried personal belongings with them. The reader might also detect an urgency to reach as wide an area as possible, a mission certainly felt in the early church. Baggage gets in the way. Finally, perhaps mindful of his own experience, Jesus urges the apostles to leave any place that rejects them. Shaking off the dust is thought to be a Jewish custom that allows one to go on without dwelling on past troubles (see Acts 13:51).

Along with these specific instructions, Jesus commissions the apostles to three particular tasks: They are to preach repentance, cast out demons, and anoint and cure the sick. Matthew and Luke record this story as well (Matthew 10; Luke 9), but Mark is the only one to associate anointing the sick with curing them. The letter of James, written about the same time or slightly before Mark's gospel, also speaks of anointing with oil (5:14). It seems clear that this was a practice in at least some of the Christian communities. The contemporary church has continued that practice in its sacrament of anointing. Through his disciples and in these three facets of the mission—healing, expelling demons and preaching conversion—Jesus restores wholeness in mind, body and soul to the whole world.

Would the three facets of mission be the same today? Why or why not?

READING I *Jeremiah 23:1—6*

Woe to the shepherds who destroy and scatter the sheep of my pasture! says the LORD. Therefore thus says the LORD, the God of Israel, concerning the shepherds who shepherd my people: It is you who have scattered my flock, and have driven them away, and you have not attended to them. So I will attend to you for your evil doings, says the LORD.

Then I myself will gather the remnant of my flock out of all the lands where I have driven them, and I will bring them back to their fold, and they shall be fruitful and multiply. I will raise up shepherds over them who will shepherd them, and they shall not fear any longer, or be dismayed, nor shall any be missing, says the LORD.

The days are surely coming, says the LORD, when I will raise up for David a righteous Branch, who shall reign as king and deal wisely, and shall execute justice and righteousness in the land. In his days Judah will be saved and Israel will live in safety. And this is the name by which he will be called: "The LORD is our righteousness."

READING II *Ephesians 2:11—22*

Roman Catholic: Ephesians 2:13–18

Remember that at one time you Gentiles by birth, whose men were called "the uncircumcision" by those who are called "the circumcision"—a physical circumcision made in the flesh by human hands—remember that you were at that time without Christ, being aliens from the commonwealth of Israel, and strangers to the covenants of promise, having no hope and without God in the world.

But now in Christ Jesus you who once were far off have been brought near by the blood of Christ. For Christ is our peace; in his flesh he has made both groups into one and has broken down the dividing wall, that is, the hostility between us. He has abolished the law with its commandments and ordinances, that he might create in himself one new humanity in place of the two, thus making peace, and might reconcile both groups to God in one body through the cross, thus putting to death that hostility through it. So Christ came and proclaimed peace to you who were far off and peace to those who were near; for through him both of us have access in one Spirit to the Father.

So then you are no longer strangers and aliens, but you are citizens with the saints and also members of the household of God, built upon the foundation of the apostles and prophets, with Christ Jesus himself as the cornerstone. In him the whole structure is joined together and grows into a holy temple in the Lord; in whom you also are built together spiritually into a dwelling place for God.

GOSPEL *Mark 6:30—34, 53—56*

Roman Catholic: Mark 6:30–34

The apostles gathered around Jesus, and told him all that they had done and taught. He said to them, "Come away to a deserted place all by yourselves and rest a while." For many were coming and going, and they had no leisure even to eat. And they went away in the boat to a deserted place by themselves. Now many saw them going and recognized them, and they hurried there on foot from all the towns and arrived ahead of them.

As Jesus went ashore, he saw a great crowd; and he had compassion for them, because they were like sheep without a shepherd; and he began to teach them many things.

When Jesus and the disciples had crossed over, they came to land at Gennesaret and moored the boat. When they got out of the boat, people at once recognized him, and rushed about that whole region and began to bring the sick on mats to wherever they heard he was. And wherever he went, into villages or cities or farms, they laid the sick in the marketplaces, and begged him that they might touch even the fringe of his cloak; and all who touched it were healed.

Practice of Prayer

Psalm 23:1—3, 3—4, 5, 6

LORD, you are my shepherd;
there is nothing I shall want.
Fresh and green are the pastures
where you give me repose.
Near restful waters you lead me,
to revive my drooping spirit.

You guide me along the right path;
you are true to your name.
If I should walk in the valley of darkness
no evil would I fear.
You are there with your crook and your staff;
with these you give me comfort.

You have prepared a banquet for me
in the sight of my foes.
My head you have anointed with oil;
my cup is overflowing.

Surely goodness and kindness shall follow me
all the days of my life.
In the LORD's own house shall I dwell
for ever and ever.

Practice of Temperance

July 24th is the birthday of Amelia Earhart, the first woman to fly solo across the Atlantic Ocean. It was a risky venture, one that could not be undertaken carelessly. A great deal of planning and teamwork went into the expedition.

All the way back to Eden, the urge to push limits has been part of human nature. People will go to great lengths to get their name in a record book. Some plan in advance. Others put themselves and others at risk by careless preparation or inadequate thought about outcomes. Temperance raises some important questions: What's worth a risk and what isn't? What is courageous and what is reckless? When should we invest our energy and when should we withhold it? Being an adventurous spirit doesn't mean being a foolish one.

Scripture Insights

Jeremiah's indictment of leaders who abandon the people is at once powerful and disturbing. The priests, rulers and false prophets in the period just before the exile had predicted that God would never allow Jerusalem to fall. All the people had to do was wait a little longer for God's vindication. Jeremiah knew that something different was going to happen: Jerusalem would be destroyed by the Babylonians, and in 587 BCE, it was. He saw that the false hopes and promises raised by the rulers had left the people of Jerusalem scattered like the sheep so many of them had pastured in the hills surrounding the city. And with no moral guidance, many Israelites had been led to sin. The leaders had driven them away from God.

God promises to gather the sheep and bring them back by raising up shepherds for them. The promise has much the same structure as the promise to raise up a prophet like Moses in Deuteronomy 18:15—20. There, the prophet will tell the people all God has said. In Jeremiah, the shepherd will shepherd (literally pasture) the people. Finally God promises to raise up a righteous Branch. The Branch will reign as a wise king who will execute justice and righteousness. This description is important; in Jewish theology, the reign of God brings justice and righteousness. Here, a king from David's family tree will become God's shepherd on earth.

Another great vision of the Davidic shepherd is the restoration of the divided Israel (Ezekiel 37:23—36). Paul sees the restoration in his time as the coming together of Jews and Gentiles in Jesus Christ. For Paul, Jesus is the righteous Branch, bringing all people near to God.

In Mark we hear again the image of shepherd. When Jesus sees the crowd hungry for guidance, he must reach out to them. But Mark gives us a different image for the shepherd of these sheep. This shepherd is not a king, or a branch of David's tree; he is a teacher—yet another description that helps the reader grasp who Jesus is for the world.

In today's world who are the "far off" and who are the "near"?

July 27, 2003

READING I 2 Kings 4:42—44

A man came from Baal-shalishah, bringing food from the first fruits to Elisha, the man of God: twenty loaves of barley and fresh ears of grain in his sack. Elisha said, "Give it to the people and let them eat." But his servant said, "How can I set this before a hundred people?" So he repeated, "Give it to the people and let them eat, for thus says the LORD, 'They shall eat and have some left.'" He set it before them, they ate, and had some left, according to the word of the LORD.

READING II Ephesians 4:1—6

Revised Common Lectionary: Ephesians 3:14–21

I therefore, the prisoner in the Lord, beg you to lead a life worthy of the calling to which you have been called, with all humility and gentleness, with patience, bearing with one another in love, making every effort to maintain the unity of the Spirit in the bond of peace. There is one body and one Spirit, just as you were called to the one hope of your calling, one Lord, one faith, one baptism, one God and Father of all, who is above all and through all and in all.

GOSPEL John 6:1—21

Roman Catholic: John 6:1–15

Jesus went to the other side of the Sea of Galilee, also called the Sea of Tiberias. A large crowd kept following him, because they saw the signs that he was doing for the sick. Jesus went up the mountain and sat down there with his disciples. Now the Passover, the festival of the Jewish people, was near. When he looked up and saw a large crowd coming toward him, Jesus said to Philip, "Where are we to buy bread for these people to eat?" Jesus said this to test Philip, for he himself knew what he was going to do. Philip answered him, "Six months' wages would not buy enough bread for each of them to get a little." One of his disciples, Andrew, Simon Peter's brother, said to him, "There is a child here who has five barley loaves and two fish. But what are they among so many people?"

Jesus said, "Make the people sit down." Now there was a great deal of grass in the place; so they sat down, about five thousand in all. Then Jesus took the loaves, and when he had given thanks, he distributed them to those who were seated; so also the fish, as much as they wanted. When they were satisfied, he told his disciples, "Gather up the fragments left over, so that nothing may be lost." So they gathered them up, and from the fragments of the five barley loaves, left by those who had eaten, they filled twelve baskets. When the people saw the sign that Jesus had done, they began to say, "This is indeed the prophet who is to come into the world."

When Jesus realized that they were about to come and take him by force to make him king, he withdrew again to the mountain by himself.

When evening came, his disciples went down to the sea, got into a boat, and started across the sea to Capernaum. It was now dark, and Jesus had not yet come to them. The sea became rough because a strong wind was blowing. When they had rowed about three or four miles, they saw Jesus walking on the sea and coming near the boat, and they were terrified. But Jesus said to them, "Here I am; do not be afraid." Then they wanted to take him into the boat, and immediately the boat reached the land toward which they were going.

Practice of Prayer

Psalm 145:10—11, 15—16, 17—18

All your creatures shall thank you, O LORD,
and your friends shall repeat their blessing.
They shall speak of the glory of your reign
and declare your might, O God,
The eyes of all creatures look to you
and you give them their food in due season.
You open wide your hand,
grant the desires of all who live.

You are just in all your ways
and loving in all your deeds.
You are close to all who call you,
who call on you from their hearts.

Practice of Fortitude

July 31 is the feast of Saint Ignatius of Loyola, founder of the Society of Jesus (Jesuits). While serving as a soldier in the Spanish army he was wounded in battle. During his recuperation, he read many books about Christ and the lives of the saints. As his physical strength was restored, his spirit underwent a radical change as well. He quit the military and vowed to dedicate his life to God's service.

It is often true that the most devastating blows to our body through disease or injury can end up fortifying our hearts and souls in ways we never could have imagined. Some of the most inspiring stories are those of people who, like Ignatius, rise from a sickbed, renewed in their faith and resolute in their desire to reach out to others.

Scripture Insights

John's gospel often gives a different version of stories told in the synoptic gospels, Matthew, Mark and Luke. His account of the Last Supper, for example, is remarkably different. In the synoptics, we hear the familiar story of breaking bread and blessing wine that is part of our liturgy. But John recalls how Jesus washed feet at the Last Supper (John 13:1–11). Eucharistic references are plentiful in John's gospel, however, especially in chapter 6. In the middle of Ordinary Time, the church takes the time to read John 6 and savor the words and actions of Jesus as he talks about the bread of life and the hunger of humankind.

That chapter opens with the multiplication of five loaves and two fish. This is one of only two stories that all four gospels relate. Jesus seems to be following in the footsteps of the great prophets like Elisha who multiplied loaves and grain, but two things set Jesus' action apart from the Old Testament prophets. First, he takes the bread and fish and gives thanks (in Greek, *eucharisteo*, from which our word eucharist comes), and then distributes them. Second, he has the disciples gather up what's left over. Twelve baskets of fragments are left, one for each of the disciples who doubted they could feed the multitude.

Some commentators refer to this passage as an institution of the eucharist because of what Jesus does with the bread and the fish. There is no cup of wine, no table ceremony, no transforming words. Nevertheless, the ritual of giving thanks and giving to others to eat is highly symbolic. Later in the chapter, Jesus uses bread as a metaphor for himself.

The crowd follows Jesus because they see the signs he does. Believing only because of outward signs is the most tenuous form of faith. At the end of the passage, the crowd wants to make Jesus king because of what they have seen. They have misunderstood Jesus' person and message. He is forced into hiding because earthly kingship is not what Jesus came for (John 18:36).

Some people wonder if the miracle was one of multiplication or getting people to share what they already had. What difference does that make?

August 3, 2003

EIGHTEENTH SUNDAY IN ORDINARY TIME
EIGHTH SUNDAY AFTER PENTECOST

READING I   *Exodus 16:2—4, 12—15*

Revised Common Lectionary: Exodus 16:2–4, 9–15

The whole congregation of the Israelites complained against Moses and Aaron in the wilderness. The Israelites said to them, "If only we had died by the hand of the LORD in the land of Egypt, when we sat by the pots filled with meat and ate our fill of bread; for you have brought us out into this wilderness to kill this whole assembly with hunger."

Then the LORD said to Moses, "I am going to rain bread from heaven for you, and each day the people shall go out and gather enough for that day. In that way I will test them, whether they will follow my instruction or not."

"I have heard the complaining of the Israelites; say to them, 'At twilight you shall eat meat, and in the morning you shall have your fill of bread; then you shall know that I am the LORD your God.'"

In the evening quails came up and covered the camp; and in the morning there was a layer of dew around the camp. When the layer of dew lifted, there on the surface of the wilderness was a fine flaky substance, as fine as frost on the ground. When the Israelites saw it, they said to one another, "What is it?" For they did not know what it was. Moses said to them, "It is the bread that the LORD has given you to eat."

READING II   *Ephesians 4:17, 20—24*

Revised Common Lectionary: Ephesians 4:1–16

Now this I affirm and insist on in the Lord: you must no longer live as the Gentiles live, in the futility of their minds. That is not the way you learned Christ! For surely you have heard about him and were taught in him, as truth is in Jesus. You were taught to put away your former way of life, your old self, corrupt and deluded by its lusts, and to be renewed in the spirit of your minds, and to clothe yourselves with the new self, created according to the likeness of God in true righteousness and holiness.

GOSPEL   *John 6:24—35*

When the crowd saw that neither Jesus nor his disciples were beside the sea, they themselves got into the boats and went to Capernaum looking for Jesus. When they found him on the other side of the sea, they said to him, "Rabbi, when did you come here?" Jesus answered them, "Very truly, I tell you, you are looking for me, not because you saw signs, but because you ate your fill of the loaves. Do not work for the food that perishes, but for the food that endures for eternal life, which the Son-of-Man will give you. For it is the Son-of-Man that God, the Father, has sealed."

Then they said to Jesus, "What must we do to perform the works of God?" Jesus answered them, "This is the work of God, that you believe in the one whom God has sent." So they said to him, "What sign are you going to give us then, so that we may see it and believe you? What work are you performing? Our ancestors ate the manna in the wilderness; as it is written, 'He gave them bread from heaven to eat.'" Then Jesus said to them, "Very truly, I tell you, it was not Moses who gave you the bread from heaven, but it is my Father who gives you the true bread from heaven. For the bread of God is that which comes down from heaven and gives life to the world." They said to him, "Sir, give us this bread always."

Jesus said to them, "I am the bread of life. Whoever comes to me will never be hungry, and whoever believes in me will never be thirsty."

116

Practice of Prayer

Psalm 78:3—4, 23—24, 25, 54

The things we have heard and understood,
the things our ancestors have told us,
these we will not hide from their children
but will tell them to the next generation:
the glories and might of the LORD
and the marvelous deeds God has done,

Yet God commanded the clouds above
and opened the gates of heaven;
rained down manna for their food,
and gave them bread from heaven.

Mere mortals ate the bread of angels,
The LORD sent them meat in abundance;
So God brought them to that holy land,
to the mountain that was won by his hand.

Practice of Temperance

Our grocery stores are stocked with every variety of food, so it is hard to visualize the Israelites awaiting their daily gift of manna and quail. God gives them food, but just enough to meet one day's need. No stockpiling was allowed or necessary. In time they came to trust in this divine provision.

Trusting in God's care is a day-to-day process: refraining from worry and curbing the urge to hoard what we fear being without. What does it take to temper worry? When have you experienced God giving you exactly enough to meet your needs?

Scripture Insights

Alongside John 6 and the discourse on the bread of life, the church hears most of the fourth and fifth chapters of Paul's letter to the Ephesians. Known as one of the captivity letters (Colossians, Philippians and Philemon are the others) because it is apparently written from prison (Ephesians 4:1), the letter to the Ephesians discusses the mystery of life in Christ. Paul's exhortation to "live lives worthy of the calling to which you have been called," which we heard last week, strikes at the heart of Christian discipleship. This week, Paul continues to call the Ephesians to a renewal in Christ—to "put away your former way of life . . . and be renewed in the spirit of your minds" (4:22–23). It was expected that baptism into the death and resurrection of Christ would bring radical life changes for early Christians. For some this meant giving up jobs and wealth; for others it meant hospitality or service. For everyone, life in Christ was life lived according to God and not according to the world. Christians were encouraged to embrace love rather than ambition, greed or power, and to focus on the treasure of heaven, rather than on earthly wealth.

Consequently this small section of the letter to the Ephesians provides the perfect prelude to the discourse on the bread of life in John's gospel. Jesus warns the crowd that they are thinking wrongly—running to see him for perishable bread (6:26). In Paul's vocabulary, the crowd sees Jesus with old eyes, with their old selves. If they saw Jesus with spiritual eyes, they would know him as the bread of life. They would seek only the bread of life. They would hear Jesus' gentle correction to their assertion that Moses gave them manna from heaven. "It is my Father who gives you the true bread from heaven . . ." (6:32). Physical hunger and thirst made the Jews rely on God in the desert. Jesus shows the crowd that hunger has much deeper implications for the soul. If they believe Jesus is food and drink, they will never be hungry or thirsty.

How would you bring the good news of Jesus as the bread of life to those without food?

READING I   *1 Kings 19:4—8*

Elijah went a day's journey into the wilderness, and came and sat down under a solitary broom tree. He asked that he might die: "It is enough; now, O LORD, take away my life, for I am no better than my ancestors."

Then he lay down under the broom tree and fell asleep. Suddenly an angel touched him and said to him, "Get up and eat." Elijah looked, and there at his head was a cake baked on hot stones, and a jar of water. He ate and drank, and lay down again.

The angel of the LORD came a second time, touched him, and said, "Get up and eat, otherwise the journey will be too much for you." Elijah got up, and ate and drank; then he went in the strength of that food forty days and forty nights to Horeb the mount of God.

READING II   *Ephesians 4:25—5:2*

Roman Catholic: Ephesians 4:30–5:2

So then, putting away falsehood, let all of us speak the truth to our neighbors, for we are members of one another. Be angry but do not sin; do not let the sun go down on your anger, and do not make room for the devil. Thieves must give up stealing; rather let them labor and work honestly with their own hands, so as to have something to share with the needy. Let no evil talk come out of your mouths, but only what is useful for building up, as there is need, so that your words may give grace to those who hear. And do not grieve the Holy Spirit of God, with which you were marked with a seal for the day of redemption. Put away from you all bitterness and wrath and anger and wrangling and slander, together with all malice, and be kind to one another, tenderhearted, forgiving one another, as God in Christ has forgiven you. Therefore be imitators of God, as beloved children, and live in love, as Christ loved us and gave himself up for us, a fragrant offering and sacrifce to God.

GOSPEL   *John 6:35, 41—51*

Roman Catholic: John 6:41–51

Jesus said to them, "I am the bread of life. Whoever comes to me will never be hungry, and whoever believes in me will never be thirsty."

Then the Judeans began to complain about him because he said, "I am the bread that came down from heaven." They were saying, "Is not this Jesus, the son of Joseph, whose father and mother we know? How can he now say, 'I have come down from heaven'?" Jesus answered them, "Do not complain among yourselves. No one can come to me unless drawn by the Father who sent me; and I will raise that person up on the last day. It is written in the prophets, 'And they shall all be taught by God.' Everyone who has heard and learned from the Father comes to me. Not that anyone has seen the Father except the one who is from God; this one has seen the Father.

"Very truly, I tell you, whoever believes has eternal life. I am the bread of life. Your ancestors ate the manna in the wilderness, and they died. This is the bread that comes down from heaven, so that one may eat of it and not die. I am the living bread that came down from heaven. Whoever eats of this bread will live forever; and the bread that I will give for the life of the world is my flesh."

Practice of Prayer

Psalm 34:2—3, 4—5, 6—7, 8—9

I will bless the LORD at all times,
God's praise always on my lips;
in the LORD my soul shall make its boast.
The humble shall hear and be glad.

Glorify the LORD with me.
Together let us praise God's name.
I sought the LORD and was heard;
from all my terrors set free.

Look towards God and be radiant;
let your faces not be abashed.
When the poor cry out the LORD hears them
and rescues them from all their distress.

The angel of the LORD is encamped
around those who fear God, to rescue them.
Taste and see that the LORD is good.
They are happy who seek refuge in God.

Practice of Justice

Diakonia is a Greek word that means service or servanthood. Although the word is frequently associated with those ordained as deacons, in the New Testament *diakonia* was regarded as the essential way of life for all baptized Christians. This week offers an opportunity to reflect on the lives of two great models of service. Saint Lawrence, whose feast is today, was a deacon in the third century. Well-known for his generosity to the poor, he was also boldly defiant of Roman authority.

Florence Nightingale devoted her life to tending the sick and improving hospital facilities and procedures. She founded the first school of nursing in England and helped to establish that profession as a noble calling. The anniversary of her death is August 13.

The call to *diakonia* can serve justice in many ways and take distinctive forms in our lives. How have you been called?

Scripture Insights

The letter to the Ephesians seems to provide a marked contrast to the other two readings today. Paul continues his exhortation to live as new people, marked by the seal of the Holy Spirit (probably a reference to baptism). Particular actions and attitudes, such as bitterness, anger and slander, are unworthy of such people. On the other hand, kindness and forgiveness are to be encouraged, even expected. For the Ephesians, the best and only example of love and forgiveness was Jesus.

Two phrases from the other two readings might give clues as to how the Ephesians and the other members of the early church were supposed to persevere in their spiritual transformation. In the first reading, the Lord provides Ezekiel with food and drink in the wilderness. The first time, God simply commands Ezekiel to eat. The second time, God adds the single phrase, "otherwise the journey will be too much for you." While the reference to Ezekiel's trip to Horeb is clear, the idea of a journey can apply also to the process of renewal—spiritual journey—apparent in Ephesians. The lesson seems clear. Eat the food that God provides and you will have strength for the journey.

John's gospel again identifies Jesus as the "living bread that came down from heaven." John adds, "Whoever eats this bread will live forever." Belief in Jesus yields eternal life. Belief is the fundamental, life-changing event. If the command of God in Ezekiel is to eat, the command of Jesus in John is to eat this bread from heaven and live forever. In baptism, the Ephesians inherit both messages. Jesus is the food they must eat for the journey. In their love and forgiveness, they reflect the eternal life Jesus gave them through his own death on the cross. The gospel of John and the letter to the Ephesians form interwoven pictures of a faith that leads to life and the discipleship that springs from that faith. Belief in Jesus Christ, as Paul is fond of saying, means the Christian is no longer a slave to sin, but is free to choose a different kind of life—one of kindness and love.

In what sense is faith in Jesus a gift of God? In what way do we have to work at it?

August 17, 2003

READING I   *Proverbs 9:1—6*

Wisdom has built her house,
    she has hewn her seven pillars.
She has slaughtered her animals,
        she has mixed her wine,
    she has also set her table.
She has sent out her young serving women,
        she calls
    from the highest places in the town,
"You that are simple, turn in here!"
    To those without sense she says,
"Come, eat of my bread
    and drink of the wine I have mixed.
Lay aside immaturity, and live,
    and walk in the way of insight."

READING II   *Ephesians 5:15—20*

Be careful then how you live, not as unwise people but as wise, making the most of the time, because the days are evil. So do not be foolish, but understand what the will of the Lord is. Do not get drunk with wine, for that is debauchery; but be filled with the Spirit, as you sing psalms and hymns and spiritual songs among yourselves, singing and making melody to the Lord in your hearts, giving thanks to God the Father at all times and for everything in the name of our Lord Jesus Christ.

GOSPEL   *John 6:51—58*

Jesus said, "I am the living bread that came down from heaven. Whoever eats of this bread will live forever; and the bread that I will give for the life of the world is my flesh."

The Judeans then disputed among themselves, saying, "How can this man give us his flesh to eat?" So Jesus said to them, "Very truly, I tell you, unless you eat the flesh of the Son-of-Man and drink his blood, you have no life in you. Those who eat my flesh and drink my blood have eternal life, and I will raise them up on the last day; for my flesh is true food and my blood is true drink. Those who eat my flesh and drink my blood abide in me, and I in them. Just as the living Father sent me, and I live because of the Father, so whoever eats me will live because of me. This is the bread that came down from heaven, not like that which your ancestors ate, and they died. But the one who eats this bread will live forever."

Practice of Prayer

Psalm 34:2—3, 10—11, 12—13, 14—15

I will bless the LORD at all times
God's praise always on my lips;
in the LORD my soul shall make its boast.
The humble shall hear and be glad.

Revere the LORD, you saints.
They lack nothing, who revere the Lord.
Strong lions suffer want and go hungry
but those who seek the LORD lack no blessing.

Come, children, and hear me
that I may teach you the fear of the LORD.
Who are those who long for life
and many days, to enjoy their prosperity?

Then keep your tongue from evil
and your lips from speaking deceit.
Turn aside from evil and do good;
seek and strive after peace.

Practice of Prudence

In T. H. White's book *The Once and Future King*, Merlin is a true figure of discretion and good sense *(prudentia)*. Knowing Arthur's royal destiny, he prepares the boy for his future role by turning him into various animals, insects and birds. As an ant, Arthur learns that large things are accomplished in small ways. As a fish, he learns the importance of having a strong backbone. Such tutelage contributes to Arthur's greatness as a king by enlarging his capacity for imagination, observation, empathy and compassion.

We all have Merlins in our lives—people who help us plunge into life in order to learn how to take on future responsibilities with grace and integrity. Who are the wisdom figures in your life? How have they challenged and inspired you to fulfill your own destiny?

Scripture Insights

Bread and wine, crucial to Jesus' teaching about himself, were staples of the Hebrew diet. They also figure prominently in the description of Wisdom's banquet in the first reading. The book of Proverbs is one of the wisdom books, with lessons drawn from life experience. It contains practical tips for living such as a parent might pass on to a child: "Go to the ant, you lazybones; consider its ways, and be wise . . . " (6:6). Proverbs also contains descriptions of Wisdom herself, who seems to be a semi-divine figure. She is the firstborn of God and present with God at the creation of the world (8:22–31). In the passage today, she sends out her servants to call everyone to her banquet so that they might gain understanding. Like last week's letter to the Ephesians, Proverbs exhorts readers to lay aside their former lives.

The similarity between Wisdom and Jesus has been noted by many scholars and readers. The gospel of John, for example, applies some of the language about Wisdom to Jesus. Thus, Jesus is firstborn of God and the one through whom everything was made. Jesus sends his disciples out to gather everyone to another and different banquet of bread and wine. But, as Jesus points out, the bread he gives is his flesh for the life of the world (6:51). Wisdom, insight and eternal life come from eating Jesus' flesh and drinking his blood.

The command of Jesus to eat his flesh and drink his blood was deeply troubling to the Jews, however, regardless of the wisdom this action may have imparted. The Mosaic Law strictly forbade drinking blood, considered to be life itself. But Jesus is pushing the crowd to see with spiritual eyes. This flesh and blood is sacramental nourishment from the one who has come from heaven. Here Jesus no longer talks about belief, but repeats that the crowd must eat and drink to receive eternal life. This points to the eucharistic meal as a way to spiritual understanding. The one who eats the bread of Jesus, like the one who eats the bread of Wisdom, comes to know God and Jesus' unity with God.

Wisdom calls the simple and those without sense to eat her meal. What does she mean? Would you ever see yourself in this category?

August 24, 2003

TWENTY-FIRST SUNDAY IN ORDINARY TIME
ELEVENTH SUNDAY AFTER PENTECOST

READING I *Joshua 24:1—2a, 14—18*

Roman Catholic: Joshua 24:1—2a, 15—17, 18b

Joshua gathered all the tribes of Israel to Shechem, and summoned the elders, the heads, the judges, and the officers of Israel; and they presented themselves before God. And Joshua said to all the people, "Now therefore revere the LORD, and serve the LORD in sincerity and in faithfulness; put away the deities that your ancestors served beyond the River and in Egypt, and serve the LORD. Now if you are unwilling to serve the LORD, choose this day whom you will serve, whether the gods your ancestors served in the region beyond the River or the gods of the Amorites in whose land you are living; but as for me and my household, we will serve the LORD."

Then the people answered, "Far be it from us that we should forsake the LORD to serve other gods; for it is the LORD our God who brought us and our ancestors up from the land of Egypt, out of the house of slavery, and who did those great signs in our sight. The LORD protected us along all the way that we went, and among all the peoples through whom we passed; and the LORD drove out before us all the peoples, the Amorites who lived in the land. Therefore we also will serve the LORD, for the LORD is our God."

READING II *Ephesians 5:21—32*

Revised Common Lectionary: Ephesians 6:10—20

Be subject to one another out of reverence for Christ. Wives, be subject to your husbands as you are to the Lord. For the husband is the head of the wife just as christ is the head of the church, the body of which he is the Savior. Just as the church is subject to Christ, so also wives ought to be, in everything, to their husbands. Husbands, love your wives, just as Christ loved the church and gave himself up for her, in order to make her holy by cleansing her with the washing of water by the word, so as to present the church to himself in splendor, without a spot or wrinkle or anything of the kind—yes, so that she may be holy and without blemish. In the same way, husbands should love their wives as they do their own bodies. He who loves his wife loves himself. For no one ever hates his own body, but he nourishes and tenderly cares for it, just as Christ does for the church, because we are members of his body. "For this reason a man will leave his father and mother and be joined to his wife, and the two will become one flesh." This is a great mystery, and I am applying it to Christ and the church.

GOSPEL *John 6:56—69*

Roman Catholic: John 6:60—69

Jesus said, "Those who eat my flesh and drink my blood abide in me, and I in them. Just as the living Father sent me, and I live because of the Father, so whoever eats me will live because of me. This is the bread that came down from heaven, not like that which your ancestors ate, and they died. But the one who eats this bread will live forever." He said these things while he was teaching in the synagogue at Capernaum.

When many of his disciples heard it, they said, "This teaching is difficult; who can accept it?" But Jesus, being aware that his disciples were complaining about it, said to them, "Does this offend you? Then what if you were to see the Son-of-Man ascending to where he was before? It is the spirit that gives life; the flesh is useless. The words that I have spoken to you are spirit and life. But among you there are some who do not believe." For Jesus knew from the first who were the ones that did not believe, and who was the one that would betray him. And he said, "For this reason I have told you that no one can come to me unless it is granted by the Father."

Because of this many of his disciples turned back and no longer went about with him. So Jesus asked the twelve, "Do you also wish to go away?" Simon Peter answered him, "Lord, to whom can we go? You have the words of eternal life. We have come to believe and know that you are the Holy One of God."

Practice of Prayer

Psalm 34:2–3, 16–17, 18–19, 20–21, 22–23

I will bless the LORD at all times
God's praise always on my lips;
in the LORD my soul shall make its boast.
The humble shall hear and be glad.

The eyes of the LORD are toward the just
and his ears toward their appeal.
The face of the LORD rebuffs the wicked
to destroy their remembrance from the earth.

They call and the LORD hears
and rescues them in all their distress.
The LORD is close to the broken-hearted;
those whose spirit is crushed God will save.

Many are the trials of the upright
but the LORD will come to rescue them,
keeping guard over all their bones,
not one of their bones shall be broken.

Evil brings death to the wicked;
those who hate the good are doomed.
The LORD ransoms the souls of the faithful.
None who trust in God shall be condemned.

Practice of Temperance

In today's first reading Joshua assembles the people and asks a pivotal question. Which god are they going to serve—the god of their enemies or the God who has stood by them? Their answer is plain. They will not forsake the God who brought them out of slavery.

Joshua's question is still pertinent, but for modern times it may need some rephrasing. When our lives spin out of control it may feel as if our "god"—of money, work, time, "stuff"—has chosen us. Like our ancestors, we too may find ourselves enslaved—by our responsibilities, wants, and ambitions. It is an act of liberation to choose God over these other demands; that is, to keep our attention on God primary so that the other factors do not become overwhelming. Holding to a spiritual perspective enables temperance; it places other aspects of life in order.

Scripture Insights

In the reading from John's gospel the disciples are grappling with a difficult teaching from Jesus that they do not entirely understand, mainly because they cannot see beyond the literal interpretation of his words.

Paul's letter to the Ephesians contains a text that is troubling for many today. The command for wives to be submissive to their husbands has been taken out of context and misused for centuries. In this section of Ephesians, Paul has been exhorting his listeners to give up all manner of vices, becoming people of love and forgiveness. He also envisions a different way for people to relate in marriage. Paul understands marriage as a metaphor for Christ's relationship with the church and develops an image to express that relationship: the church as a body with Christ as its head. Paul uses this image to frame his understanding of the marriage covenant.

Marriage was seen as a metaphor for God's relationship with Israel long before Paul used it to describe Christ and the church. Paul adds the element of mutual reverence and love, using the image of the head and body to include interdependence in the hierarchical marriage relationship of that time. The body and the head work together in life. This is the obedience that Paul advocates for wife and husband—one that allows them to live as a united whole. Paul adds that the head must love the body, countering the notion of wives as property common in Paul's time. The husband must love his wife as Christ loves the church. If such love is the foundation of the husband's part in the marriage, he cannot abuse or neglect, cannot be faithless, cruel or cold. These are the vices that followers of Christ give up. Just as disciples become new people, husbands and wives become a new unity in the marriage covenant, practicing kindness and forgiveness. In the same way, Christ and his church become a single entity in the new covenant.

How can mutual respect and self-sacrificing love be expressed in the marriage covenant today?

August 31, 2003

TWENTY-SECOND SUNDAY IN ORDINARY TIME
TWELFTH SUNDAY AFTER PENTECOST

READING I   Deuteronomy 4:1—2, 6—9

Roman Catholic: Deuteronomy 4:1–2, 6–8

So now, Israel, give heed to the statutes and ordinances that I am teaching you to observe, so that you may live to enter and occupy the land that the LORD, the God of your ancestors, is giving you. You must neither add anything to what I command you nor take away anything from it, but keep the commandments of the LORD your God with which I am charging you. You must observe them diligently, for this will show your wisdom and discernment to the peoples, who, when they hear all these statutes, will say, "Surely this great nation is a wise and discerning people!" For what other great nation has a deity so near to it as the LORD our God is whenever we cry out? And what other great nation has statutes and ordinances as just as this entire law that I am setting before you today?

But take care and watch yourselves closely, so as neither to forget the things that your eyes have seen nor to let them slip from your mind all the days of your life; make them known to your children and your children's children.

READING II   James 1:17—27

Roman Catholic: James 1:17–18, 21b-22, 27

Every generous act of giving, with every perfect gift, is from above, coming down from the Father of lights, with whom there is no variation or shadow due to change. In fulfillment of the divine purpose God gave us birth by the word of truth, so that we would become a kind of first fruits of God's creatures.

You must understand this, my beloved: let everyone be quick to listen, slow to speak, slow to anger; for your anger does not produce God's righteousness. Therefore rid yourselves of all sordidness and rank growth of wickedness, and welcome with meekness the implanted word that has the power to save your souls.

But be doers of the word, and not merely hearers who deceive themselves. For if any are hearers of the word and not doers, they are like those who look at themselves in a mirror; for they look at themselves and, on going away, immediately forget what they were like. But those who look into the perfect law, the law of liberty, and persevere, being not hearers who forget but doers who act—they will be blessed in their doing.

If any think they are religious, and do not bridle their tongues but deceive their hearts, their religion is worthless. Religion that is pure and undefiled before God, the Father, is this: to care for orphans and widows in their distress, and to keep oneself unstained by the world.

GOSPEL   Mark 7:1—8, 14—15, 21—23

Now when the Pharisees and some of the scribes who had come from Jerusalem gathered around Jesus, they noticed that some of his disciples were eating with defiled hands, that is, without washing them. (For the Pharisees, and all the Jewish people, do not eat unless they thoroughly wash their hands, thus observing the tradition of the elders; and they do not eat anything from the market unless they wash it; and there are also many other traditions that they observe, the washing of cups, pots, and bronze kettles.) So the Pharisees and the scribes asked Jesus, "Why do your disciples not live according to the tradition of the elders, but eat with defiled hands?" He said to them, "Isaiah prophesied rightly about you hypocrites, as it is written,

'This people honors me with their lips,
but their hearts are far from me;
in vain do they worship me,
teaching human precepts as doctrines.'

You abandon the commandment of God and hold to human tradition."

Then Jesus called the crowd again and said to them, "Listen to me, all of you, and understand: there is nothing outside a person that by going in can defile, but the things that come out are what defile." For it is from within, from the human heart, that evil intentions come: fornication, theft, murder, adultery, avarice, wickedness, deceit, licentiousness, envy, slander, pride, folly. All these evil things come from within, and they defile a person."

Practice of Prayer

Psalm 15:2—3, 3—4, 4—5

Those who walk without fault,
those who act with justice
and speak the truth from their hearts,
those who do not slander with their tongue,

those who do no wrong to their kindred,
who cast no slur on their neighbors,
who hold the godless in disdain,
but honor those who fear the LORD;

those who keep their word, come what may,
who take no interest on a loan
and accept no bribes against the innocent.
Such people will stand firm for ever.

Practice of Justice

Jesus had patience for just about everybody but hypocrites. Besieged by those wanting his time and healing touch, he generally responded with tenderness. But with those who complained about neglecting outer observances, he rarely concealed his disapproval. True justice, he taught, looked past human actions and into the heart.

It's easy to confuse the trivial for the essential. Keeping score of others' offenses against taste or decorum can be absorbing, but it may be simply a way to soothe our own egos, not part of the real work of justice. We should consider the stinging words in today's gospel: "For it is from within, from the human heart, that evil intentions come . . . " (Mark 7: 21) The just assessment looks past the outer rules, into the hearts of our neighbors, and it does not omit examining our own hearts.

Scripture Insights

Today all three readings are concerned with the disposition of the heart and its connection with outer actions. Moses begins the first of his exhortations to the Israelites before they cross the Jordan into Canaan. The law of God is just, more so than the laws of any other nation. Obedience to the law of God, says Moses, will show Israel's wisdom and discernment. But hearing the word and desiring it with the heart must come first. Conversion of the heart always has primary importance for Moses and the rest of the prophets. Moses spoke of circumcision of the heart as a sign of the interiorization of the covenant (Deuteronomy 10:16). Isaiah told the Israelites that God despised the festivals, sacrifices and rituals because the Israelites were not caring for the orphan and the widow. They were going through the motions of obedience without care for God and God's justice. Their attitude was apparent in their lack of compassion.

James understands the implication of "hearing" the law for the Jews. To hear is to obey. According to James, a good Christian is in the same position. One cannot be a hearer of the word without doing right as well and following the law without a faithful heart has no place in the covenant relationship.

In Mark's gospel, Jesus speaks precisely to the last point. The Pharisees are concerned with outward appearances, not inner conversion. When Jesus quotes Isaiah, he reminds them that such scrupulous behavior without the necessary conversion of heart is not true worship of God. Jesus is not attacking the Jewish law here. His point is about the systematic judgment of the scribes and Pharisees that does not ask first what is the disposition of the heart, but, rather, whether every letter of the law has been observed. Like Moses, Isaiah and the other prophets before him, Jesus knows that lip service and outward obedience without inner transformation are not a sign of covenant relationship.

What examples do we see today in church or society of outward obedience and inward rebellion?

READING I   *Isaiah 35:4—7a*

Say to those who are of a fearful heart,
    "Be strong, do not fear!
Here is your God.
    Your God will come with vengeance,
with terrible recompense.
    God will come and save you."

Then the eyes of the blind shall be opened,
    and the ears of the deaf unstopped;
then the lame shall leap like a deer,
    and the tongue of the speechless sing for joy.
For waters shall break forth in the wilderness,
    and streams in the desert;
the burning sand shall become a pool,
    and the thirsty ground springs of water.

READING II   *James 2:1—10, 14—17*

Roman Catholic: James 2:1–5

My brothers and sisters, do you with your acts of favoritism really believe in our glorious Lord Jesus Christ? For if a person with gold rings and in fine clothes comes into your assembly, and if a poor person in dirty clothes also comes in, and if you take notice of the one wearing the fine clothes and say, "Have a seat here, please," while to the one who is poor you say, "Stand there," or, "Sit at my feet," have you not made distinctions among yourselves, and become judges with evil thoughts? Listen, my beloved brothers and sisters. Has not God chosen the poor in the world to be rich in faith and to be heirs of the dominion promised to those who love God? But you have dishonored the poor. Is it not the rich who oppress you? Is it not they who drag you into court? Is it not they who blaspheme the excellent name that was invoked over you?

You do well if you really fulfill the royal law according to the scripture, "You shall love your neighbor as yourself." But if you show partiality, you commit sin and are convicted by the law as transgressors. For whoever keeps the whole law but fails in one point has become accountable for all of it.

What good is it, my brothers and sisters, if you say you have faith but do not have works? Can faith save you? If a brother or sister is naked and lacks daily food, and one of you says to them, "Go in peace; keep warm and eat your fill," and yet you do not supply their bodily needs, what is the good of that? So faith by itself, if it has no works, is dead.

GOSPEL   *Mark 7:24—37*

Roman Catholic: Mark 7:31–37

Jesus set out and went away to the region of Tyre. He entered a house and did not want anyone to know he was there. Yet he could not escape notice, but a woman whose little daughter had an unclean spirit immediately heard about him, and she came and bowed down at his feet. Now the woman was a Gentile, of Syrophoenician origin. She begged him to cast the demon out of her daughter. Jesus said to her, "Let the children be fed first, for it is not fair to take the children's food and throw it to the dogs." But she answered him, "Sir, even the dogs under the table eat the children's crumbs." Then he said to her, "For saying that, you may go—the demon has left your daughter." So she went home, found the child lying on the bed, and the demon gone.

Then Jesus returned from the region of Tyre, and went by way of Sidon towards the Sea of Galilee, in the region of the Decapolis. They brought to him a deaf man who had an impediment in his speech; and they begged him to lay his hand on him. Jesus took him aside in private, away from the crowd, and put his fingers into his ears, and he spat and touched his tongue. Then looking up to heaven, Jesus sighed and said to him, "Ephphatha," that is, "Be opened." And immediately his ears were opened, his tongue was released, and he spoke plainly. Then Jesus ordered them to tell no one; but the more he ordered them, the more zealously they proclaimed it. They were astounded beyond measure, saying, "He has done everything well; he even makes the deaf to hear and the mute to speak."

Practice of Prayer

Psalm 146:7, 8—9, 9—10

It is the LORD who keeps faith for ever,
who is just to those who are oppressed.
It is God who gives bread to the hungry,
the LORD, who sets prisoners free,
the LORD who gives sight to the blind,
who raises up those who are bowed down,
the LORD, who protects the stranger
and upholds the widow and orphan.

The LORD will reign for ever,
Zion's God, from age to age.

Practice of Justice

In the first line of his classic novel, *War and Peace*, Leo Tolstoy raises an essential question. If humans can work together to produce something as horrifying as war, couldn't they channel that same energy into doing something monumentally good?

The role of a prophet is not only to deliver messages of caution; it is also to envision a better world. The pursuit of justice is not only about preventing horrible wrongs; it is also about hope, about who we can be and what we can accomplish when we embrace God's guidance and power.

Reread today's first reading and consider what makes you "fearful of heart." What hope for our world do you find in the prophet's view of justice?

Scripture Insights

Isaiah's vision of the coming day of God reveals a world turned upside down. The blind see, the deaf hear, the mute speak and waters spring up in the desert. This is a world of the unexpected and surprising. It is a result that is as unsettling as it is joyful, for it is not what nature has intended. In the presence of the divine, anything needed is provided; anything broken is made whole. The laws of nature, created by God, are suspended when God comes in glory.

Mark's gospel describes the living fulfillment of Isaiah's prophecy when Jesus touches the deaf and mute man so that he hears and speaks. As in the other healing stories, Jesus demonstrates mastery over the limits of the human body. Already he has made the lame walk (Mark 2) and the dead live (Mark 5). The next time he heals (Mark 8:22–26), he will cure a blind man. Where Jesus walks, life in its wholeness abounds. The astonishment of the people suggests that they remember the prophecy of Isaiah and wonder if this might be the sign that God has come to save them.

In what way might these texts illuminate the epistle from James? James addresses a particular fault of a Christian community in the first century. The people show favoritism to the rich and well-dressed. James reminds them that God's preference is for the poor and disenfranchised. God did, after all, rescue poor Israel from wealthy Egypt. In that act, God displayed a fondness for turning things upside down. James reminds the church that God's power is not limited to healing the sick or sending manna. God also has control over economic and social injustices. A society that allows these things will be surprised, unsettled and ultimately changed at the coming day of the Lord. Just as God will heal our broken bodies, God will heal the broken relationships caused by unjust uses of wealth as well. That will be good news to some, but for those who define themselves by their wealth and the privilege it buys them, it will be a painful transformation.

How do we follow God in making a preferential option for the poor?

*S*eptember 14, 2003

READING I   *Numbers 21:4b — 7a*

From Mount Hor the Israelites set out, but the people became impatient on the way. They spoke against God and against Moses, "Why have you brought us up out of Egypt to die in the wilderness? For there is no food and no water, and we detest this miserable food." Then the LORD sent poisonous serpents among the people, and they bit the people, so that many Israelites died.

The people came to Moses and said, "We have sinned by speaking against the LORD and against you; pray to the LORD to take away the serpents from us."

READING II   *Philippians 2:6 — 11*

Revised Common Lectionary: 1 Corinthians 1:18–24

Christ Jesus, though he was in the form of God, did not regard equality with God as something to be exploited, but relinquished it all, taking the form of a slave, being born in human likeness. And being found in human form, he humbled himself and became obedient to the point of death—even death on a cross.

Therefore God also highly exalted him and gave him the name that is above every name, so that at the name of Jesus every knee should bend, in heaven and on earth and under the earth, and every tongue should confess that Jesus Christ is Lord, to the glory of God, the Father.

GOSPEL   *John 3:13 — 17*

Jesus said: "No one has ascended into heaven except the one who descended from heaven, the Son-of-Man. And just as Moses lifted up the serpent in the wilderness, so must the Son-of-Man be lifted up, that whoever believes in him may have eternal life.

"For God loved the world in this way, that God gave the Son, the only begotten one, so that everyone who believes in him may not perish but may have eternal life. Indeed, God did not send the Son into the world to condemn the world, but in order that the world might be saved through him."

Practice of Prayer

Psalm 78:1—2, 34—35, 36—37, 38

Give heed, my people, to my teaching;
turn your ear to the words of my mouth.
I will open my mouth in a parable
and reveal hidden lessons of the past.

When God slew them they would seek him,
return and seek him in earnest.
They remembered that God was their rock,
God, the Most High their redeemer.

But the words they spoke were mere flattery;
they lied to God with their lips.
For their hearts were not truly sincere;
they were not faithful to the covenant.

Yet the one who is full of compassion
forgave them their sin and spared them.
So often God held back the anger
that might have been stirred up in rage.

Practice of Prudence

Within days of the shootings at Columbine High School, a carpenter erected fifteen crosses in a park across from the campus, setting off a storm of controversy. Some objected to religious symbols on civic property. More were offended by the number of crosses: thirteen for the students and teacher killed by two young gunmen, and two for the gunmen, who killed themselves as police arrived. Those two crosses were later removed.

The cross is a powerful symbol. What was it intended to signify here? How did observers interpret it?

The crosses for the gunmen were probably meant as a sign of forgiveness and inclusion. As time passed, many came to see them as victims as well—destroyed by inner forces beyond their moral capacity. But when the crosses were erected, few held that view. Did the crosses for the killers force the people to consider a compassionate view they might otherwise have ignored? Or did the sight of the crosses for the killers actually harden hearts? Was this action the most effective and prudent way to accomplish the good intended?

Scripture Insights

Consider the contrasts in Philippians and in John: between Jesus relinquishing himself and God exalting him, and between Jesus lifted up like the serpent and Jesus saving the world. These juxtapositions are as challenging as they are compelling. What savior would take the form of a slave? What power can there be in crucifixion and death? How can we believe that someone who dies brings eternal life?

Moses lifted up the serpent in the desert so that the people might look at what was killing them. In their prayer to God, they opened themselves to God's grace and so recovered. When they looked at the serpent, they lived. In John's gospel, Jesus is lifted up like the serpent. John's clear reference to the Numbers passage and his repetition (three times) of the "lifting up" of the Son of Man (see 8:28 and 12:32—34) are indicative of the way he contrasts the old and new covenants. Jesus, like the serpent, is a figure of horror. When the witnesses to the crucifixion gather below the cross, they confront the reasons for death—greed, hatred, envy and fear. But in the self-giving of Jesus on the cross, they receive more than human life. They receive the gift of God's never-ending love and grace, which makes life eternal. The church lives forever in the presence of God.

John is the only evangelist to discuss why God sends Jesus to the world. Matthew, Mark and Luke tie Jesus to the fulfillment of the prophecies of old, but John speaks about the love of God for the world. Moses told Israel that God chose them, not because they were the greatest nation in the world, but because God loved them (Deuteronomy 7:8). John places Jesus' birth into the world in that same context of love from God. Jesus is the center of God's new relationship with human beings. He was never meant to condemn the world, but to save it, and so, as the hymn from Philippians tells us, Jesus' self-sacrificing love was not a sign of weakness and slavery but a sign of his lordship over heaven and earth.

To relinquish self seems contradictory in a culture that emphasizes self-esteem and self-promotion. How do Christians follow this example of Jesus?

September 14, 2003

READING I   Isaiah 50:4—9a

The Lord GOD has given me
    the tongue of a teacher,
that I may know how to sustain
    the weary with a word.
Morning by morning the Lord GOD wakens—
    wakens my ear
    to listen as those who are taught.
The Lord GOD has opened my ear,
    and I was not rebellious,
    I did not turn backward.
I gave my back to those who struck me,
    and my cheeks to those who pulled out the
    beard;
I did not hide my face
    from insult and spitting.

The Lord GOD helps me;
    therefore I have not been disgraced;
therefore I have set my face like flint,
    and I know that I shall not be put to shame;
    the one who vindicates me is near.
Who will contend with me?
    Let us stand up together.
Who are my adversaries?
    Let them confront me.
It is the Lord GOD who helps me;
    who will declare me guilty?

READING II   James 3:1—12

Not many of you should become teachers, my brothers and sisters, for you know that we who teach will be judged with greater strictness. For all of us make many mistakes. Anyone who makes no mistakes in speaking is perfect, able to keep the whole body in check with a bridle. If we put bits into the mouths of horses to make them obey us, we guide their whole bodies. Or look at ships: though they are so large that it takes strong winds to drive them, yet they are guided by a very small rudder wherever the will of the pilot directs.

So also the tongue is a small part of the body, yet it boasts of great exploits. How great a forest is set ablaze by a small fire! And the tongue is a fire. The tongue is placed among our bodily parts as a world of iniquity; it stains the whole body, sets on fire the cycle of nature, and is itself set on fire by hell. For every species of beast and bird, of reptile and sea creature, can be tamed and has been tamed by the human species, but no one can tame the tongue—a restless evil, full of deadly poison. With it we bless the Lord and Father, and with it we curse those who are made in the likeness of God. From the same mouth come blessing and cursing. My brothers and sisters, this ought not to be so. Does a spring pour forth from the same opening both fresh and brackish water? Can a fig tree, my brothers and sisters, yield olives, or a grapevine figs? No more can salt water yield fresh.

GOSPEL   Mark 8:27—38

Jesus went on with his disciples to the villages of Caesarea Philippi; and on the way he asked his disciples, "Who do people say that I am?" And they answered him, "John the Baptist; and others, Elijah; and still others, one of the prophets." Jesus asked them, "But who do you say that I am?" Peter answered him, "You are the Messiah." And he sternly ordered them not to tell anyone about him.

Then he began to teach them that the Son-of-Man must undergo great suffering, and be rejected by the elders, the chief priests, and the scribes, and be killed, and after three days rise again. He said all this quite openly. And Peter took him aside and began to rebuke him. But turning and looking at his disciples, Jesus rebuked Peter and said, "Get behind me, Satan! For you are setting your mind not on divine things but on human things."

Jesus called the crowd with his disciples, and said to them, "If any want to become my followers, let them deny themselves and take up their cross and follow me. For those who want to save their life will lose it, and those who lose their life for my sake, and for the sake of the gospel, will save it. For what will it profit them to gain the whole world and forfeit their life? Indeed, what can they give in return for their life? Those who are ashamed of me and of my words in this adulterous and sinful generation, of them the Son-of-Man will also be ashamed when he comes in the glory of his Father with the holy angels."

Practice of Prayer

Psalm 116:1—6, 9

Alleluia!

I love the LORD, for the LORD has heard
the cry of my appeal.
The LORD was attentive to me
in the day when I called.

They surrounded me, the snares of death,
with the anguish of the tomb;
they caught me, sorrow and distress.
I called on the LORD's name.

O LORD, my God, deliver me!

How gracious is the LORD, and just;
our God has compassion.
The LORD protects the simple hearts;
I was helpless so God saved me.

I will walk in the presence of the LORD
in the land of the living.

Practice of Fortitude

In 1955, Rosa Parks, an African American woman, refused to give up her seat on a bus to a white man. After being arrested, she asked the police officer a simple question: "Why do you push us around?" Four days later, a boycott of the city bus system by Montgomery's African Americans began. It lasted 381 days and set off a chain of events that eventually led to the passage of desegregation laws across the United States.

Since that day, Rosa Parks has spoken of the fatigue that led her to defy the bus driver's demand and to break an unjust law. She was physically tired after a long day's work and emotionally tired of a lifetime of discrimination. Rosa Parks reminds us that sometimes our bodies can be wiser than our minds. Some of our greatest shows of fortitude often emerge from staying put!

Scripture Insights

Halfway through Mark's gospel, Jesus' first prediction of his death and resurrection shocks the most loyal of disciples. When Peter confesses Jesus as Messiah, he probably held the traditional belief that the Messiah would be a great king or warrior, come to save the Jews from Rome. (Kings required anointing and the word *messiah* means anointed.) Mighty kings are not put to death like common criminals. God's anointed one certainly would not be defeated by outside forces. Jesus' teaching contradicted everything the Jews believed about the Messiah. It is no wonder that Peter begins to rebuke him.

This teaching of Jesus sheds light on why he repeatedly asks that no one speak of his miracles or his identity. Without the proper understanding of who the Messiah really is, people will never believe in Jesus beyond his miracles. They will not be able to look at the crucified Jesus and see their salvation. Jesus' warning to Peter not to set his mind on human things is a warning to Mark's readers as well. True messianic activity does not lie in conquering nations, but in dying for the sake of the world.

In the first reading, the servant of God in the prophecy of Isaiah proclaims that God has given him the tongue of a teacher to sustain the weary. The secret of the teacher's authority, though, lies in how well he listens to God ("The Lord GOD wakens my ear"), even if it leads to suffering and death. Jesus teaches his disciples well about the suffering and death of the Son of Man because he has listened well to the Father's command and understands the love of God for God's people. Jesus is also able to teach his followers the cost of discipleship—to deny themselves and be ready to lose their lives for the sake of the gospel. It is another lesson Jesus himself has learned. "Get behind me," he tells Peter. In part he is saying to Peter, "Follow my example." He then repeats that invitation and lesson for the crowd and for the entire church community, both then and now.

When have you felt called to deny yourself for the sake of the gospel?

LET·ME·SEE AGAIN!

Preparation for the Word

Blessed are you, Lord, God of all creation,
in the longer nights and the beauty of darkness.
May your Holy Spirit busy our minds,
train our mouths, excite our hearts
as we wrap ourselves in the words of scripture.
Here Jesus draws closer to his passion,
tells puzzling parables to friends and foes,
preaches persistence and a strange prudence,
has compassion for those who suffer,
and warns all to be on the watch.
For the world stands ever under your judgment,
    O God.

To this gospel and to the Hebrew Scriptures
and to the urgent letters of the apostles,
make us now attend.
We pray in Jesus' name who is Lord
    for ever and ever.
Amen.

Thanksgiving for the Word

We give you thanks,
loving God and judge of the world,
for the spiral of seasons and what they bring:
scriptures made more dear to us in repetition.
We give you thanks for the years of our lives:
we are climbing Jacob's ladder
between earth and heaven,
each rung your word, ever old, ever new.

Let your word be foundation and destination,
our firm ground and that for which
    we ever reach.
Then, Lord of the harvest, harvest us home
to await with all the saints the resurrection
    of the dead
and the life of the world to come.
We pray in Jesus' name who is Lord
    for ever and ever.
Amen.

Weekday Readings

September 22: *Ezra 1:1–6; Luke 8:16–18*
September 23: *Ezra 6:7–8, 12b, 14–20; Luke 8:19–21*
September 24: *Ezra 9:5–9; Luke 8:1–6*
September 25: *Haggai 1:1–8; Luke 9:7–9*
September 26: *Haggai 1:15b-2:9; Luke 9:18–22*
September 27: *Zechariah 2:5–9, 14–15a; Luke 9:43b–45*

September 29: Feast of Michael, Gabriel and Raphael
   Deuteronomy 7:9–10, 13–14; John 1:47–51
September 30: *Zechariah 8:20–23; Luke 9:51–56*
October 1: *Nehemiah 2:1–8; Luke 9:57–62*
October 2: *Nehemiah 8:1–4a, 5–6, 7b–12; Matthew 18:1–5, 10*
October 3: *Baruch 1:15–22; Luke 10:13–16*
October 4: *Baruch 4:5–12, 27–29; Luke 10:17–24*

October 6: *Jonah 1:1—2:1, 11; Luke 10:25–37*
October 7: *Jonah 3:1–10; Luke 10:38–42*
October 8: *Jonah 4:1–11; Luke 11:1–4*
October 9: *Malachi 3:13–20a; Luke 11:5–13*
October 10: *Joel 1:13–15; Luke 11:15–26*
October 11: *Joel 4:12–21; Luke 11:27–28*

October 13: *Romans 1:1–7; Luke 11:29–32*
October 14: *Romans 1:16–25; Luke 11:37–41*
October 15: *Romans 2:1–11; Luke 11:42–46*
October 16: *Romans 3:21–30; Luke 11:47–54*
October 17: *Romans 4:1–8; Luke 12:1–7*
October 18: Feast of Saint Luke
   2 Timothy 4:10–17b; Luke 10:1–9

October 20: *Romans 4:20–25; Luke 12:13–21*
October 21: *Romans 5:12, 15b, 17–19, 20b–21; Luke 12:35–38*
October 22: *Romans 6:12–18; Luke 12:39–48*
October 23: *Romans 6:19–23; Luke 12:49–53*
October 24: *Romans 7:18–25a; Luke 12:54–59*
October 25: *Romans 8:1–11; Luke 13:1–9*

October 27: *Romans 8:12–17; Luke 13:10–17*
October 28: Feast of Saints Simon and Jude
   Ephesians 2:19–22; Luke 6:12–19
October 29: *Romans 8:26–30; Luke 13:22–30*
October 30: *Romans 8:31b–39; Luke 13:31–35*
October 31: *Romans 9:1–5; Luke 14:1–5*
November 1: Solemnity of All Saints
   Revelation 7:2–4, 9–14; 1 John 3:1–3; Matthew 5:1–12a

November 3: *Romans 11:29–36; Luke 14:12–14*
November 4: *Romans 12:5–16a; Luke 14:15–24*
November 5: *Romans 13:8–10; Luke 14:25–33*
November 6: *Romans 14:7–12; Luke 15:1–10*
November 7: *Romans 15:14–21; Luke 16:1–8*
November 8: *Romans 16:3–9, 16, 22–27; Luke 16:9–15*

November 10: *Wisdom 1:1–7; Luke 17:1–6*
November 11: *Wisdom 2:23–3:9; Luke 17:7–10*
November 12: *Wisdom 6:1–11; Luke 17:11–19*
November 13: *Wisdom 7:22–8:1; Luke 17:20–25*
November 14: *Wisdom 13:1–9; Luke 17:26–37*
November 15: *Wisdom 18:14–16; 19:6–9; Luke 18:1–8*

November 17: *1 Maccabees 1:10–15, 41–43, 54–57, 62–64;*
   Luke 18:35–43
November 18: *2 Maccabees 6:18–31; Luke 19:1–10*
November 19: *2 Maccabees 7:1, 20–31; Luke 19:11–28*
November 20: *1 Maccabees 2:15–29; Luke 19:41–44*
November 21: *1 Maccabees 4:36–37, 52–59; Luke 19:45–48*
November 22: *1 Maccabees 6:1–13; Luke 20:27–40*
November 23: *Deuteronomy 1:1–6, 8–20; Luke 21:1–4*

November 25: *Deuteronomy 2:31–45; Luke 21:5–11*
November 26: *Deuteronomy 5:1–6, 13–14, 15–16, 23–28;*
   Luke 21:12–19
November 27: Thanksgiving Day
   Sirach 50:22–24; 1 Corinthians 1:3–9; Luke 17:11–19
November 28: *Deuteronomy 7:2–14; Luke 21:29–33*
November 29: *Deuteronomy 7:15–27; Luke 21:34–36*

September 21, 2003

READING I   *Wisdom 2:12, 17—20*

Revised Common Lectionary: Jeremiah 11:18–20

The wicked say:
"Let us lie in wait for the righteous man,
because he is inconvenient to us and opposes
    our actions;
he reproaches us for sins against the law,
and accuses us of sins against our training.
Let us see if his words are true,
and let us test what will happen at the end
    of his life;
for if the righteous man is God's child, he will
help him,
and will deliver him from the hand
    of his adversaries.
Let us test him with insult and torture,
so that we may find out how gentle he is,
and make trial of his forbearance.
Let us condemn him to a shameful death,
for, according to what he says,
    he will be protected."

READING II   *James 3:13 — 4:3, 7 — 8a*

Roman Catholic: James 3:16–4:3

Who is wise and understanding among you? Show by your good life that your works are done with gentleness born of wisdom. But if you have bitter envy and selfish ambition in your hearts, do not be boastful and false to the truth. Such wisdom does not come down from above, but is earthly, unspiritual, devilish. For where there is envy and selfish ambition, there will also be disorder and wickedness of every kind. But the wisdom from above is first pure, then peaceable, gentle, willing to yield, full of mercy and good fruits, without a trace of partiality or hypocrisy. And a harvest of righteousness is sown in peace for those who make peace.

Those conflicts and disputes among you, where do they come from? Do they not come from your cravings that are at war within you? You want something and do not have it; so you commit murder. And you covet something and cannot obtain it; so you engage in disputes and conflicts. You do not have, because you do not ask. You ask and do not receive, because you ask wrongly, in order to spend what you get on your pleasures.

Submit yourselves therefore to God. Resist the devil, and the devil will flee from you. Draw near to God, and God will draw near to you.

GOSPEL   *Mark 9:30—37*

Jesus and the disciples went on and passed through Galilee. He did not want anyone to know it; for he was teaching his disciples, saying to them, "The Son-of-Man is to be betrayed into human hands, and they will kill him, and three days after being killed, he will rise again." But they did not understand what he was saying and were afraid to ask him.

Then they came to Capernaum; and when Jesus was in the house he asked them, "What were you arguing about on the way?" But they were silent, for on the way they had argued with one another who was the greatest. He sat down, called the twelve, and said to them, "Whoever wants to be first must be last of all and servant of all." Then he took a little child and put it among them; and taking it in his arms, he said to them, "Whoever welcomes one such child in my name welcomes me, and whoever welcomes me welcomes not me but the one who sent me."

Practice of Prayer

Psalm 54:3—4, 5, 6—8

O God, save me by your name;
by your power, uphold my cause.
O God, hear my prayer;
listen to the words of my mouth.

For the proud have risen against me,
ruthless foes seek my life.
They have no regard for God.

But I have God for my help.
The Lord upholds my life.
Let the evil recoil upon my foes;
you who are faithful, destroy them.

I will sacrifice to you with willing heart
and praise your name, O LORD, for it is good.

Practice of Temperance

Today's second reading describes cravings out of control. Greed, lust, envy and gluttony destroy any interior sense of peace and well-being. This war within us then threatens our relationships with others and disturbs the stability of the community. The inner storms of individuals magnified to the global scale of the warfare of nations can be truly catastrophic.

Temperance is a virtue, and not just because it puts a healthy hold on our appetites. We can join a self-help group for that purpose. Temperance opens us to "the wisdom from above" by aligning attitudes and actions with the desires of God. The result is greater harmony with ourselves and with the world. What cravings are at war within us? How can the practice of temperance help us make peace within ourselves?

Scripture Insights

Among biblical texts, the letter of James is one of the most direct in its description of the causes of war and injustice. James does not blame the devil, unjust authority or outside forces. "Those conflicts and disputes among you, where do they come from? Do they not come from your cravings that are at war within you?"(4:1) Envy, greed and ambition are at the heart of much of the world's trouble. According to James, these are precisely the emotions that bind someone to the world, rather than to God (4:4). Writing to Christians in the first century, James focuses on Christian conduct—utter devotion to the things of God.

James' identification of the sin in our lives provides a lens through which we might view all three readings. His manner of teaching resembles wisdom literature, from which the first reading comes. The picture of the wicked sketched in the verses we read today is fleshed out in the entire second chapter of Wisdom. There we are shown wild desire for the things of this world. When godless people realize that someone who is righteous indicts their ambition and greed, they want to torture the righteous one because he opposes them. They want free rein to do whatever they wish. The last verse of the chapter speaks directly to James' concern. "But by the devil's envy, death entered the world, and those who belong to his company experience it" (Wisdom 2:24).

In Mark's gospel, the disciples argue about who is the greatest among them. This dispute, set between a prophecy about the crucifixion and a teaching about the presence of Christ in the most unimportant of people, underscores the disciples' ignorance of Jesus' mission. Envy demands a better position, greed desires wealth, and ambition seeks power. Jesus' life, death and teaching contradict all three. The apostles show they are still tied to the values of the world. To be true disciples of Christ, they must set aside envy and ambition and open themselves to the fruits of wisdom and the Spirit.

What does James mean when he says: "You do not have because you do not ask. You ask and do not receive, because you ask wrongly . . . "?

September 28, 2003

TWENTY-SIXTH SUNDAY IN ORDINARY TIME
SIXTEENTH SUNDAY AFTER PENTECOST

READING I   Numbers 11:25—29

Revised Common Lectionary: Numbers 11:4–6, 10–16, 24–29

Then the LORD came down in a cloud of dust and spoke to Moses, and took some of the spirit that was on him and put it on the seventy elders; and when the spirit rested upon them, they prophesied. But they did not do so again.

Two men remained in the camp, one named Eldad, and the other named Medad, and the spirit rested on them; they were among those registered, but they had not gone out to the tent, and so they prophesied in the camp. And a youth ran and told Moses, "Eldad and Medad are prophesying in the camp." And Joshua son of Nun, the assistant of Moses, one of his chosen ones, said, "My lord Moses, stop them!" But Moses said to him, "Are you jealous for my sake? Would that all the LORD's people were prophets, and that the LORD's spirit be given to them all!"

READING II   James 5:1— 6

Revised Common Lectionary: James 5:13–20

Come now, you rich people, weep and wail for the miseries that are coming to you. Your riches have rotted, and your clothes are moth-eaten. Your gold and silver have rusted, and their rust will be evidence against you, and it will eat your flesh like fire. You have laid up treasure for the last days. Listen! The wages of the laborers who mowed your fields, which you kept back by fraud, cry out, and the cries of the harvesters have reached the ears of the Lord of hosts. You have lived on the earth in luxury and in pleasure; you have fattened your hearts in a day of slaughter. You have condemned and murdered the righteous one, who does not resist you.

GOSPEL   Mark 9:38—50

Roman Catholic: Mark 9:38–43, 45, 47–48

John said to Jesus, "Teacher, we saw some man casting out demons in your name, and we tried to stop him, because he was not following us." But Jesus said, "Do not stop him; for no one who does a deed of power in my name will be able soon afterward to speak evil of me. Whoever is not against us is for us. For truly I tell you, whoever gives you a cup of water to drink because you bear the name of Christ will by no means lose the reward.

"If any of you put a stumbling block before one of these little ones who believe in me, it would be better for you if a great millstone were hung around your neck and you were thrown into the sea. If your hand causes you to stumble, cut it off; it is better for you to enter life maimed than to have two hands and to go to hell, to the unquenchable fire. And if your foot causes you to stumble, cut it off; it is better for you to enter life lame than to have two feet and to be thrown into hell. And if your eye causes you to stumble, tear it out; it is better for you to enter the dominion of God with one eye than to have two eyes and to be thrown into hell, where their worm never dies, and the fire is never quenched.

"For everyone will be salted with fire. Salt is good; but if salt has lost its saltiness, how can you season it? Have salt in yourselves, and be at peace with one another."

Practice of Prayer

Psalm 19:8, 10, 12—13, 14

The law of the LORD is perfect,
it revives the soul.
The rule of the LORD is to be trusted,
it gives wisdom to the simple.

The fear of the LORD is holy,
abiding for ever.
The decrees of the LORD are truth
and all of them just.

So in them your servant finds instruction;
great reward is in their keeping.
But can we discern all our errors?
From hidden faults acquit us.

From presumption restrain your servant
and let it not rule me.
Then shall I be blameless,
clean from grave sin.

Practice of Justice

In the song "Botswana," John Stewart sings about the victims of poverty and starvation in Africa. Haunted by "pictures of the children with the flies in their eyes," he describes his struggle with the vast imbalance between abundance and need in our world. While children starve, the rich "fire up the Porsches" in plush neighborhoods. It is a scorching indictment of the unjust systems that keep so many in wretched need while others have far more than enough. Stewart's song asks, "Do pictures of children with flies in their eyes make even God cry?" (Shanachie Entertainment Corporation, 1993.) What images of injustice haunt you? How can you respond?

Scripture Insights

In his letter, James defines the actions of a believer and also defines the actions that lead one away from God. For James, wealth ties people to the world's values. He is particularly critical of the rich whose wealth was acquired through fraud and injustice. Verse 5:4 reminds us of two places in the Pentateuch: "The wages of the laborers who mowed your fields . . . cry out. . . ." is an echo of Abel's blood that cries out from the earth in Genesis 4:10 after Cain murders him. The cries of the harvesters reach the ears of the Lord of Hosts just as the cries of the widows and orphans do in Exodus 22:22. Those who are oppressed and marginalized have the attention of God. James makes it clear that wealth gained through the suffering of the innocent condemns those who have it. They will weep in misery.

While James urges his readers to humility, gentleness, mercy and righteousness (see last week's reading), Jesus warns his followers not to be a "stumbling block" to the "little ones" who believe in Jesus. He is warning listeners that their own actions are an example, good or bad. His second teaching echoes the language of the first: Remove whatever causes you to stumble. Hands, feet and eyes are often the instruments of sin. Jesus' graphic illustration reminds the disciples that they must be ready to let go of everything, including their pride, in order to enter the kingdom of God.

The hell that Jesus names in Mark's gospel is not the Hebrew *Sheol,* but a place outside Jerusalem believed to have been a site of child sacrifice to pagan gods in its earlier history, later converted to a dump in which fire burned continuously. In the original text, it is called Gehenna. Later it became the model for the Christian concept of hell as a place of fire. Isaiah's description of the bodies of those who rebelled against God also influenced this text: "Their worm shall not die; their fire shall not be quenched . . . " (Isaiah 66:24). Discipleship leads to life; any other path means death.

What causes you to stumble? What are the stumbling blocks you put in front of others?

October 5, 2003

READING I *Genesis 2:18—24*

The Lord God said, "It is not good that the man should be alone; I will make him a helper as his partner." So out of the ground the Lord God formed every animal of the field and every bird of the air, and brought them to the man to see what he would call them; and whatever the man called every living creature, that was its name. The man gave names to all cattle, and to the birds of the air, and to every animal of the field; but for the man there was not found a helper as his partner.

So the Lord God caused a deep sleep to fall upon the man, and while he slept, took one of his ribs and closed up its place with flesh. And the rib that the Lord God had taken from the man the Lord God made into a woman and brought her to the man.

Then the man said,

"This at last is bone of my bones
    and flesh of my flesh;
this one shall be called Woman,
    for out of Man this one was taken."

Therefore a man leaves his father and his mother and clings to his wife, and they become one flesh.

READING II *Hebrews 2:9—11*

Revised Common Lectionary: Hebrews 1:1–4; 2:5–12

Jesus for a little while was made lower than the angels, now crowned with glory and honor because of the suffering of death, so that by the grace of God he might taste death for everyone.

It was fitting that God, for whom and through whom all things exist, in bringing many children to glory, should make the pioneer of their salvation perfect through sufferings. For the one who sanctifies and those who are sanctified all have one origin. For this reason Jesus is not ashamed to call them brothers and sisters, saying, "I will proclaim your name to my brothers and sisters, in the midst of the congregation I will praise you."

GOSPEL *Mark 10:2—16*

Some Pharisees came, and to test Jesus they asked, "Is it lawful for a husband to divorce his wife?" Jesus answered them, "What did Moses command you?" They said, "Moses allowed a husband to write a certificate of dismissal and to divorce her." But Jesus said to them, "Because of your hardness of heart Moses wrote this commandment for you. But from the beginning of creation, 'God made them male and female.' 'For this reason a man shall leave his father and mother and be joined to his wife, and the two shall become one flesh.' So they are no longer two, but one flesh. Therefore what God has joined together, let no one separate." Then in the house the disciples asked Jesus again about this matter. He said to them, "Whatever man divorces his wife and marries another commits adultery against her; and if she divorces her husband and marries another, she commits adultery."

People were bringing little children to Jesus in order that he might touch them; and the disciples spoke sternly to them. But when Jesus saw this, he was indignant and said to them, "Let the little children come to me; do not stop them; for it is to such as these that the dominion of God belongs. Truly I tell you, whoever does not receive the dominion of God as a little child will never enter it." And Jesus took them up in his arms, laid his hands on them, and blessed them.

Practice of Prayer

Psalm 128:1—2, 3, 4—5, 6

O blessed are you who fear the LORD
and walk in God's ways!

By the labor of your hands you shall eat.
You will be happy and prosper;
your wife like a fruitful vine
in the heart of your house;
your children like shoots of the olive,
around your table.
Indeed thus shall be blessed
those who fear the LORD.
May the LORD bless you from Zion
all the days of your life!
May you see your children's children
in a happy Jerusalem!

On Israel, peace!

Practice of Justice

On October 4 we celebrate the memorial of Saint Francis of Assisi, patron saint of Italy, founder of the Franciscan order, advocate of the poor and lover of all creatures. This gentle man of poverty sought out God's presence in every lowly place. His attitude of patient, loving attention to all creatures has inspired many who choose the work of caring for animals as caretakers or as political advocates.

Human self-absorption and arrogance often result in the neglect of our stewardly duties toward the animals who share our earth: disrespect for the needs of other species, and more grievously, willful mistreatment.

Many who love animals gather on the memorial of Saint Francis to honor the connectedness of all life by blessing animals. Communities often bless pets and service animals such as seeing-eye dogs and police horses, sometimes farm animals, and sometimes (collectively, *in absentia*) wildlife. Have you ever felt a bond with an animal? Have you ever felt called to care for or speak for creatures at risk?

Scripture Insights

When the Pharisees test Jesus, they question him on points of the law. Rabbinical discussion frequently included arguments about how the law was to be interpreted. Those promoting a particular viewpoint would use scripture to persuade others. In the question of divorce, Jesus tests the Pharisees' knowledge of Mosaic law and then counters their answer with his own interpretation and biblical text. Quoting Genesis 1:27 and Genesis 2:24, Jesus points to the intimate relationship of men and women from the beginning of creation. Both are created in God's image, destined to live in relationship with one another. For Jesus, marriage is a blessed relationship and the proper arena in which to fulfill the original biblical commands to be fruitful and multiply.

Jewish law provided for a certificate of divorce (Deuteronomy 24:1), but Jesus sees this as a compromise for human weakness. He does not specifically condemn divorce, but lays out the ideal on which all marriages are based. The implication is that divorce is an aberration and a sign of the brokenness of the world. In later discussion with the disciples, Jesus defines remarriage as an occasion of adultery against a spouse.

Jesus protests the easy ending of a marriage in his society. His teaching protects women, who could be dismissed from a marriage with a piece of paper, and promotes the idea that adultery is a sin against a woman as much as against a man. Jesus also makes a woman's responsibility equal to a man's in marriage, forbidding wives to divorce their husbands or commit adultery by marrying another. The Mosaic law had not considered either possibility. Most important, Jesus focuses on the sanctity of marriage rather than on the lawfulness of divorce for any reason. He raises the understanding of marriage from a civil institution to a state of life blessed by God.

As in marriage, Jesus expects more care than the law required in other relationships. What might he say about the casual way some conduct friendships? About the indifference of some employers for employees?

October 12, 2003

TWENTY-EIGHTH SUNDAY IN ORDINARY TIME
EIGHTEENTH SUNDAY AFTER PENTECOST

READING I   *Wisdom 7:7—11*

I prayed, and understanding was given me;
I called on God, and the spirit of wisdom
    came to me.
I preferred her to scepters and thrones,
and I accounted wealth as nothing in
    comparison with her.
Neither did I liken to her any priceless gem,
because all gold is but a little sand in her sight,
and silver will be accounted as clay before her.
I loved her more than health and beauty,
and I chose to have her rather than light,
because her radiance never ceases.
All good things came to me along with her,
and in her hands uncounted wealth.

READING II   *Hebrews 4:12—16*

Roman Catholic: Hebrews 4:12–13

Indeed, the word of God is living and active,
sharper than any two-edged sword, piercing until
it divides soul from spirit, joints from marrow; it
is able to judge the thoughts and intentions of the
heart. And before God no creature is hidden, but
all are naked and laid bare to the eyes of the one to
whom we must render an account.

Since, then, we have a great high priest who
has passed through the heavens, Jesus, the Son of
God, let us hold fast to our confession. For we do
not have a high priest who is unable to sympathize with our weaknesses, but we have one who
in every respect has been tested as we are, yet
without sin. Let us therefore approach the throne
of grace with boldness, so that we may receive
mercy and find grace to help in time of need.

GOSPEL   *Mark 10:17— 31*

Roman Catholic: Mark 10:17–30

As Jesus was setting out on a journey, a man ran
up and knelt before him, and asked him, "Good
Teacher, what must I do to inherit eternal life?"
Jesus said to him, "Why do you call me good? No
one is good but God alone. You know the commandments: 'You shall not murder; You shall not
commit adultery; You shall not steal; You shall not
bear false witness; You shall not defraud; Honor
your father and mother.'" The man said to Jesus,
"Teacher, I have kept all these since my youth."
Jesus, looking at him, loved him and said, "You
lack one thing; go, sell what you own, and give the
money to the poor, and you will have treasure in
heaven; then come, follow me." When the man
heard this, he was shocked and went away griev-
ing, for he had many possessions.

Then Jesus looked around and said to his disciples, "How hard it will be for those who have
wealth to enter the dominion of God!" And the
disciples were perplexed at these words. But Jesus
said to them again, "Children, how hard it is to
enter the dominion of God! It is easier for a camel
to go through the eye of a needle than for someone
who is rich to enter the dominion of God." They
were greatly astounded and said to one another,
"Then who can be saved?" Jesus looked at them
and said, "For mortals it is impossible, but not for
God; for God all things are possible."

Peter began to say to Jesus, "Look, we have left
everything and followed you." Jesus said, "Truly I
tell you, there is no one who has left house or
brothers or sisters or mother or father or children
or fields, for my sake and for the sake of the good
news, who will not receive a hundredfold now in
this age—houses, brothers and sisters, mothers
and children, and fields, with persecutions—and
in the age to come eternal life. But many who are
first will be last, and the last will be first."

Practice of Prayer

Psalm 90:12—13, 14—15, 16—17

Make us know the shortness of our life
that we may gain wisdom of heart.
LORD, relent! Is your anger for ever?
Show pity to your servants.

In the morning, fill us with your love;
we shall exult and rejoice all our days.
Give us joy to balance our affliction
for the years when we knew misfortune.

Show forth your work to your servants;
let your glory shine on their children.
Let the favor of the Lord be upon us:
give success to the work of our hands
(give success to the work of our hands).

Practice of Prudence

When New York became the first state to ban the use of cell phones while driving, there was a flurry of argument about the matter. Some applauded the decision as a judicious move promoting public safety. Others dissented, leery of one more restriction on individual freedom. One newspaper columnist raised an interesting question: Isn't there a difference between reckless driving and distracted driving? Should the latter, foolish though it might be, be against the law?

Prudence is defined in the *Catechism of the Catholic Church* as the "charioteer" of the virtues. "It guides the other virtues by setting rule and measure" (# 1806). For the prudent person, using a cell phone while driving is only an example of a much larger issue. The bigger concern is whether he or she is choosing wisely, acting justly and holding to what is best for the good of all.

Scripture Insights

Legend connects the book of Wisdom with Solomon, who succeeded his father, King David, on the throne of Israel. In the story of Solomon (1 Kings 3:4—9), the young king prays to God not for riches or power, but for an understanding heart to govern the people. God grants his request and also rewards him with riches and glory beyond compare. In the passage from Wisdom, we hear the narrator (usually thought to be Solomon) tell how he prayed for wisdom, desiring her more than any earthly treasure. The author writes in the style of much of the wisdom literature (Proverbs, Job and Ecclesiastes, for instance). Unlike the prophets who got their message from visions or the voice of God, the lessons in the wisdom literature are drawn from life experience.

Wisdom (in Hebrew, *hokmah,* and in Greek, *Sophia*) was paired with understanding and discernment. Wisdom is feminine; she is depicted as the reflection of God and image of God's goodness (Wisdom 7:26). She is also God's master crafter and the first of God's acts (Proverbs 8:22). In Wisdom 10, she is cast as God in the retelling of stories from Genesis and Exodus. Some scholars have called her the feminine face of God. Whatever her identity, ancient writers saw great beauty and treasure in Wisdom. They considered her a pathway to God. Thus the wisdom literature is full of prayers for wisdom.

The Wisdom reading provides a nice counterpoint to the gospel where Jesus discusses the price of discipleship. "Riches" in the gospel means everything related to worldly wealth, possessions and relationships. None of these can stand in the way of the service of God. When the disciples look at the implications of the word "rich" and realize there are many ways of being rich, they cry out in frustration, "Then who can be saved?" For Jesus, the answer is not in doubt. Rich or poor, God must be the center of life, but the rich must work especially hard to overcome attachments to their worldly goods. He might have recited Wisdom's prayer for them.

What attachments, of any sort, distract you from your spiritual work?

October 19, 2003

TWENTY-NINTH SUNDAY IN ORDINARY TIME
NINETEENTH SUNDAY AFTER PENTECOST

READING I   Isaiah 53:4—12

Roman Catholic: Isaiah 53:10–11

Surely he has borne our infirmities
    and carried our diseases;
yet we accounted him stricken,
    struck down by God, and afflicted.
But he was wounded for our transgressions,
    crushed for our iniquities;
upon him was the punishment
        that made us whole,
    and by his bruises we are healed.
All we like sheep have gone astray;
    we have all turned to our own way,
and the LORD has laid on him
    the iniquity of us all.

He was oppressed, and was afflicted,
    yet did not open his mouth;
like a lamb that is led to the slaughter,
    and like a ewe that is silent before the shearers,
    so he did not open his mouth.
By a perversion of justice he was taken away.
    Who could have imagined his future?
For he was cut off from the land of the living,
    stricken for the transgression of my people.
They made his grave with the wicked
    and his tomb with the rich,
although he had done no violence,
    and there was no deceit in his mouth.

Yet it was the will of the LORD to crush him
        with pain.
When you make his life an offering for sin,
    he shall see his offspring, and shall prolong
        his days;
through him the will of the LORD shall prosper.
    Out of his anguish he shall see light;
he shall find satisfaction through his knowledge.
    The righteous one, my servant, shall make
        many righteous,
    and shall bear their iniquities.
Therefore I will allot him a portion with the great,
    and he shall divide the spoil with the strong;

because he poured out himself to death,
    and was numbered with the transgressors;
yet he bore the sin of many,
    and made intercession for the transgressors.

READING II   Hebrews 4:14—16

Revised Common Lectionary: Hebrews 5:1–10

Since, then, we have a great high priest who has passed through the heavens, Jesus, the Son of God, let us hold fast to our confession. For we do not have a high priest who is unable to sympathize with our weaknesses, but we have one who in every respect has been tested as we are, yet without sin. Let us therefore approach the throne of grace with boldness, so that we may receive mercy and find grace to help in time of need.

GOSPEL   Mark 10:35—45

James and John, the sons of Zebedee, came forward to Jesus and said to him, "Teacher, we want you to do for us whatever we ask of you." And Jesus said to them, "What is it you want me to do for you?" And they said to him, "Grant us to sit, one at your right hand and one at your left, in your glory." But Jesus said to them, "You do not know what you are asking. Are you able to drink the cup that I drink, or be baptized with the baptism that I am baptized with?" They replied, "We are able." Then Jesus said to them, "The cup that I drink you will drink; and with the baptism with which I am baptized, you will be baptized; but to sit at my right hand or at my left is not mine to grant, but it is for those for whom it has been prepared."

When the ten heard this, they began to be angry with James and John. So Jesus called them and said to them, "You know that among the Gentiles those whom they recognize as their rulers are domineering, and their great ones are tyrants over them. But it is not so among you; but whoever wishes to become great among you must be your servant, and whoever wishes to be first among you must be slave of all. For the Son-of-Man came not to be served but to serve, and to give his life a ransom for many."

Practice of Prayer

For the word of the LORD is faithful
and all his works done in truth.
The LORD loves justice and right
and fills the earth with love.

The LORD looks on those who fear him,
on those who hope in his love,
to rescue their souls from death,
to keep them alive in famine.

Our soul is waiting for the LORD.
The Lord is our help and our shield.

May your love be upon us, O LORD,
as we place all our hope in you.

Practice of Prudence

In the gospel reading, the request James and John make of Jesus seems incredible in the light of what we know about Jesus and his kingdom. But they do not know what they are asking. Jesus recognizes that immediately. He tries to suggest the gravity of the cup and the baptism he will endure, but they miss his meaning as thoroughly as they have missed the teachings about the nature of his kingship. Their imprudence—first in failing to consider the limits of their understanding, and second in making such an audacious request before their sure-to-be-offended peers—is truly astounding.

To misunderstand, to desire honor and attention—these are human. But prudence can help us sort out our thoughts and desires in the privacy of our minds. Prayerful reflection, an act of prudence, gives us the benefit of God's direction before we blunder into situations we don't understand.

Scripture Insights

The first reading is probably familiar to us as the Good Friday reading about the suffering servant of God. From early times, the Christian church has applied this image to Jesus. The prophecy of a servant who would redeem Israel through suffering is unique among prophetic books. To say that Isaiah predicted the coming of Jesus is not accurate, but Isaiah did see the world turned upside down by God's victory and the restoration of Israel. Mountains would be made low, crooked made straight, rivers run in the desert, and those who were humiliated and brought low would be raised up. In Isaiah's imagination and poetry, the suffering servant enhanced the "new creation" God was working out.

Those who witnessed the crucifixion and resurrection of Jesus Christ were trying to describe something they had never experienced. Children who are learning to speak do much the same thing. Early Christian communities found the most apt descriptions for Jesus in the words and prophecies of the Hebrew scriptures. For them, Jesus was the fulfillment of those scriptures because what they read there fit their experience of Jesus so closely. As Christians we need the Hebrew scriptures to explain the identity of Jesus. The words of Isaiah help us understand the object of our belief; in turn, our belief provides some illumination on the words spoken so long before Jesus.

The New Testament quotes Isaiah more than any other Old Testament book except for the Psalms. It is Isaiah's strong poetry and imagination, as well as his insight into God's actions in history that make his prophecy such a rich resource for understanding who Jesus is in the life of the world. Isaiah's description of the suffering one also paints a sobering picture for any disciple who would drink the cup Jesus drinks and follow in his footsteps for the sake of God and the world.

Read all four of the servant songs in Isaiah (42:1—4; 49:1—6; 50:4—9) and discuss the characteristics of each servant. What features of our world would concern each of these servants?

READING I   *Jeremiah 31:7—9*

Thus says the LORD:
Sing aloud with gladness for Jacob,
    and raise shouts for the chief of the nations;
proclaim, give praise, and say,
    "Save, O LORD, your people,
    the remnant of Israel."
See, I am going to bring them from the land
        of the north,
    and gather them from the farthest parts
        of the earth,
among them the blind and the lame,
    those with child and those in labor, together;
    a great company, they shall return here.
With weeping they shall come,
    and with consolations I will lead them back,
I will let them walk by brooks of water,
    in a straight path in which they shall
        not stumble;
for I have become as a father to Israel,
    and Ephraim is my firstborn.

READING II   *Hebrews 5:1—6*

Revised Common Lectionary: Hebrews 7:23–28

Every high priest chosen from among mortals is put in charge of things pertaining to God on their behalf, to offer gifts and sacrifices for sins. The high priest is able to deal gently with the ignorant and wayward, since he himself is subject to weakness; and because of this he must offer sacrifice for his own sins as well as for those of the people. And one does not presume to take this honor, but takes it only when called by God, just as Aaron was.

So also Christ did not glorify himself in becoming a high priest, but was appointed by the one who said to him, "You are my Son, today I have begotten you"; as God says also in another place, "You are a priest forever, according to the order of Melchizedek."

GOSPEL   *Mark 10:46—52*

As Jesus and his disciples and a large crowd were leaving Jericho, Bartimaeus son of Timaeus, a blind beggar, was sitting by the roadside. When he heard that it was Jesus of Nazareth, he began to shout out and say, "Jesus, Son of David, have mercy on me!" Many sternly ordered him to be quiet, but he cried out even more loudly, "Son of David, have mercy on me!" Jesus stood still and said, "Call him here." And they called the blind man, saying to him, "Take heart; get up, he is calling you." So throwing off his cloak, he sprang up and came to Jesus. Then Jesus said to him, "What do you want me to do for you?" The blind man said to him, "My teacher, let me see again." Jesus said to him, "Go; your faith has made you well." Immediately he regained his sight and followed Jesus on the way.

Practice of Prayer

Psalm 126:1—2, 2—3, 4—5, 6

When the LORD delivered Zion from bondage,
it seemed like a dream.
Then was our mouth filled with laughter,
on our lips there were songs.

The heathens themselves said: "What marvels
the LORD worked for them!"
What marvels the LORD worked for us!
Indeed we were glad.

Deliver us, O LORD, from our bondage
as streams in dry land.
Those who are sowing in tears
will sing when they reap.

They go out, they go out, full of tears,
carrying seed for the sowing;
they come back, they come back, full of song,
carrying their sheaves.

Practice of Temperance

Halloween is a holiday that sometimes teaches the cost of intemperance. Over-excitement and stomachaches from too much candy are minor examples. When "tricks" go too far, property damage can result. What is meant to be a holiday for childlike fun can become an occasion of excess. Ironically, it takes place on the eve of a day devoted to the saints—models of self-discipline.

Not that sainthood is unremittingly dull. It's just focused. Soren Kierkegaard defined a saint as someone who can will the one thing. Their dedication comes not from self-suppression, but from an adherence to interior discipline that enables them to focus on the one thing of greatest importance: love of God.

This year, through your kindness, hospitality and temperate playfulness, be a "saintly" presence for each child who comes to your door.

Scripture Insights

Jesus' departure from Jericho signals the beginning of his final journey to Jerusalem and the passion that awaits him there. Mark takes a break from his terse writing style to describe the healing of the blind Bartimaeus in detail.

In both Old and New Testament, blindness is often a symbol of ignorance, particularly the ignorance of unbelief and lack of insight (Isaiah 6:9–10; Matthew 15:14; Romans 2:19). The servant of the Lord was to open the eyes of the blind (Isaiah 42:7). Thus healing blindness became a mark of the Messiah.

The story of Bartimaeus (the name in Hebrew or Aramaic means son of Timaeus—it is translated for the Greek-speaking audience) is the story of a simple healing by Jesus, another example of his election by God and his compassion for others. A deeper interpretation focuses on the beggar's shout to the "Son of David" and on his identification of Jesus as "my teacher" (*Rabboni*—the same word used by Mary Magdalene in John 20:16). This suggests that the one who is blind sees more clearly than those who are sighted. Still another emphasis can be placed on the closing line, "Immediately he regained his sight and followed Jesus on the way." Coming just before the entry into Jerusalem and the passion, the story of Bartimaeus provides a sterling example of Christian discipleship, particularly after the difficult teachings on divorce, ambition and riches. Finally, note the question Jesus asks: "What do you want me to do for you?" It is the same question he asked James and John when they wanted to be placed at his right and left hand. In both cases, the availability and vulnerability of Jesus as he awaits the answer gives some indication of the openness we must have toward others who call on us. The faith of Bartimaeus, his willingness to speak the deepest desire of his heart and his immediate response of following Jesus remains a constant source of inspiration for the church.

Jeremiah names the blind, the lame and the pregnant among those whom the Lord will gather back to Jerusalem. Why would these people be singled out in Jeremiah's prophecy?

READING I   Wisdom 3:1—9

The souls of the righteous are in the hand of God,
and no torment will ever touch them.
In the eyes of the foolish they seemed to have died,
and their departure was thought to be a disaster,
and their going from us to be their destruction;
but they are at peace.

For though in the sight of others
    they were punished,
their hope is full of immortality.
Having been disciplined a little,
    they will receive great good,
because God tested them and found them worthy;
like gold in the furnace God tried them,
and like a sacrificial burnt offering
    God accepted them.

In the time of their visitation they will shine forth,
and will run like sparks through the stubble.
They will govern nations and rule over peoples,
and the Lord will reign over them forever.
Those who trust in God will understand truth,
and the faithful will abide with the Lord in love,
because grace and mercy are upon
    God's holy ones,
and God watches over the elect.

READING II   Romans 5:5—11

and hope does not disappoint us, because God's
love has been poured into our hearts through the
Holy Spirit that has been given to us.

For while we were still weak, at the right time
Christ died for the ungodly. Indeed, rarely will anyone die for a righteous person—though perhaps
for a good person someone might actually dare to
die. But it is proof of God's own love for us in that
while we still were sinners Christ died for us.

Much more surely then, now that we have been
justified by his blood, will we be saved through him
from the wrath of God. For if while we were enemies, we were reconciled to God through the death
of the Son of God, much more surely, having been
reconciled, will we be saved by the life of the Son of
God. But more than that, we even boast in God
through our Lord Jesus Christ, through whom we
have now received reconciliation.

GOSPEL   Matthew 5:1—12

When Jesus saw the crowds, he went up the mountain and sat down; and his disciples came to him.
Then Jesus began to speak, and taught them, saying:

"Blessed are the poor in spirit, for theirs is the
dominion of heaven. Blessed are those who
mourn, for they will be comforted. Blessed are the
meek, for they will inherit the earth. Blessed are
those who hunger and thirst for righteousness, for
they will be filled. Blessed are the merciful, for
they will receive mercy. Blessed are the pure in
heart, for they will see God. Blessed are the peace-
makers, for they will be called children of God.

"Blessed are those who are persecuted for
righteousness' sake, for theirs is the dominion of
heaven. Blessed are you when people revile you
and persecute you and utter all kinds of evil
against you falsely on my account. Rejoice and be
glad, for your reward is great in heaven, for in the
same way they persecuted the prophets who were
before you."

Practice of Prayer

Psalm 23:1—3a, 3b—4, 5, 6

LORD, you are my shepherd;
there is nothing I shall want.
Fresh and green are the pastures
where you give me repose.
Near restful waters you lead me,
to revive my drooping spirit.

You guide me along the right path;
You are true to your name.
If I should walk in the valley of darkness
no evil would I fear.
You are there with your crook and your staff;
with these you give me comfort.

You have prepared a banquet for me
in the sight of my foes.
My head you have anointed with oil;
my cup is overflowing.

Surely goodness and kindness shall follow me
all the days of my life.
In the LORD's own house shall I dwell
for ever and ever.

Practice of Fortitude

"Blessed are they who mourn, for they will be comforted" (Matthew 5:4). For anyone who has lived through the unexpected death of a loved one, this beatitude can be especially hard to embrace. In the first few days, weeks, months or even years, it seems as if comfort is completely out of reach. Mourning can be an extremely lonely time. Friends and relatives who drew closer at the time of the funeral return to their normal routines, seemingly unaware of the mourner's unending sorrow.

The words of Jesus promise relief, carrying the hope that one will eventually move beyond the constant hurt that fills each day. On this feast of All Souls, reflect on a time of loss when you drew strength from your faith and from the love of others. Are there mourners who need your attention now?

Scripture Insights

All Souls is the second of the church's great feasts of remembrance for the dead. All Saints, November 1, celebrates those whose lives are known to us and who may, perhaps, have an official feast of their own during the liturgical year. All Souls, on the other hand, celebrates every soul who has died and has been gathered in by God, whether we know them or not.

The church chooses three readings to teach us about death in God. The book of Wisdom opens with an exhortation to seek justice and an assurance that "the souls of the righteous are in the hand of God." The vision of reward after death suggests the beginnings of a belief in resurrection, which the Pharisees of the New Testament confessed. There is comfort in the understanding that the grace and mercy of God surround us, even in death.

The reading from Romans describes the source of eternal life even for those who are sinful. The death of Jesus justifies all people before God, including God's enemies. Not only does this prove God's love for the world, but it opens us to an understanding of that love even for those we feel may not deserve it. God's compassion is not limited to those who are perfect in their obedience.

Finally, the gospel takes us to Matthew's Sermon on the Mount. The poor in spirit, the ones who mourn, the lowly and all the rest are precisely the people who are not known except by those who love them and by God. Their deaths are generally unremarked. There are rarely miracles attached to their names. They will not be named saints by the church, but the dignity of their lives among us challenges us to live in a more disciplined and faithful manner. The great communion of saints in the church incorporates all those who have gone before us and who pray with us when we turn to God. Fathers, grandmothers, sisters and brothers who have died remind us of the hope to which we are called and become the sign of unity with God for all creation when this world ends.

In what ways can we celebrate the communion of saints outside this particular feast?

November 2, 2003

ROMAN CATHOLIC: SEE PAGES 146—147
THE TWENTY-FIRST SUNDAY AFTER PENTECOST

READING I   Deuteronomy 6:1—9

Moses said to the people, Now this is the commandment—the statutes and the ordinances—that the LORD your God charged me to teach you to observe in the land that you are about to cross into and occupy, so that you and your children and your children's children, may fear the LORD your God all the days of your life, and keep all the decrees and the commandments of the LORD your God that I am commanding you, so that your days may be long. Hear therefore, O Israel, and observe them diligently, so that it may go well with you, and so that you may multiply greatly in a land flowing with milk and honey, as the LORD, the God of your ancestors, has promised you.

Hear, O Israel: The LORD is our God, the LORD alone. You shall love the LORD your God with all your heart, and with all your soul, and with all your might. Keep these words that I am commanding you today in your heart. Recite them to your children and talk about them when you are at home and when you are away, when you lie down and when you rise. Bind them as a sign on your hand, fix them as an emblem on your forehead, and write them on the doorposts of your house and on your gates.

READING II   Hebrews 9:11—14

When Christ came as a high priest of the good things that have come, then through the greater and perfect tent (not made with hands, that is, not of this creation), he entered once for all into the Holy Place, not with the blood of goats and calves, but with his own blood, thus obtaining eternal redemption. For if the blood of goats and bulls, with the sprinkling of the ashes of a heifer, sanctifies those who have been defiled so that their flesh is purified, how much more will the blood of Christ, who through the eternal Spirit offered himself without blemish to God, purify our conscience from dead works to worship the living God!

GOSPEL   Mark 12:28—34

One of the scribes came near and heard Jesus and the Sadducees disputing with one another, and seeing that Jesus answered them well, asked him, "Which commandment is the first of all?" Jesus answered, "The first is, 'Hear, O Israel: the Lord our God, the Lord is one; you shall love the Lord your God with all your heart, and with all your soul, and with all your mind, and with all your strength.' The second is this, 'You shall love your neighbor as yourself.' There is no other commandment greater than these."

Then the scribe said to Jesus, "You are right, Teacher; you have truly said that 'God is one, and besides God there is no other'; and 'to love God with all the heart, and with all the understanding, and with all the strength,' and 'to love one's neighbor as oneself,'—this is much more important than all whole burnt offerings and sacrifices." When Jesus saw that the scribe answered wisely, he said to him, "You are not far from the dominion of God." After that no one dared to ask him any question.

Practice of Prayer

Psalm 119:1—8

They are happy whose life is blameless,
who follow God's law!
They are happy who do God's will,
seeking God with all their hearts,
who never do anything evil
but walk in God's ways.
You have laid down your precepts
to be obeyed with care.

May my footsteps be firm
to obey your statutes.
Then I shall not be put to shame
as I heed your commands.
I will thank you with an upright heart
as I learn your decrees.
I will obey your statutes
do not forsake me.

Practice of Prudence

This week Americans go to the polls to elect candidates for national and local offices. Surrounding this sober duty is a razzle-dazzle process in which candidates use every attention-grabbing device they can afford to attract voters to their message. In fact, the week before an election can sometimes feel like a replay of Halloween. Prudent voters must filter out a lot of noise before they can sort through the information they need to make decisions. And even then, the factors to consider seem vast and complex—personalitites and aptitudes, current domestic and international economic and political conditions, unforeseen, perhaps unimaginable events.

As we survey the possibilities, we may find it helpful to reflect on Mark's description of Jesus calmly penetrating to the essence of the law in this week's gospel reading. Sifting and sorting is indeed the work of prudence. It is not only a rational process, but one into which we invite Holy Wisdom.

Scripture Insights

Before the Jews crossed the Jordan River into Canaan, Moses gathered them together so that he could teach them for the last time. God had told Moses he would die before he reached the Promised Land, so Moses wanted to review all the laws that God had given him on Sinai, to remind the people of the love God had for them and the obedience expected of them. The book of Deuteronomy is presented as that teaching. The Hebrew name for Deuteronomy, *Devarim,* is taken from the first sentence: "These are the words of Moses . . . " Some scholars suggest that a more appropriate title might be Memoirs, because Moses recounts the details of the Exodus and the wilderness wandering to the new generation who will occupy the land.

In the beginning of chapter 6, after he has recalled the Ten Commandments and God's covenant, Moses calls attention to a great commandment that encompasses all others for the Jews. It is so important that it is accorded its own name, the Shema (which means "hear"). All Jews learn this by heart and teach it to their children. The most devout write it on parchment and place it in small boxes that they wear on their foreheads and at their wrists so that it is always before them, literally as well as figuratively. The Shema is recited in synagogues and is a guide for behavior among Jews today.

Jesus could have given no other response to the scribe who asked him about the greatest commandment. He expands his answer to include what he considered to be the second great law. "Love your neighbor as yourself" is not original with Jesus. It is in Leviticus 19:18 among various codes of behavior. Jesus lifts it out and emphasizes it, giving it new meaning and a place of importance among the other laws of the community.

"Love God" and "Love your neighbor" were the two standards by which early Christians were to judge their actions.

Imagine keeping the words of these two laws literally on our foreheads, at our wrists and at our doorways. What might be the effect of this practice?

READING I   *Ezekiel 47:1—2, 8—9, 12*

Then he brought me back to the entrance of the temple; there, water was flowing from below the threshold of the temple toward the east (for the temple faced east); and the water was flowing down from below the south end of the threshold of the temple, south of the altar. Then he brought me out by way of the north gate, and led me around on the outside to the outer gate that faces toward the east; and the water was coming out on the south side. He said to me, "This water flows toward the eastern region and goes down into the Arabah; and when it enters the sea, the sea of stagnant waters, the water will become fresh. Wherever the river goes, every living creature that swarms will live, and there will be very many fish, once these waters reach there. It will become fresh; and everything will live where the river goes. On the banks, on both sides of the river, there will grow all kinds of trees for food. Their leaves will not wither nor their fruit fail, but they will bear fresh fruit every month, because the water for them flows from the sanctuary. Their fruit will be for food, and their leaves for healing."

READING II   *1 Corinthians 3:9c—11, 16—17*

You are God's field, God's building. According to the grace of God given to me, like a skilled master builder I laid a foundation, and someone else is building on it. Each builder must choose with care how to build on it. For no one can lay any foundation other than the one that has been laid; that foundation is Jesus Christ.

Do you not know that you are God's temple and that God's Spirit dwells in you? Anyone who destroys God's temple will be destroyed by God. For God's temple is holy, and you are that temple.

GOSPEL   *John 2:13—22*

The Passover of the Jewish people was near, and Jesus went up to Jerusalem. In the temple he found people selling cattle, sheep, and doves, and the money changers seated at their tables. Making a whip of cords, he drove all of them out of the temple, both the sheep and the cattle. He also poured out the coins of the money changers and overturned their tables. He told those who were selling the doves, "Take these things out of here! Stop making my Father's house a marketplace!" His disciples remembered that it was written, "Zeal for your house will consume me." The Judeans then said to him, "What sign can you show us for doing this?" Jesus answered them, "Destroy this temple, and in three days I will raise it up." The Judeans then said, "This temple has been under construction for forty-six years, and will you raise it up in three days?" But Jesus was speaking of the temple of his body.

After he was raised from the dead, his disciples remembered that he had said this; and they believed the scripture and the word that Jesus had spoken.

Practice of Prayer

Psalm 46:3, 4, 5—6, 8, 11

God is for us a refuge and strength,
a helper close at hand, in time of distress,
so we shall not fear though the earth should rock,
though the mountains fall into the depths
   of the sea;

The waters of a river give joy to God's city,
the holy place where the Most High dwells.
God is within, it cannot be shaken;
God will help it at the dawning of the day.

Come, consider the works of the LORD,
the redoubtable deeds God has done on the earth.

Practice of Justice

It is common in many cities to see a homeless person standing on a street corner asking for spare change. Some see them as freeloaders. If they had enough gumption, they could get a job. Others are aware of factors such as mental illness that make the plight of the homeless much more complex.

For most, panhandlers raise a dilemma: Will the money be used for food, or to support a drug habit? How can you know what the person really needs? You have ten seconds to decide. Some people formulate a policy for themselves; others act on intuition.

Justice is a two-pronged process. It aims to alleviate the immediate pain of those in need through acts of charity and generosity. It also strives to change societal structures that keep people locked in a cycle of poverty. Both approaches are worthy. The second is certainly more difficult, but will ultimately be more effective.

Scripture Insights

St. John Lateran is the cathedral of Rome and the site of several councils of the church. Less familiar than, say, St. Peter's in Vatican City, St. John's is the church of the pope as the bishop of Rome. Churches remind us that God is present in the world. When we enter the church's space and time, we bring the world with us; when we go back into the world, we bring God with us.

The key word used in today's texts is *temple*, the gathering place for the faithful in Old Testament and very early Christian times. In the gospel, the merchants were bringing the world's values into the sacred space of the temple where God's values should reign. In this first part of the gospel of John, Jesus defends the temple as a place of prayer. In the second part of the gospel, Jesus uses the word "temple" as a metaphor for his own body. His body defines sacred space and time and calls attention to the presence of God in the world. This temple might be killed, but will be raised up in three days. But those listening could not see beyond the literal understanding of the word.

Paul also uses the word temple metaphorically to speak of our bodies as temples of the Holy Spirit. As such, we are to behave as though the presence of God shines through us.

Finally, Ezekiel shows us a mystical vision of the temple in the day of the Lord. Water from this temple brings life to the whole earth. It is a symbol of wholeness and restored relationship between Israel and God. John would adapt this vision in the last chapters of Revelation.

The words *temple* and *church* continue to have multiple meanings today. We mean the building, the people, and the dwelling place of God in eternity. Church is the means of relationship with God and the people of God. A feast devoted to a church allows us to reflect on who and what church is for us.

How do church buildings mediate your experience of God? Of other aspects of church?

November 9, 2003

READING I   *1 Kings 17:8—16*

The word of the LORD came to Elijah, saying, "Go now to Zarephath, which belongs to Sidon, and live there; for I have commanded a widow there to feed you." So Elijah set out and went to Zarephath. When he came to the gate of the town, a widow was there gathering sticks; he called to her and said, "Bring me a little water in a vessel, so that I may drink." As she was going to bring it, he called to her and said, "Bring me a morsel of bread in your hand." But she said, "As the LORD your God lives, I have nothing baked, only a handful of meal in a jar, and a little oil in a jug; I am now gathering a couple of sticks, so that I may go home and prepare it for myself and my son, that we may eat it, and die."

Elijah said to her, "Do not be afraid; go and do as you have said; but first make me a little cake of it and bring it to me, and afterwards make something for yourself and your son. For thus says the LORD the God of Israel: The jar of meal will not be emptied and the jug of oil will not fail until the day that the LORD sends rain on the earth."

She went and did as Elijah said, so that she as well as he and her household ate for many days. The jar of meal was not emptied, neither did the jug of oil fail, according to the word of the LORD spoken by Elijah.

READING II   *Hebrews 9:24—28*

Christ did not enter a sanctuary made by human hands, a mere copy of the true one, but he entered into heaven itself, now to appear in the presence of God on our behalf. Nor was it to offer himself again and again, as the high priest enters the Holy Place year after year with blood that is not his own; for then he would have had to suffer again and again since the foundation of the world.

But as it is, Christ has appeared once for all at the end of the age to remove sin by the sacrifice of himself. And just as it is appointed for mortals to die once, and after that the judgment, so Christ, having been offered once to bear the sins of many, will appear a second time, not to deal with sin, but to save those who are eagerly waiting for him.

GOSPEL   *Mark 12:38—44*

As Jesus taught, he said, "Beware of the scribes, who like to walk around in long robes, and to be greeted with respect in the marketplaces, and to have the best seats in the synagogues and places of honor at banquets! They devour widows' houses and for the sake of appearance say long prayers. They will receive the greater condemnation."

Jesus sat down opposite the treasury, and watched the crowd putting money into the treasury. Many rich people put in large sums. A poor widow came and put in two small copper coins, which are worth a penny. Then Jesus called his disciples and said to them, "Truly I tell you, this poor widow has put in more than all those who are contributing to the treasury. For all of them have contributed out of their abundance; but she out of her poverty has put in everything she had, all she had to live on."

Practice of Prayer

Psalm 146:1b—4, 6c—10b

My soul, give praise to the LORD;
I will praise the LORD all my days,
make music to my God while I live.

Put no trust in the powerful,
mere mortals in whom there is no help.
Take their breath, they return to clay
and their plans that day come to nothing.

It is the Lord who keeps faith for ever,
who is just to whose who are oppressed.
It is God who gives bread to the hungry,
the LORD, who sets prisoners free,

the LORD who gives sight to the blind,
who raises up those who are bowed down,
the LORD, who protects the stranger
and upholds the widow and orphan.

It is the LORD who loves the just
but thwarts the path of the wicked.
The LORD will reign for ever,
Zion's God, from age to age.

Practice of Fortitude

His paintings now adorn t-shirts and coffee mugs, so it is hard to fathom the controversy that initially raged around Claude Monet and his fellow Impressionists. Defying academic art, they discovered a new way of seeing the world, concentrating on the way light transforms solid objects. They captured on canvas a moment's "impression" of light and color. The critics and public resisted this new vision and the Impressionsts' work was excluded from French salons and exhibits. But the power of their new insight gave them the fortitude to continue working

Monet's birthday is November 14. Celebrate it by looking at art or taking a walk. Let his paintings teach you how to see the transformative power of light on the objects around you. And let that remind you of the fortitude of this painter in the midst of rejection and criticism.

Scripture Insights

The story of Elijah's encounter with the widow of Zarephath shows us the radical trust of two faithful servants of God. We also see the importance of generosity, particularly to strangers. Both Jews and the early Christians believed that strangers might be messengers of God in disguise (see Romans 12:13 and Hebrews 13:1). Both built generosity and hospitality into their moral codes. The Jewish prophets were constantly exhorting the people to look after the strangers, the widows and the orphans—in short, the disenfranchised of society. The law paid special heed to the stranger in a strange land, whose plight resembled that of the Jews themselves in Egypt. Christians were given the parable of the sheep and goats (Matthew 25) and told that loving the neighbor as oneself was the second greatest commandment. It is not surprising that the story of a Jewish prophet and a generous widow should grace the pages of the Old Testament.

Consider carefully, however, the faith that both the widow and Elijah must have. The widow gives up the last of her grain and the little oil she has to feed Elijah. Even though Elijah promises plenty, her leap of faith and her incredible generosity in sharing the last of what she has are amazing. By the same token, Elijah had to trust that God would take care of the situation. He must rely on the hospitality of a stranger for his meal. In this case a peculiar reversal has taken place. Normally, Elijah, who is a Jew and a man, would have been taking care of the widow. This was the law; he was bound to do so. Here, he had to be humble enough to let a widow take care of him, knowing he was taking her last bit of grain and oil. Elijah does not know where his next meal is coming from either. The promise he makes on God's behalf is all he has to give her. Her generosity and his faith and humility come together to allow God to work.

How does it feel to be dependent on someone else, or to have someone dependent on you? How do you maintain an attitude of humility and generosity in either of those situations?

November 16, 2003

THIRTY-THIRD SUNDAY IN ORDINARY TIME
TWENTY-THIRD SUNDAY AFTER PENTECOST

READING I   Daniel 12:1—3

"At that time Michael, the great ruler, the protector of your people, shall arise. There shall be a time of anguish, such as has never occurred since nations first came into existence. But at that time your people shall be delivered, everyone who is found written in the book. Many of those who sleep in the dust of the earth shall awake, some to everlasting life, and some to shame and everlasting contempt. Those who are wise shall shine like the brightness of the sky, and those who lead many to righteousness, like the stars forever and ever."

READING II   Hebrews 10:11—14, [15—18,] 19—25

Roman Catholic: Hebrews 10:11–14, 18

Every priest stands day after day at his service, offering again and again the same sacrifices that can never take away sins. But when Christ had offered for all time a single sacrifice for sins, "he sat down at the right hand of God," and since then has been waiting "until his enemies would be made a footstool for his feet." For by a single offering he has perfected for all time those who are sanctified.

And the Holy Spirit also testifies to us, for after saying, "This is the covenant that I will make with them after those days, says the Lord: I will put my laws in their hearts, and I will write them on their minds," then is added, "I will remember their sins and their lawless deeds no more." Where there is forgiveness of these, there is no longer any offering for sin.

Therefore, my friends, since we have confidence to enter the sanctuary by the blood of Jesus, by the new and living way that Christ opened for us through the curtain (that is, through his flesh), and since we have a great priest over the house of God, let us approach with a true heart in full assurance of faith, with our hearts sprinkled clean from an evil conscience and our bodies washed with pure water. Let us hold fast to the confession of our hope without wavering, for the one who has promised is faithful. And let us consider how to provoke one another to love and good deeds, not neglecting to meet together, as is the habit of some, but encouraging one another, and all the more as you see the Day approaching.

GOSPEL   Mark 13:24—32

Revised Common Lectionary: Mark 13:1–8

Jesus said: "In those days, after that suffering, the sun will be darkened, and the moon will not give its light, and the stars will be falling from heaven, and the powers in the heavens will be shaken. Then they will see 'the Son-of-Man coming in clouds' with great power and glory. Then the Son-of-Man will send out the angels, and gather his elect from the four winds, from the ends of the earth to the ends of heaven.

"From the fig tree learn its lesson: as soon as its branch becomes tender and puts forth its leaves, you know that summer is near. So also, when you see these things taking place, you know that he is near, at the very gates. Truly I tell you, this generation will not pass away until all these things have taken place. Heaven and earth will pass away, but my words will not pass away.

"But about that day or hour no one knows, neither the angels in heaven, nor the Son, but only the Father.

Practice of Prayer

Psalm 16:5, 8, 9—10, 11

O LORD, it is you who are my portion and cup.
it is you yourself who are my prize.

I keep you, LORD, ever in my sight;
since you are at my right hand, I shall stand firm.

And so my heart rejoices, my soul is glad;
even my body shall rest in safety.
For you will not leave my soul among the dead,
nor let your beloved know decay.

You will show me the path of life,
the fullness of joy in your presence,
at your right hand happiness for ever.

Practice of Temperance

Anne Frank was a young woman who spoke her mind. Her diary gave her an outlet for her fears, dreams and frustrations during the two years she spent hiding from the Nazis in an Amsterdam attic. It helped her cope with the difficulties of living with her family and four other people in such a confined space. She wrote of having to learn to temper her own particular wants and to hold her tongue when her attic-mates were particularly annoying. She was often unsuccessful, and her writing is a poignant confession of her struggles to bear up.

Anne Frank's story has been read by millions of people across the globe. It shows us the concrete human consequences of a terrible episode in world history. This description of a small group of people just trying to survive in desperate circumstances is made all the more touching by Anne's candid revelations about her own daily struggle with tolerance and self discipline.

Scripture Insights

Apocalyptic literature arose in periods of strife and persecution. Two examples are the latter half of Daniel, written around 150 BCE, and the Revelation of John, written during the Roman persecution of Christians at the end of the first century CE. Presented as God's revelations to the faithful who live in fear, they exhort people to remain true to God, who will not desert them. Usually a cataclysmic battle ensues between the forces of evil and God, who is the ultimate victor. A glorious ending is painted for those who remain true to God. Apocalyptic literature uses symbols easily recognizable to the audience, but often strange to subsequent generations. Many of our images of heaven come from scenes at the end of Daniel and Revelation.

The reading from Daniel shows a shift in Jewish thinking about life after death. In the Pentateuch and the prophets there was no afterlife. People lived on in the memories of their descendants, and punishment and reward were carried out in subsequent generations. This is why God talks about blessing being carried into the thousandth generation of those who love God, while curses last through the third or fourth generation. (Notice the disparity in duration.) With the advent of unceasing persecution, however, some Jews developed a theology that allowed for God's reward or punishment to take place after death, when "those who sleep in the earth will rise." The idea of an afterlife would eventually call up images of fire, heavenly cities, deep pits and the names of the faithful written in the book of life.

There is a flavor of the apocalytic in Mark's gospel this week. Cosmic reversals will occur, the Son of Man will come in the clouds to gather the elect, and heaven and earth will pass away. But Jesus assures us that his words will not pass away and the Father will be in control.

How do you read the references to sin, judgment, reward and punishment in today's texts?

November 23, 2003

CHRIST THE KING
THE REIGN OF CHRIST

READING I   Daniel 7:9 —10, 13 —14

Roman Catholic: Daniel 7:13–14

As I watched,
thrones were set in place,
    and an Ancient One sat down on the throne,
whose clothing was white as snow,
    the hair of whose head like pure wool;
whose throne was fiery flames,
    and its wheels were burning fire.
A stream of fire issued
    and flowed out from the presence
        of the Ancient of Days,
whom a thousand thousands served,
    and ten thousand times ten thousand stood
        in attendance.
The court sat in judgment,
    and the books were opened.

As I watched in the night visions,
I saw one like a human being
    coming with the clouds of heaven.
And he came to the Ancient One,
    before whom he was presented.
To him was given dominion
    and glory and kingship,
that all peoples, nations, and languages
    should serve him.
His dominion is an everlasting dominion
    that shall not pass away,
and his reign is one
    that shall never be destroyed.

READING II   Revelation 1:4b — 8

Roman Catholic: Revelation 1:5–8

Grace to you and peace from the one who is and who was and who is to come, and from the seven spirits who are before God's throne, and from Jesus Christ, the faithful witness, the firstborn of the dead, and the ruler of the rulers of the earth. To the one who loves us and freed us from our sins by his blood, and made us to be a dominion, priests serving his God and Father, to Jesus Christ be glory and dominion forever and ever. Amen.

Look! He is coming with the clouds;
    every eye will see him,
even those who pierced him;
    and on his account all the tribes of the earth
    will wail.
So it is to be. Amen.

"I am the Alpha and the Omega," says the Lord God, who is and who was and who is to come, the Almighty.

GOSPEL   John 18:33 — 37

Roman Catholic: John 18:33b — 37

Pilate entered the headquarters again, summoned Jesus, and asked him, "Are you the King of the Jews?" Jesus answered, "Do you ask this on your own, or did others tell you about me?" Pilate replied, "I am not Jewish, am I? Your own nation and the chief priests have handed you over to me. What have you done?" Jesus answered, "My kingdom is not from this world. If my kingdom were from this world, my followers would be fighting to keep me from being handed over to the Judeans. But as it is, my kingdom is not from here." Pilate asked him, "So you are a king?" Jesus answered, "You say that I am a king. For this I was born, and for this I came into the world, to testify to the truth. Everyone who belongs to the truth listens to my voice."

Practice of Prayer

Psalm 93:1, 1—2, 5

The LORD is king, with majesty enrobed;
the LORD is robed with might,
and girded round with power.

The world you made firm, not to be moved;
your throne has stood firm from of old.
From all eternity, O LORD, you are.

Truly your decrees are to be trusted.
Holiness is fitting to your house,
O LORD, until the end of time.

Practice of Virtue

Practicing virtue isn't about being good. It goes far beyond concern for external rules and standards of behavior. Outward practices of virtue are best developed from the inside and involve a growing freedom to love God and all that God has created.

The word "cardinal" comes from the Latin derivative *cardo,* which means "hinge." All other virtues hinge upon the cardinal ones—prudence, justice, temperance and fortitude. The end of one liturgical year and the beginning of another offers an opportunity to consider the movements of these four virtues in our lives. What experiences have made you conscious of your growth in these virtues? Have you developed any strategies for cultivating them? How do they enable you to love God and neighbor more freely?

Scripture Insights

The solemnity of Christ the King closes the liturgical year with a paradox. Two images of royalty and power confront us. Daniel's visions portray a powerful being who looks like a human being. The original Aramaic says "son of man," but this is not the semi-divine figure of the early first century. In the Hebrew scriptures, the phrase "son of man" refers to a human being. What appears to Daniel, however, is no ordinary human being. The power accorded him is greater than any king's power; his kingship is over the whole earth. The figure shares God's power in both the service of peoples and everlasting kingship.

Readers and writers of the New Testament found the Daniel passage and the title "Son of Man" to be profoundly significant in their discussion of Jesus. Much of the image of Jesus' glorious reign at the end of time has its roots in Daniel's vision.

The paradox arises in the passage from John's gospel. Jesus is brought before Pilate, scourged, insulted, spat upon. He endures interrogation about his kingship and kingdom that Pilate has no possibility of understanding because Pilate's definition of kingship belongs to the world. It is too narrow to contain the broken man who stands before him. If Pilate had looked at the Jewish understanding of kingship found in Deuteronomy 17, he would have understood better. The king of Israel was not to plan battles, attack nations or make laws. He was not to protect the people. The sole duty of the king was to read the law of God and obey it. He was to provide the example of what it meant to follow God's commandment. In this context, Jesus was truly king in a way the world could not understand.

The church chooses to portray the broken king on a cross as a symbol of faith, love and obedience: Deuteronomy's definition. Yet Christians also revere the visions described in the books of Daniel and Revelation, of Christ sitting at the right hand of the Father and reigning gloriously at the end of time. This paradox is the legacy of the incarnation.

What is your image of kingship? What are the qualities of a king that you would apply to Jesus?

Information on the License to Reprint from At Home with the Word 2003

The low bulk rate prices of *At Home with the Word 2003* are intended to make quantities of the book affordable. Single copies are $8.00 each; 5–99 copies, $6.00 each; 100 or more copies, $4.00. We encourage parishes to buy quantities of this book.

However, Liturgy Training Publications makes a simple reprint license available to parishes that would find it more practical to reproduce some parts of this book. Scripture Insights, Practice of Prudence, Temperance, Fortitude or Justice, prayers titled Preparation for the Word and Thanksgiving for the Word and lists of Weekday Readings may be duplicated for the parish bulletin or reproduced in other formats. These may be used every week or as often as the license holder chooses.

The license granted is for the period beginning with the First Sunday of Advent—December 1, 2002—through the solemnity of Christ the King—November 23, 2003.

Please note that the license does *not* cover scripture readings or psalms (Practice of Prayer). See the acknowledgments page at the beginning of this book for the names of the copyright holders of these texts.

The materials reprinted under license from LTP may not be sold, may not be used in connection with any program or event for which a fee is charged and may be used only among the members of the community obtaining the license. The license may not be purchased by a diocese for use in its parishes.

No reprinting may be done by the parish until the license is signed by both parties and the fee is paid. Copies of the license agreement will be sent on request. The fee varies with the number of copies to be reproduced on a regular basis:

Up to 100 copies: $100
101 to 500 copies: $300
501 to 1000 copies: $500
More than 1000 copies: $800

For further information, call the reprint permissions department at 773-486-8970, ext. 268, or fax your request to 773-486-9158, attn: reprint permissions.